W9-ATB-836

ANTIQUES

Traditional techniques of the master craftsmen
furniture, glass, ceramics, gold, silver and much more

Edited by Elizabeth Drury

DOUBLEDAY & COMPANY INC.
GARDEN CITY, NEW YORK
1986

Copyright © 1986 by Roxby
Art Publishing Limited

All rights reserved. No part of this
book may be reproduced or
transmitted in any form or by any means,
electrical or mechanical,
including photocopying, recording or
by an information storage or
retrieval system, without permission
in writing from the publisher.

Doubleday & Company Inc.
Garden City, New York

Made by Roxby Art Publishing Limited
a division of Roxby Press Limited
98 Clapham Common North Side
London SW4 9SG

Editor: Elizabeth Drury
Art Direction: Raymond Gautier Design
Design: Hilary Krag
Illustration: Aziz Khan and Simon Roulstone
Picture Research: Mary-Jane Coles
Typesetting: Tradespools Limited
Reproduction: F. E. Burman Limited
Printing and Binding: Tonsa, San Sebastian, Spain

Contributing Authors
Introduction: Philippa Glanville
Woodwork: Philip Astley-Jones, Frances Collard,
Elizabeth Drury, Carolyn Eardley,
Ian Hedley and Yvonne Jones
Glass: David Watts
Ceramics: Henry Sandon
Metalwork: Judith Banister, Dorothy Bosomworth,
W. K. Gale, Philippa Glanville, Anthony North,
Shelley Nott and David Watts

Library of Congress Cataloging-in-Publication Data

Antiques: traditional techniques of the master
craftsmen - furniture, glass, ceramics,
gold, silver, and much more.

Bibliography: p. 218
Includes index.
1. Decorative arts—Technique. I. Drury, Elizabeth.
NK1130.A5   1986   745   85-6828
ISBN 0-385-23128-8

First American Edition 1986

CONTENTS

Illustration of a marquetry-cutter's donkey from Art du Menuisier *by Jacob-André Roubo, 1772.*

FOREWORD

This book explains the techniques that were used in the past to fashion and decorate wood, glass, pottery and porcelain, gold and silver, and metals such as pewter, copper and brass. Craftsmen working in the traditional manner, turning wood, moulding clay with their hands to form pots, hammering the plates for armour or acid etching glass, were creating the articles that are today described as 'antiques'.

On a simple level, the purpose of compiling such a work was to clarify what is meant by the terms 'marquetry' and 'ormolu', 'embossing' and 'chasing', among many others. They may be familiar to perusers of sale-room catalogues, and those who read the labels in museums, but their meaning may not be so completely understood by an amateur as to be applied correctly to other objects. The numerous illustrations of pieces with accompanying descriptions contribute greatly to such an understanding.

The main purpose, though, is to show how, over the centuries, craftsmen have actually practised their trades and exercised their skills: how bronze was cast and enamel was attached to metal by firing, how pottery was both made and ornamented with liquid clay known as 'slip'; what their tools looked like and how they sat or stood – or lay, in the case of the blade-makers – while they worked.

A glance through the succeeding pages reveals that there are similarities in the treatment of one material and another. Their surfaces could be painted or gilded, for example; or incised, either substantially, as in some woodcarving, or delicately, to create a linear design, as in engraving on glass or on metalwork.

The differences are important, too: the way in which the type of glass known as 'cristallo' is dissimilar in weight and appearance to the later lead glass, for example, and japanning has a different depth and texture to the Oriental lacquer that it was intended to imitate.

Comparisons of this kind may lead to conclusions as to the date and place of origin of a piece, and set it in a historical and geographical context. Above all they serve to extend an understanding of the nature of a great many objects that are today admired and valued, and an admiration for the craftsmen who made them.

ELIZABETH DRURY

INTRODUCTION

BY HAMMER AND HAND
ALL ARTS DO STAND

That unity of hand and eye, understanding of materials, application of precisely judged strength, epitomized by the Blacksmiths' Company motto, are essential to all crafts. The right tools, simple in construction but subtly and almost infinitely varied in their effect, and heat, applied to modify and shape the raw material, are the factors common to the diverse techniques described in the following pages.

Two systems co-existed, one on a small scale supplying the limited high-class and wealthy market with highly refined and luxurious objects, often with a considerable degree of hand-work and heavy dependence on expensive raw materials; this section used traditional techniques and had an insatiable appetite for novelty in design in response to shifts in fashion. The Boulle workshops in Paris were among those producing work for a small number of rich patrons.

The alternative system, which supplied the far larger general market, was organized to produce articles as cheaply as possible with the minimum of attention from the individual craftsman; the tendency has always been for this sector to throw up innovations in technology, and to find cheaper substitutes for expensive raw materials in order to decrease costs or to increase output. There were several ways of doing this. The specialist spoon-maker of the sixteenth century already attached standard cast finials supplied by outworkers to his products, just as the eighteenth-century delft tile-maker used stencils for the rapid decoration of hundreds of tiles a day, a far cry from the free-hand painters working in the porcelain factories at Meissen, Chelsea or Copenhagen.

By concentrating processes in the hands of skilled specialists, the benefits of these two contrasting organizations could be enjoyed. A large and fashionable Georgian furniture-maker, Seddons of Aldersgate Street, London, employed 400 apprentices on the basic construction of their furniture, but had in the same large building gilders, ormolu makers, mirror workers and upholsterers, each capable of working in the refined Anglo-French style favoured by Henry Holland for the Prince of Wales.

Advances in technology were slow to come in to the luxury end of these crafts; while rolling mills enabled Matthew Boulton's Soho manufactory to turn out long runs of inexpensive die-struck and loaded candlesticks made from thin sheet silver, his aristocratic customers still expected personally designed and hand-raised objects with heavy cast detail. At the upper end of every craft, designers were essential to interpret the customer's wishes and produce a design for the craftsmen.

Whatever the process, this one skill was a prerequisite – someone capable of designing, or perhaps modelling, the original. Modellers were usually anonymous: Johann Joachim Kändler, at the Meissen factory, and the other Kändler, Frederick, who was both a goldsmith and modeller in London from about 1727, are unusual in that their names are known. The dependence, in the luxury trade at least, on trained designers was satisfied from the late seventeenth century by schools of drawing. In early Georgian London the St Martin's Lane Academy provided a pool in which engravers, goldsmiths, modellers, sculptors and artists could swim together and learn from each other, a fruitful source of the Rococo style. But this was a far cry from the craftsman. For him changes in design were troublesome and originality to be avoided. The most convenient method was also the quickest and the most economical, and it was essential to be able to reproduce copies from a carefully carved and finished mould.

Casting was a crucial skill for all metalworkers, and for the

Left: Detail of a wall painting from the study of Francesco I de' Medici, Palazzo Vecchio, Florence, planned by Georgio Vasari (1511–74) and completed 1570/72. Jewellers and goldsmiths are depicted in unlikely proximity. The products of their skills are ranged along a shelf, below which working drawings are pinned, and tools are hung above and beside the furnaces. This painting, one of a series showing craftsmen at work, is indicative of a new attitude to – and curiosity about – technical matters.

Left: Detail of a lithograph of glassmaking at William Ford's glassworks, Edinburgh, c.1840. The methods of the traditional flint glassblowers at work here were being supplemented by two- and three-part moulds and, from the mid-nineteenth century, by press-moulding, to produce much cheaper glass for the mass market. However, the older working method shown here of a two-man team survived in some traditional English glasshouses well into the twentieth century.

ornament applied to some woodwork, whether a run of simple iron firebacks or lead pilgrim badges, or sets of sophisticated ormolu furniture or clock mounts. In porcelain and fine stoneware, too, moulds in several parts were essential to produce both figures and certain standard tablewares. Aaron Wood made pattern blocks for the Staffordshire salt-glaze manufacturers in the late 1750s, but these were used also by the porcelain factories at Liverpool, Worcester and Bow.

Moulds, and the models from which they were taken, were valuable and were frequently re-used or shared between different workshops. Wooden models, carved for Wedgwood, are still at Barlaston. Lead plaquettes which circulated throughout northern Europe in the sixteenth century were a convenient means of publicizing the designs of Peter Flötner. These were reproduced both by London goldsmiths and by Nuremberg pewterers.

The craftsman's dependence on good models was always a handicap, craftsmen in America sometimes resorting to taking castings from imported English-made pieces. In the nineteenth century, to provide good models for young craftsmen, the firm of Elkington's developed the electrotyping process in conjunction with the Museum of Science and Art (the Victoria and Albert Museum). They copied famous objects of all periods, but particularly of the Roman period and of the fifteenth and sixteenth centuries (then regarded as the high peaks of European artistic achievement), and distributed them cheaply as models to schools and colleges of design.

Almost all traditional western European crafts described in this book were stimulated by external factors. The most significant source was trade with India and China, which brought raw materials, new techniques and new design ideas.

Exotic materials gave new opportunity to the cabinet-maker, using wood from the East Indies or South America, or a little earlier, cane for furniture from the East Indies. Japanning as a cheap imitation of lacquer was another response to the enormous excitement generated among European customers by Far Eastern decorative art. New techniques included above all the secret of making porcelain. It had been palely imitated in tin-glazed earthenware in Persia and later in western Europe from the late Middle Ages; the secret was finally cracked by Böttger for Meissen. Even more significant for the crafts of both the potter and the goldsmith was the introduction of new drinks – tea, coffee and chocolate – which meant an entirely new range of products and also a new class of consumer.

Before the seventeenth century, specialist knowledge of materials and technology was regarded as part of the mystery of each craft, to be learned and handed on secretly and not written down. Outsiders, especially aliens, were often excluded from membership of craft guilds. Conversely, knowledge of new technologies was valuable and travelled only in the heads of its practitioners, so that, for example, Henry VIII, needing an armour workshop, had to import his armourers from Innsbruck and, later, glassmakers skilled at making Venetian *cristallo* from Murano, against the wishes of the Venetian authorities. The Innsbruck-trained armourers

Left: Sheet of German designs for silver tableware, c.1720–40. The engraver crammed into this suite of designs for silver as many variant forms of ornament as possible as models for the goldsmith. Ornament for goldsmiths ignored frontiers, and similar designs to these are found chased and engraved on silver in France and England from about 1720. Engraved ornaments often appeared long after the designs occurred on plate: ideas circulated in the form of sketches, in journeymen's heads and as actual objects which were then copied.

Above: French engraved design for a marquetry table-top in the manner of André-Charles Boulle (1642–1732), early eighteenth century.
Left: English paper stencil, cut from a letter, for a japanned tray. It was in use at the Star Japan Co., in Bilston, in the late nineteenth century.
Right: Designs for japanning from A Treatise of Japanning and Varnishing by John Stalker and George Parker, 1688. This handbook, published in Oxford, shows the speed with which imported ornament and techniques could be assimilated. The East India Company started importing Oriental lacquer in the 1660s, and by the 1680s numerous imitations were being made and a repertoire of 'Chinese' ornament was established.

had the secret of making a kind of steel, a secret not shared by English ironworkers before the seventeenth century.

The shift from craft practices not written down at the time, and therefore hard to reconstruct today, to a science-based technology was already occurring in some crafts in the sixteenth century. Metallurgy was in the forefront, since it was essential both for success in warfare and for their economic stability for princes to understand the production of guns and coinage. Handbooks describing metallurgical techniques, glassmaking and goldsmithing were written by Biringuccio, before the end of the sixteenth century, and more were to appear under the stimulus of the scientific enlightenment of the seventeenth and eighteenth centuries. For example, in England the gentlemen of the Royal Society busied themselves with such industrial techniques as brassmaking enamelling, varnishing, the rolling press, making gunpowder, the history of refining, and ironmaking among many others. Diderot aimed his encyclopedia at a newly active class of gentlemen entrepreneurs anxious to benefit financially from investment in expanding French industries. Societies such as the Lunar Society of Birmingham, which included active scientists such as Erasmus Darwin, Joseph Priestley and James Watt, were a forum where ideas were exchanged on the application of steam power to machinery.

With economic pressure for workshops to specialize, the general level of training declined. The Goldsmiths' Company of London complained as early as 1607 that many journeymen were no longer more than hammermen capable of only the simplest tasks. Standard designs and decoration were the norm for furniture-makers, porcelain manufacturers, glass-makers and goldsmiths, who shared common designs taken from sheets of engraved ornament such as those by Lock and Copland. Originality was expensive and might not sell.

A tendency towards specialization was particularly evident in the pottery industry. Wedgwood in 1790 employed about 160 people at Etruria, divided into departments according to the ware produced. A long list of specialist skills – hollow-ware pressers, turners of flatware and of hollow-ware, handlers, biscuit-oven firers, brushers, placers, firemen, girl colour grinders, painters, enamellers and gilders, and so on – indicates that this was still a process in which the object was handled many times, although there was machinery to speed up certain stages.

Because of the desire to emulate the rich surface effects of precious metals, those working in all the materials discussed in the succeeding chapters – whether making furniture, armour, porcelain or glass – from time to time used gilding or silvering, or inlay, in imitation of gold and silver. Other decorative surfaces included etching with acid, blueing for steel, burnishing and applying colours in various ways. Glass and pottery in particular lent themselves to rich, decorative effects, and in the nineteenth and early twentieth centuries magnificent multi-coloured glass has been made both for the mass market

and for the individual, discerning patron, for example by Gallé and Tiffany.

Innovations in technique occurred away from the traditional craft organization, which could become a stranglehold. Boulton, for example, deliberately set up beyond the reach of the Goldsmiths' Company of London and refused to take apprentices in the time-honoured way, but took in young lads to train who had some skill with their hands. The traditional picture of the goldsmith as a master working side by side with his journeymen is almost certainly inaccurate for England by the late sixteenth century, when the leading goldsmiths at least were businessmen, merchants, bankers, concerned with the Mint and with property dealing while retaining managers to supervise their workshops. Many were indeed not manufacturers at all, but retailers who organized sub-contractors rather than producing anything themselves. In ceramics and in glassmaking a similar picture is emerging: the early investors in the London delft factories were businessmen rather than artist-craftsmen. Ravenscroft and Dwight were gentlemen scientists, more interested in the research into new materials than in the commercial application of their techniques, and it is significant that the stoneware industry moved rapidly to Nottingham from London. These examples are drawn mainly from England because in the change from craft organization to a recognizably industrial structure England led the way. This was because it was centralized, because it had at least in London a very substantial community to produce credit and a mass market for the consumer goods, and because it had cheap sources of power in water and coal, which by the end of the eighteenth century were being heavily exploited in the interests of what traditionally had been workshop-based crafts.

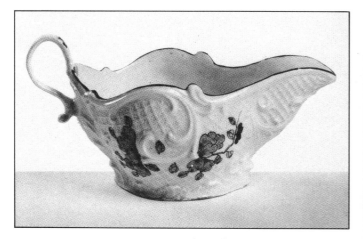

Above: Soft-paste porcelain sauce-boat, Longton Hall, Staffordshire, c.1759–60.
Right: Salt-glazed stoneware sauce-boat, Staffordshire, c.1759–65; stoneware mould, or 'block', for a sauce-boat modelled by Aaron Wood (1717–85), c.1757–65. Blocks provided the models from which plaster moulds were taken. The porcelain and stoneware manufacturers then used those to form their wares.

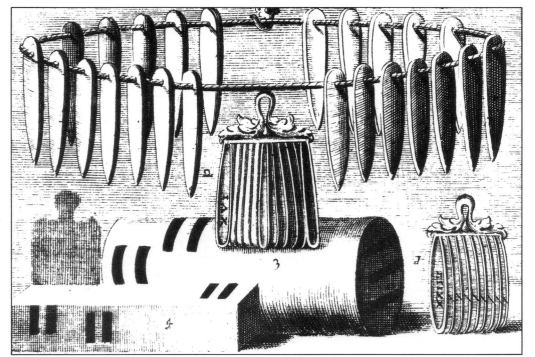

Left: Detail of an illustration showing assaying equipment from Description of Leading Ore Processing and Mining Methods by Lazarus Ercker, 1574. The 24 gold touch needles on the wire were graded in purity from one carat of gold to 23 of silver up to 24 carat of pure gold. The smaller sets were of graded copper and silver, for testing silver. The piece to be tested was rubbed on the touchstone (left). The streak was then compared for colour with the streak left by the needle closest to it and the standard ascertained.

Below: Goldsmith's shop, the frontispiece to A New Touch-stone for Gold and Silver Wares by W. Badcock, 1679. The processes include hammering – or forging – plate, refining metal in the furnace, assaying plate and, at the back, marking assayed plate, a task carried out by the Warden of the Goldsmiths' Company.

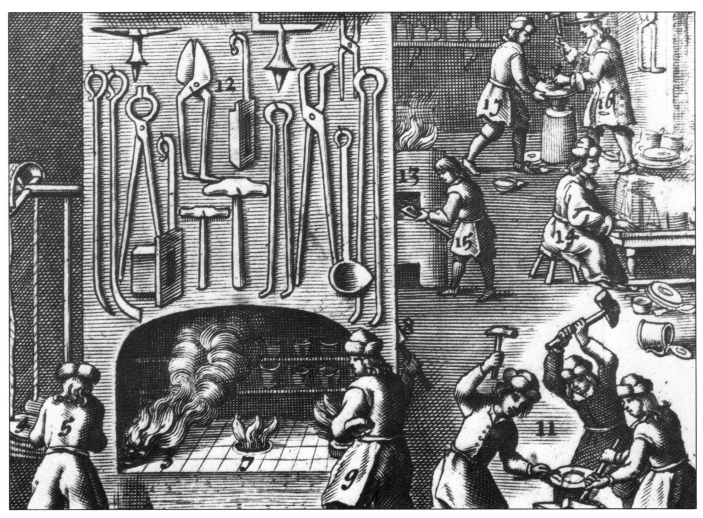

WOODWORK

In the late Middle Ages, when the guild system came into being, woodworkers had already begun to develop particular skills: the cooper who made casks practised a separate trade from the bowyer who made bows and the fletcher who made arrows; the joiner undertook different work from the carpenter who was employed on the wooden structure of buildings. They served different apprenticeships and worked for different rates of pay.

As the craft developed, the tendency towards specialization increased. By the middle of the eighteenth century joining, turning, carving and gilding, veneering, upholstering and the other techniques used in making and decorating furniture were carried out by different craftsmen.

The history of furniture-making is related to the rise in demand for household furnishings and the desire that these should be objects of an ornamental as well as utilitarian nature. It is also the story of the craftsmen's gradual understanding and mastery of their prime material: wood.

Trees are divided into two main types: softwoods and hardwoods. Softwoods are coniferous, needle-leaved trees and generally evergreen. Hardwoods are broad leaved and generally deciduous, and they are subdivided into temperate varieties such as oak and walnut and equatorial varieties such as mahogany and satinwood. Confusingly, there are soft types of wood, such as lime, which come from hardwood trees and hard types of wood, such as yew, which come from softwood trees. The timbers most often used in furniture-making are from hardwoods. Yew is one of the exceptions; and pine is another, used particularly in the construction of the 'carcase', or framework (see p. 34), and for inexpensive furniture.

In general the firm heartwood from the core of the tree is used in preference to the younger softwood lying between the heartwood and the bark. The softwood is more likely to warp, and it is more vulnerable to decay.

Until the early fourteenth century, pieces of furniture such as chests were made from heavy planks hewn from logs by a process known as 'riving'. An iron wedge was driven into the log towards the centre, roughly on the line of the medullary rays radiating from the heart of the tree. The split was then extended down its length with other wedges until the log fell in two. Further riving was done on the two parts until planks of the required thickness were obtained. By the nature of the splits, the planks were wedge shaped in section, and they were usually squared up with an adze before being used.

Left: English black japanned bureau cabinet, c.1725. Japanning was a form of decoration that imitated the appearance of Oriental lacquer, though different materials were used. It first became popular in Europe in the late seventeenth century and in America in the mid-eighteenth century.

Left: English turned cup in lignum vitae. The bowl, stem and foot would have been shaped on a foot-operated pole lathe. The 'rose' pattern was cut into the surface by a process known as 'engine-turning' in which the procedure was reversed, the work remaining still while the cutting-edge was moved to create the repeat design.

TIMBER

Lighter planks than those that resulted from the process of riving were produced when the logs were sawn. The sawpit of the late Middle Ages continued to be used for supplying rural craftsmen with timber even after steam-powered machinery had been introduced into sawmills in the mid-nineteenth century. The log lay across planks resting on the ground on either side of the pit, and it was sawn through by two men pulling alternately on a two-handled saw. The 'top sawyer' – usually the owner of the sawpit – worked above ground, while the 'bottom sawyer' had the uncomfortable job of working in the pit below in a continuous shower of sawdust.

When 'converting' logs into the planks by sawing, two basic methods were employed: through-and-through, or plain, sawing, in which the log was sawn in parallel cuts along its length, and quarter sawing, in which the log was first quartered and the quarters then converted in one of a variety of ways. Taking the log as a circle, the planks were either cut radially (as in riving) or tangentially to the circle. The way in which the planks were converted determined both the stability and the appearance of the timber.

Living trees, and newly felled timber, hold up to 50% of their weight in 'free' water, contained within the cells; some swamp-grown trees hold up to 200%. Before it can be used, the timber must be dried, or 'seasoned', and the moisture content reduced to approximately that of the atmosphere in which the furniture will eventually stand. Seasoning strengthens the wood, lessens its susceptibility to some forms of decay and decreases its tendency to shrink or expand once it has been shaped and the various components assembled. Trees are usually felled in the winter when the moisture content is at its lowest.

The traditional method of seasoning timber was by air-drying. The planks were stacked under cover with spacers between them so that the air could circulate freely, and dry the planks evenly and at a rate which would not stress the timber fibres. The free water drained off first. At fibre saturation point, the moisture that remained was 'bound' water in the cell walls, and as this dried out the timber began to shrink.

Shrinkage occurs in two directions: along the annual rings, which record the tree's growth, and between the rings. The shrinkage along the rings is always the greater, averaging twice that between the rings. There is no movement along the 'grain', the term used to describe the disposition of the fibres through which, in a living tree, the sap rises.

Seasoned timber is hygroscopic: it absorbs and gives out moisture so that the moisture content of the wood corresponds to that of the atmosphere. Because movement is greater along the annual rings than between them, tangentially sawn planks are more affected by changes in atmospheric conditions than radially sawn planks. In the former any movement in the timber occurs evenly; in the latter it can cause serious distortion in the form of warping.

Radially sawn planks, as well as possessing greater stability, have a more interesting 'figure', or surface pattern. The annual

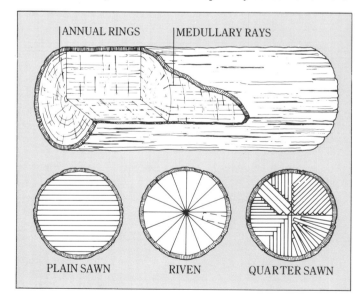

Above: Section through a log and various methods of converting timber. With riving and quarter sawing the planks are radially cut; with plain sawing some are cut radially and some tangentially.
Right: Cupping, caused by the annual rings shrinking, and bowing, caused by the plank bending under its own weight when the timber is stacked for seasoning without spacers.
Far right: Illustration of a sawpit from The Young Tradesman or Book of English Trades, *1839.*

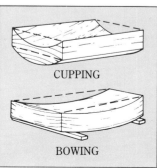

rings are composed of narrow, dark-coloured bands representing slow, winter growth and wider bands of light-coloured timber representing fast, summer growth. These appear as dark and light stripes. The medullary rays in, for example, radially sawn oak appear as flecks. Tangentially sawn planks are characterized by the U- or V-shaped grain markings seen particularly in mahogany and rosewood.

Other types of figure are produced by cutting through growth irregularities. The timber so derived is relatively unstable and it is more often used as a 'veneer', a wood applied to the surface in thin sheets (see p.36), than in the solid.

Because of the difficulty of moving heavy logs and planks, furniture-makers, until the middle of the seventeenth century, mainly used timbers that were available to them locally. At that date furniture had begun to assume a new importance: chests, chairs and tables were fundamental to an increasingly peaceful, comfortable and civilized way of living. More time and money were spent on the manufacture of these objects, and this included the acquisition of materials from farther afield as well as the practice of more complicated techniques.

In Britain oak was one of the most common indigenous trees. Being straight grained, it was comparatively easy to rive, and its hardness and durability were also important to the furniture-maker. Certainly, most surviving pieces of furniture made in Britain from the Middle Ages until the mid-seventeenth century are made of oak. The darker bog oak came from trees of great age or which had been immersed in water,

Above: English parquetry breakfast table, nineteenth century. The table-top is composed of lozenges of veneer of various woods, including rosewood, burr walnut, snakewood, coromandel, calamander and satinwood.
Left: American block-front knee-hole desk made of mahogany, 1760–85. This type of block-front furniture, with flattened curves and carved shell ornament, is particularly associated with Newport, Rhode Island, and the Goddard and Townsend families of cabinet-makers.

particularly peat water. With other native woods such as holly, box and yew, it was used in the sixteenth and seventeenth centuries in inlays (see p.39).

Elsewhere in Europe chestnut was used as well as oak, but by the sixteenth century these were being superseded by walnut for high-quality pieces. The close texture permitted intricate carving, and by the middle of the succeeding century it was much in demand for veneers because of its fine colour and figure. It was easier to obtain on the Continent than in Britain, though many trees were destroyed by the hard winter of 1709. In 1720 export of walnut from France was prohibited in response to the shortage of timber, and from that time a variety of walnut grown in Virginia, Maryland and Pennsylvania was imported into Britain.

Furniture-making in America generally corresponded to British practices with a delay of approximately a decade. Thus, walnut was slower to replace oak, which continued to be used throughout the first quarter of the eighteenth century; and mahogany was slower to supplant walnut as the most used and admired timber.

Mahogany became popular in Europe as the stocks of seasoned walnut dwindled in the 1730s and 1740s. There were many advantages to working in mahogany. It was durable and resistant to decay; it had great depth of colour, whether a light-reddish hue or rich and dark; it was an excellent medium for

carving and at the same time suitable for veneers; and the great size of the trees meant that it could be obtained in wide planks for use as table-tops or the solid sides of cabinets with veneered fronts.

Initially mahogany came to Britain from Jamaica, and later from the other West Indian islands of San Domingo and Cuba. By the end of the eighteenth century Honduras, in Central America, was the main source of supply. The soil and climate of each of these accounted for the particular characteristics of the timber. Cuban mahogany possessed the finest figure – 'roe' and 'fiddle-back' being two of the best-known types – and it was the one most often used in veneering. It was also, like the San Domingo variety, suitable for carving, and was popular for chair-making (see p.24). San Domingo mahogany, by contrast, had little figure, and this was also the case with the lighter, softer timber from Honduras (sometimes known as 'baywood'). The mahogany used in France came from the East, from Ceylon and Malabar. A type found as a veneer is termed '*bois satiné*', but it is not the timber described in English as 'satinwood'.

Satinwood was never used as extensively in America as it was in Europe, where the clear, yellow colour was much admired from about 1765. It came from India and Ceylon, and also from the West Indies. The popularity of satinwood coincided with the introduction of a wide variety of exotic

Left: American oak chair table, seventeenth century, the chair back pivoting to form a table-top. The medullary rays in the four planks at the top appear as strongly marked flecks, a characteristic of radially sawn oak. The two lower ones were sawn tangentially and the rays, because they are edge on, are not visible.
Above: German walnut cupboard, mid-eighteenth century. In this piece

walnut was used both in the solid and as a 'veneer', with a thin sheet of timber applied to the surface.

Left: Spanish oak and walnut coffer, seventeenth century. Walnut is closer grained than oak and for this reason a more satisfactory timber for carving. The roundels of geometric ornament are typical of 'chip carved' decoration.

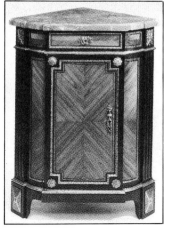

Right: French encoignure, or corner cupboard, signed by G. Durand, nineteenth century. The door panel is quarter veneered in kingwood, a timber imported from South America. The mounts are ormolu.
Far right: French secrétaire à abattant with a dark grey marble top and ormolu mounts, c.1810. The fall front, a feature of this type of upright writing desk, is veneered in finely figured mahogany.

woods in 'marquetry', a type of surface pattern formed by veneers of different shapes and colours which first became popular in the previous century (see p.39). Among them were black or purplish-brown rosewood, often with a variegated figure; the somewhat similar purpleheart; kingwood, which is related to rosewood; and tulipwood, which is yellow, shading to red. Hard, black ebony had been used in the seventeenth century in early cabinet-making (see p.32), and it was later used in 'stringing', a narrow decorative band of inlay. This might also be executed in stained, or 'ebonized', wood.

With the expansion of world-wide trade in the early nineteenth century, an increasing number of exotic timbers became available. While light-coloured indigenous woods such as maple and birch were popular for bedroom, and sometimes drawing-room, furniture, darker exotic timbers were favoured for the library and dining-room, and these might include rosewood and the heavily striped wood, calamander.

THE CRAFT OF THE JOINER

In the late fifteenth century the most important piece of household furniture was the chest, which was used for storing clothes and valuables. At that period a type of construction was developed that was an improvement on simply nailing the planks together at the corners – this had been the combined work of the carpenter and of the blacksmith who made the hinges and bands which secured the planks. Timber movement across the grain caused the nailed pieces to split; the new design of chest was panelled, and it had a frame made with pieces of wood joined lengthwise. The vertical members, known as 'stiles' and 'muntins', and the horizontal ones, or 'rails', were held together by a type of joint known as a 'mortise and tenon'. The craftsman who made this furniture was known as a 'joiner'.

The mortise is a rectangular hole and the tenon a corresponding projection on another member which fits into it. The mortise and tenon joint was used by the Ancient Egyptians, who invented many of the basic techniques employed in making and decorating furniture. It was rediscovered in Italy and from there its use spread throughout Europe.

The simplest type of mortise and tenon joint had a plain, or 'bare-faced', tenon. The mortise either extended right through the timber, so that the end of the tenon was visible, or it was 'stopped'. In this last type of mortise, the recess did not extend to the other side so the end of the tenon was concealed.

The bare-faced tenon could be 'top shouldered' or 'bottom shouldered', or both. This hid any defect in the top or bottom of the mortise which might have occurred when it was cut. The top shoulder gave additional strength to the joint which was particularly useful in the case of a corner joint. The term 'bridle joint' is given to a type of shouldered tenon with the mortise left open. It was often used for mirror-frames, especially ones with mitred corners (which form a right angle, the line of the junction bisecting the angle), and to connect the intermediate members to the main structure.

A 'shouldered tenon' is a tenon that has been 'edge shouldered' on one or two sides. This had the same effect as top and bottom shouldering and, if the features were used in combination, they added strength and stability to the joint.

On the type of chest that was new in the late-fifteenth century the framework supported panels of wood. The 'haunched' mortise and tenon was used when a groove ('rebate', or 'rabbet') in the frame was required for the panel. The groove had to extend the length and width of the frame. By making the tenon as thick as the groove was wide, and the depth of the haunch as deep as the groove, the groove was neatly hidden once the tenon was fitted into the mortise. The panels could be fitted into the middle, and they were sometimes reduced in thickness at the edges – or 'fielded' – leaving the centre thicker for carved decoration; alternatively they could be fitted into grooves so that the surface was flush

Far left: Work by J. Bourdichon, fifteenth century. The joiner is shown planing the surface of a panel. Linenfold wallpanelling, as illustrated in the foreground, first appeared in the Low Countries during the course of the fifteenth century.
Above: English oak chest, early sixteenth century. The panels were fitted into grooves in the frame, which consisted of vertical and horizontal 'members', or parts, joined together with mortise and tenon joints. An unusual feature is the horizontal placing of the linenfold panels.
Left: Detail of a Hispano-Flemish oak cupboard, early sixteenth century. The carving and beading applied to the surface is more elaborate than the decoration of the chest above; this is also an example of panel and frame construction.

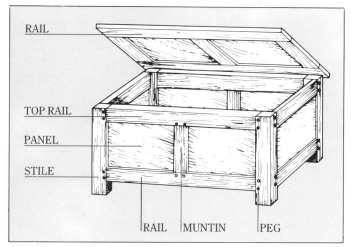

Left: English oak cupboard, c.1660. The two drawers and four cupboards make this a more complicated example of panel and frame construction. The half-balusters applied to the frame would have been turned and then split.
Below: Panel and frame construction of a chest similar to the one illustrated on the opposite page. The mortise and *tenon joints used for the frame are secured by 'dowels', or pegs; the panels are set into the frame in grooves. Panel and frame construction allows for some movement of the timber.*
Bottom: Four methods of joining the panel to the frame; halved and bridled joints and mortise and tenon joints used in panel and frame construction.

RAIL

TOP RAIL

PANEL

STILE

RAIL   MUNTIN   PEG

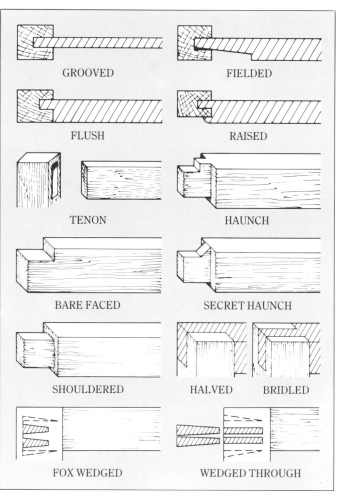

GROOVED   FIELDED

FLUSH   RAISED

TENON   HAUNCH

BARE FACED   SECRET HAUNCH

SHOULDERED   HALVED   BRIDLED

FOX WEDGED   WEDGED THROUGH

with the framework, or raised.

Other joints used at the same period for frame-making included 'wedged' joints. The basic types were known as 'wedged through' and 'fox wedged'. With the wedged-through joint the joiner began as if to make an ordinary through mortise and tenon, but then opened out the entrance at the top and bottom of the mortise and made two saw cuts in the tenon. When the tenon had been placed in the mortise, wedges were driven into the saw cuts, forcing the edges out against the tapered mortise and locking the two together. The tenon and wedges were generally made too long and were trimmed when the wedges had been hammered home. For decorative purposes, the wedges were sometimes made of wood of a contrasting colour.

The fox-wedged joint was similar to the wedged-through joint, but both the mortise and the tenon were stopped. This meant that the wedges had to be fitted loosely into the saw cuts in the tenon. The tenon was then hammered into the mortise, forcing the tenon edges out to lock them in the same way as in the wedged-through joint. If the wedges were too thick, the tenon jammed in the mortise before it was fully home; if the wedges were too slack, the mortise and tenon would lock together but too loosely.

Saws, planes and chisels were the joiner's tools. Glue was not used to any great extent until the early eighteenth century, and to render joints strong and permanent holes were drilled through both parts and slightly tapering pegs, or 'dowels', of green wood driven in. The holes in the mortise were made slightly off-centre of the holes in the tenon so that when the dowels were driven home the tenon was forced closer to the mortise. A 'horn', or block of waste wood, was left on by some joiners to protect the joint during the forming of the mortise.

THE CRAFT OF THE TURNER

Turning is a method of shaping and ornamenting wood by applying a cutting-tool to the surface as the piece is rotated on a lathe. The technique is an ancient one, used by the Egyptians perhaps as long ago as the twelfth century BC and later by the Greeks and Romans. In Medieval Germany turners in Cologne had established their own guild, independent of other wood-workers, by 1180. Since then the craft of turning – or turnery – has been practised continuously, though since the beginning of the eighteenth century mainly in the rural areas of Europe and America.

A simple form of lathe was the 'pole' lathe, so called because it was driven by the springiness of a long, tapering pole. When the lathe was set up in the open, close to a source of timber, the branch of a live sapling might be used; otherwise the pole was bolted to the workshop ceiling. A length of cord was tied to the thin end of the pole or branch. The middle of the cord was looped around a 'mandrel', or axis to which the work was secured, or the piece of timber itself, which was held in a horizontal position by spikes or screws in the vertical 'headstock' and 'tailstock', and the other end attached to a foot treadle. The cord was kept under tension so that the pole bent under the strain. When the foot treadle was depressed the cord rotated the piece towards the turner, and when it was released the spring in the pole caused the piece to rotate away from him. Sometimes, to give a better grip, a leather strap was used instead of a cord.

The cutting of the timber was done on the downstroke, and on the upstroke the blade was removed. With one hand the turner held the blade down on the tool rest and guided it, and the other hand he used to steady the tool.

Before the invention of wheel lathes which were hand driven by an assistant, and power lathes, the pole lathe was the type most commonly used for 'spindle turning'. This term describes the making of objects that are greater in length than in diameter – the legs and 'stretchers', or horizontal bars, for tables and chairs, balusters and bed posts, and small items such as lace bobbins and chessmen. Sometimes the basic shaping was done by the turner and the article was finished by the carver (see p. 44).

Beech was the timber often used for this kind of work. The logs were split by riving, and the wedge-shaped 'billets' trimmed with an axe and then with a draw-knife to as near as possible the eventual shape of the piece. The timber in its green state was easier both to rive and turn than seasoned timber. Until the end of the seventeenth century a great deal of turned furniture was made from seasoned oak, which was extremely hard to work.

In 'bowl turning' the diameter of the article exceeded its length and a pole lathe of slightly different construction was needed. It had more space between the lathe bed and the 'centres', securing the work at either side, to accommodate a deeper piece of timber; the tailstock was set lower so that the turner could cut right round to the base of the work. For turning a large object such as a table-top the headstock was swung round so that it faced away from the main structure to give greater clearance.

A particular skill was the cutting of a series of successively smaller bowls from one piece of timber. As many as six could be made, with the turner first forming the outside of the largest bowl and then reversing the block on the lathe to cut the channel between this and the next bowl. When the cutting was sufficiently deep, the block was removed from the lathe and, with the use of a curved wedge and hammer, this first bowl was separated from it and set aside to be finished later. The process of cutting a curving channel was repeated to shape the smaller bowls, each operation producing an item of diminished size.

For making the domestic articles that are now described as 'treen' a variety of woods were used, including beech, elm, holly and box, and, in the seventeenth century, *lignum vitae* imported from the West Indies. Sycamore was commonly used for dairy wares as it imparted no taste or smell. From the sixteenth century some of the grander table wares imitated the shapes of pewter (see p. 212).

Far left: Illustration of a wood-turner working at a pole lathe from a book of trades published in Zurich in 1548 by Johann Stumf. The turner is shown shaping a bowl by applying a cutting-tool to the piece of timber as it revolves. Pressure on the foot treadle caused the pole to bend and the cord to rotate towards him; when he lifted his foot from the treadle, the spring in the pole caused the cord to return and the work to rotate away from him. Beside him on the bench, and on the floor, are the finished articles.
Left: English turned coffee- and spice-mill, c.1760. The mill, made in three parts, is of lignum vitae.

Left: English turned egg-cups and stand, c.1800. Though such pieces were generally made in mahogany, this example is in fruitwood.
Below: English turned standing cup and cover, early seventeenth century. The wood used for this piece was maple. The fine, clearly engraved decoration is of heraldic beasts and devotional verses.

THE CRAFT OF THE CHAIR-MAKER

Throughout the Middle Ages and until the beginning of the sixteenth century the armchair was a symbol of precedence and authority. Its use was reserved for the head of the household and honoured guests. Seating for those of lower rank was in the form of stools and benches, and even chests.

One of the earliest types of chair made for ordinary domestic use evolved from the chest. The back stiles were extended upwards to head height, and the back and sides were panelled. Developing from this, the lid of the chest became a fixed seat, and the panelled sides of the chest disappeared so that the seat was supported on four legs.

Another precursor of the square-framed chair was the stool: the trestle stool with solid end uprights and the joint stool. This had four turned legs attached with mortise and tenon joints to rails at the top, and at the bottom to stretchers. The seat was fixed with wooden pegs. The English backstool was a natural evolution from the joint stool, the back stiles extending upwards and linked by a panel or carved back rails.

The X-frame chair, equally, was developed from the stool: in this case a stool of the light, folding type known as a 'fold-stool' illustrated in manuscripts of the tenth century. By the seventeenth century some X-frame chairs were made with fixed parts.

Left: English upholstered and painted oak X-frame chair of state, c.1610. The upholstered X-frame chair derived from a type of Medieval folding stool with the back and seat of leather or canvas. This would originally have been accompanied by a footstool and two flanking stools, similarly upholstered.
Below: English joint stool of carved and turned oak with legs of fluted baluster form, sixteenth century. Visible here are the dowels securing the mortise and tenon joints.

In the course of the sixteenth century greater emphasis began to be placed on comfort. To this upholstery made an important contribution (see p.28). Altering the angle of the chair back from the vertical to a more relaxing inclining position was one improvement, which usually involved sloping the back legs backwards; another was to shape the back to suit the curve of the sitter's back.

The shape of the seat was also altered, becoming narrower at the back. An early example of this feature is to be found on a type of sixteenth-century French chair known as a '*caquetoire*', because it was popular with ladies who wished to gossip and chatter (*caqueter*). Round seats were introduced in the seventeenth century in Dutch, so-called 'Burgomeister', chairs.

Caning for seats and chair backs was made from split rattan imported into Europe from the Malay peninsular. It was first used by the Dutch, who by the seventeenth century had established profitable trading connections with the East.

Since the sixteenth century numerous different types of chair have been devised. Their manufacture involved the skills of joining, turning, carving or bending (see p.26), or a combination of these. National or regional differences depend chiefly on the type of timber employed; constructional features such as the point at which the top rail was joined to the back uprights and the legs to the back uprights and seat rail, and whether or not angle blocks were used to strengthen the seat frame from behind; and the manner in which the chair was decorated.

Particular attention was paid to the design of the back and the legs. A type of leg introduced in the seventeenth century and popular throughout Europe and in America in the eighteenth century was the cabriole. Resembling a goat's hind leg, the upper part swells out at the knee and the curve swings in towards the foot, where it flares out again. Different forms of foot include the turned bun, the paw, claw-and-ball and the scroll. The leg was formed from a piece of timber of square section, and it involved considerable wastage of the material. A template was used to saw the four sides to the required outline curve. The remaining shaping was done with a

Above: English caquetoire *in the French style, late sixteenth or early seventeenth century. The chair is made of dark Brazilian mahogany, also known as 'cherry mahogany' or 'bullet-wood'. Distinctive features of the* caquetoire *are the splayed seat, narrow back and arms which bow outwards.*
Left: American mahogany settee, 1800–15. Settees with caned seats and backs, based on the English model, are characteristic of the seat furniture produced in the Federal period. It has fine carving on the back and arms, and on the legs, and it would originally have been fitted with a long seat cushion, perhaps with two cylindrical cushions placed parallel with the arms at each end.

spokeshave and rasp, and the detail was carved (see p.47).

A technique for shaping timber used in chair-making was bending. The advantages of bending timber were that there was less wastage of timber than in the processes of sawing or carving from the solid, or turning, and that the finished piece was comparatively strong because the grain ran along the length of the bend.

Originally saplings were used on account of their suppleness. They were bent by tying their ends together until the wood had dried. Later it was found that mature timber could be used if it were first boiled or steamed. It was shaped around a template in a 'former', which resembled a peg-board, and either it was left in the former until it had dried or the ends were tied together as before and the piece removed to dry.

A subsequent development was to use a steel strap in place of the pegs and wedges. The strap, with two handles attached, was placed behind the piece of timber and used to pull the

timber against the former. This method reduced the number of breakages as the strap applied pressure evenly along the length of the timber.

Normally the timber was bent in the rough and shaped with a spokeshave or draw-knife when it was dry. Varieties of timber that bend well are ash, elm, yew, birch, oak, beech, hickory and walnut. Sometimes it was necessary to shape the curve in two or three stages.

An example of a component shaped by bending is the bow back of a Windsor chair. In Britain the earliest reference to a Windsor chair dates from the late seventeenth century. Simple in design and economical in the making, it was quite unlike the highly carved, ornate chairs of that period. Locally grown timber was employed, and it was common for three or four different timbers to be used for a single chair. As their popularity increased, better-quality chairs were made in yew and mahogany.

Below: English and American types of Windsor chair.
Right: American comb-back Windsor chair, with drawers in the arm and under the seat, attributed to E. B. Tracy, Connecticut, c.1780–1800. The chair was originally painted green, a traditional colour for Windsor chairs.

EARLY COMB BACK

FAN BACK

AMERICAN ROD BACK

WIDE COMB BACK

AMERICAN ARROW BACK

AMERICAN ARCH BACK

MAKING A COUNTRY CHAIR
1. The seat was hollowed out with an adze, the workman securing the work with his feet and swinging the blade towards him.
2. The timber for the bow back was boiled or steamed and bent around a 'former'.
3. The bow back, central splat – cut with a bow saw – and sticks on either side of it were assembled, holes having been drilled in the bow back and in the seat.

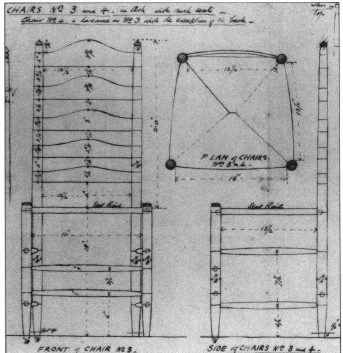

Left: American Shaker ladderback armchair, mid-nineteenth century. Furniture made in the Shaker communities was spare and unornamented, and simple in construction. The slatted back, which is a feature of most of the chairs that were produced commercially, was based on a traditional English farmhouse type.
Above: Design for rush-seated turned chairs by Ernest W. Gimson (1864– 1919), English, 1904. This is a measured drawing, in ink on tracing paper, giving the full-size details for the chairs. *Gimson rarely made furniture himself, but from designs such as this craftsmen at his workshop at Sapperton in Gloucestershire were able to carry out his ideas.*

Windsor chairs became popular in America in the middle of the eighteenth century, although their existence was recorded at the beginning of the century. In Britain they were made for poor to middle-class households, but in America they appeared in the homes of the rich as well.

A characteristic feature of the Windsor chair is the solid seat. It could be up to 2 inches (5 cm) thick and was the basis on which the whole chair was constructed. Holes were drilled underneath to take the legs, and on the top to take the back spindles and arms. As the holes were round, the assembly of the chair was similar to that of dowelling. Sometimes the holes in the seat were drilled right through and the ends of the legs and spindles split and wedged when fitted to ensure a secure fit; sometimes they were fox wedged, which meant that the hole was not drilled right through and the wedge was placed in the leg before hammering home. The seat was hollowed out with an adze, the hollow part being known as the 'saddle'.

The legs were generally turned, but some better-quality Windsor chairs had cabriole legs at the front. Turned work was generally in the form of a simple vase shape with beads top and bottom. Eventually stretchers were added to the legs to give them more strength – usually three forming an H, all being thicker in the centre than at the ends. A minor variation was the 'cow-horn', or 'crinoline', stretcher. This joined the two front legs in a deep backward curve to accommodate the fashion for wide skirts.

The principal variations are to be found in the shapes of the backs – not all of them formed by bending – and the 'splats'. These were flat centrepieces replacing one or two spindles. Splats were often vase shaped in outline and pierced. A paper or wooden pattern was used, and the design was cut with a bow saw.

The manufacture of the Windsor chair started as a cottage industry, one man making the complete chair. Later, the work was generally shared between several craftsmen: the turner who turned the legs, stretchers and back spindles; the workman who shaped the seats (known in parts of England as the 'bottomer'); the workman who did the bending; the benchman who sawed the splats and arms; the framer who assembled the parts; the workman who did the finishing. This pattern of work led in the nineteenth century to mass production.

UPHOLSTERY

Seat furniture in the Middle Ages was often covered with material. Sometimes it was loosely covered giving a draped effect, and occasionally the folds were attached to the frame by nails. By 1600 fixed upholstery had developed in which the use of large dome-headed nails, braid and short fringes were combined to hold the top cover in place. The fabric was much more important than the woodwork: for grand chairs needle-work, damask, satin, velvet, taffeta, and cloth of gold and silver were all used as top covers, while simpler seats could be covered with a range of woollen and worsted materials. 'Turkeywork', a pile fabric made in England in imitation of Oriental carpets and exported to the Continent and America, was popular from the early seventeenth century, and, from about 1640, leather.

Trimmings were suited to the materials of the top covers so that silk, silver and silver-gilt fringes and braids were used for grander chairs and wool or worsted for simpler ones. The nails would often be brass and, for grander chairs, they might be gilded and arranged in decorative patterns.

From the mid-seventeenth century upholstery covers and trimmings changed as new ideas on comfort and fashion were developed in Holland and France. Lavish silks, damasks, brocades and Italian cut velvets were used, and with them elaborate fringes, galloons (gold or silver threads), tassels and braids. A greater understanding of upholstery techniques produced more sophisticated effects, and for the first time seat furniture was upholstered to match the bed hangings in grand apartments, a fashion which originated in France.

From the 1680s until about 1730 the coverings of rich material on grand chairs were detachable and made in two parts. They slipped over the back and seat and were held in place with hooks and eyes at the corners or, later with tabs and eyelets which hooked on to studs under the seat rail. These covers, which were removed and stored when the furniture was not in use in order to protect them, were to develop into the loose protective covers of the later eighteenth century. In France in the eighteenth century there was strict court etiquette governing the correct moment for their removal, which usually depended on the rank of those present. The covers were made of rich fabrics with elaborate trimmings, or of lighter fabrics, and they were intended to go over the permanent coverings.

The rise in popularity of needlework seat covers coincided with the introduction of the winged armchair in the early eighteenth century. From the 1730s there was a great increase in the variety of worsted fabrics, and new fabrics such as caffoy, calamanco and worsted damask all began to appear. Seat furniture with open backs was, from the 1750s, uphol-stered either in horsehair, now available as a woven fabric, or in leather, particularly for dining-rooms, or in chintz for chairs with painted decoration. Pattern books, published in increas-ing numbers in the 1750s and 1760s, gave basic guidelines on upholstery, particularly on close nailing and tufting patterns.

In the early eighteenth century a single row of nails was used to fix the top covers, following the line of the frame. In the middle of the century double close nailing became fashionable, with two rows of nails around the seat rails and outlining the backs. The nailing was usually done over a tape to prevent damage to the cover. In England the nails usually had circular domed heads, while in France a variety of shapes was used.

Left: English settee with needlework upholstery, c.1745. The fabric on seat furniture was often valued more highly than the woodwork.
Above: French open armchair upholstered in green velvet, with large decorative silvered nails and tassels of red, green and yellow silk, mid-seventeenth century. This is a grand example of a type of chair typically shown in Jacobean portraits.

An alternative, used in England, France and America, was a decorative metal strip around the edge of the seat.

In England and America from about 1740 tufts similar to those used on mattresses began to be used to conceal the stitches keeping the padding of the upholstery in place. These would otherwise have shown through the top cover. Tufting did not produce a deep quilted effect as in nineteenth-century buttoning, of which it was a forerunner, but made shallow indentations in the surface of the chair back and seat. Tufting was mainly confined to top covers of a single colour; on needlework covers it would have distorted the design.

During the Middle Ages cushions were used to alleviate the discomfort of hard wooden or stone seats, and at a later date in Italy and Spain chairs were sometimes fitted with fixed padding with the stitching arranged in decorative patterns. An alternative was loose padding in the form of quilted covers, which also existed before 1600, the covers secured by tapes or ribbons. It was not until the sixteenth century, however, that upholstered chairs became common.

There were two basic types of upholstered chair: X-framed and square framed. The sixteenth-century version of the X-framed chair was more solid than the Medieval one, with a firm back rail and an upholstered seat of a rudimentary form. The square-framed chair, later called a 'backstool', or 'farthingale' chair, originally had a completely unpadded back with just a piece of cloth stretched between the uprights or a very lightly padded area under the cloth. It was comparatively easy to pile a mass of stuffing (straw, feathers or hair) on to the seat and hold it down with a cover nailed round the seat. This produced a domed effect, which later in the seventeenth century was

Left: French fauteuil, *or armchair, with a drop-in seat and tapestry upholstery, mid-eighteenth century. Above: English chair in the French style with red silk damask upholstery, c.1760. The tufts concealed the stitches which kept the stuffing in place, and they were also a decorative* feature. *Usually arranged in alternate rows of three, two and three, the centre tuft of the top row was sometimes raised to follow the line of the shaped chair rail, as here. Below: English day-bed with Genoa velvet upholstery, c.1695.*

occasionally shaped with squared edges. On chairs of the farthingale type a gap was always left between the bottom of the back and the top of the seat, and, while the uprights of the back were covered to match the main upholstery, the lower framework of the legs and the stretchers were normally left uncovered, although they were sometimes painted and gilded on grand chairs.

There were great technical advances from 1660, and by 1700 all the techniques employed in seat upholstery up to the early twentieth century – except springing – had been devised. However, methods were still crude and it was not until the later eighteenth century that sophisticated effects were achieved by shaping stuffing.

European and American practices varied slightly, but the basic method used to upholster a chair – which could be elaborated for sofas – was to start with a lattice of webbing nailed across the seat frame. This was fixed under stress to achieve a taut effect. Webbing was formed of strips of woven hemp – normally its natural unbleached colour, although in the eighteenth century coloured threads were sometimes introduced. The strips were usually about 2 inches (5 cm) wide and positioned so as to form a lattice with square spaces in between on English chairs. In France wider strips, usually

about 4 inches (10 cm) wide, were laid side by side and interwoven with no spaces between which gave a stronger support. These differences are quite obvious on eighteenth-century seat furniture and may well have existed before 1700. In America leather was occasionally used instead of webbing, and in some country-made pieces in England and elsewhere in Europe lengths of rope were used.

Padding – usually curled horsehair but sometimes sheep's wool, chaff, hay, straw or shavings – was built up in a thicker layer along the front seat rail, where it was most vulnerable to pressure, in the form of a roll enclosed in linen. The roll was attached to the rail and stitched firmly around the top to give a solid edge. Smaller rolls were then placed along the other rails and the central well filled with loose horsehair, which was tied down to the webbing. The hair was covered with a piece of linen or canvas which was tacked down to the side rails, firstly at the back so that the hair could be given its final shape, then down the sides and around any arm supports and finally across the front. Although there was a fashion in England at the end of the eighteenth century for double layers of stuffing, each under a linen or canvas cover, the introduction of a layer of wadding immediately under the top cover was a nineteenth-century innovation so that last-minute adjustments could be

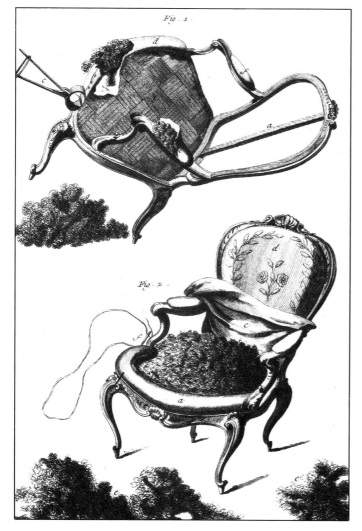

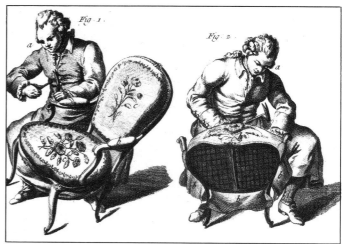

Left: Illustration from Diderot's Encyclopédie, *1751–72. It shows the webbing attached to the chair frame interlaced to form a solid layer and the curled horsehair enclosed in linen which was used to pad the front rail, where the most pressure was exerted. (Fig. 1). Horsehair was also used as the filling for the central well, and a piece of material its shown ready to be tacked down over this (Fig. 2).*
Above: Illustration from the Encyclopédie *showing the upholsterer nailing the seat covers.*
Right: English chair, c.1760. The seat is cut away to show the original stuffing. The front roll, with its linen cover folded back, is made of straw; the hair in the centre well is cut back to show the webbing. The horsehair cover and nails are modern copies of the original ones.

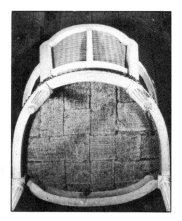

Right: French fauteuil *with needlework upholstery, c.1690. The long fringes around the seat, together with the continuing use of large nails and braid, were features characteristic of that period. Large-scale embroideries were particularly suited to chair backs of such grand dimensions.*
Above: Underside of a French fauteuil, *late eighteenth century. The wide strips of woven hemp, laid with no spaces between them, typifies the French method of webbing. Also shown is the original checked material, which hid the webbing, on to which the stuffing and covering of the back were mounted.*

made to the shape of the stuffing.

Chair and sofa backs were upholstered in the same way but required less webbing, and the padding was attached to canvas or linen nailed to the back. Drop-in seats and backs, popular from the early eighteenth century, were stuffed in the same way but did not require the roll along the front rail since the upholstery fitted inside the frame.

In France from the 1750s seat furniture tended to be fitted with alternative coverings for the different seasons. Loose seats, backs and armrests were all made so that they were removable, enabling their covers to be changed.

The main development in seat upholstery in the early nineteenth century was the introduction of the spring. Patents were taken out from as early as 1707. Spiral springs were adopted experimentally by upholsterers for seat furniture in the 1820s in England, France and Austria, and by the following decade they had generally superseded the traditional form of stuffing.

THE CRAFT OF THE CABINET-MAKER

The 'cabinet' is a piece of furniture that originated in Italy in the early sixteenth century. In one of its earliest forms it was an oblong box, fitted with drawers and closed with doors, which stood on a table. The small size of the drawers suggests that they were intended for jewellery and other precious objects.

In Italy and in the Low Countries the cabinet gradually became more elaborate, developing into a work of art in its own right as well as an object for the storage and display of valuables. It now had its own base in the form of legs or a stand, and the top had drawers and doors and alcoves, or pigeon-holes. In the Low Countries carved or painted panels were sometimes incorporated, and there might be doors which opened to reveal the highly ornamented interiors. Italian examples were more often enriched with ivory and tortoiseshell, silver, copper and brass inlays, and panels of *pietre dure*. Produced by the Opificio delle Pietre Dure in Florence, these were made up of small pieces of hardstone such as rock crystal, lapis lazuli and chalcedony, ground to shape and arranged in decorative patterns.

By the mid-seventeenth century in Italy, the Low Countries and Germany there were craftsmen who had mastered the techniques of 'veneering' (see p.36), in which thin sheets of wood and other materials were glued on to a solid carcase, and 'marquetry' (see p.39), a veneer composed of interlocking pieces forming a pattern. Veneering permitted the most economical use of rare and expensive timbers and also types or cuts of timber which in the solid were unstable. It became possible, for example, to exploit the decorative qualities of fragile sheets of cross grain in a technique known as 'oystering'.

Later in the century such cabinets were imported into France. Italian and Flemish craftsmen were commissioned to carry out work, notably for the two cardinals, Richelieu and Mazarin, and Frenchmen were sent abroad to learn the foreigners' skills. The new type of furniture that resulted in France from the introduction of designs and expertise was often veneered in ebony, and for this reason the makers became known as '*ébénistes*'.

With the restoration of the monarchy in 1660 England, too, was open to influences from the Low Countries. Makers of the new and grander furniture, the principal characteristic of which was the use of walnut veneers, became known as 'cabinet-makers'. The work of an *ébéniste* was comparable, therefore, to the work of a cabinet-maker, both making pieces that were beyond the capabilities of a joiner (although in France the distinction between the *menuisier* and the *ébéniste* was not formally recognized until 1745, and until the Revolution they belonged to the same guild).

A successful cabinet-maker took on several assistants in his workshop. André-Charles Boulle in France, Thomas Chippendale in England and Duncan Phyfe in America had working for them craftsmen – journeymen and apprentices – who specia-

Above: Flemish cabinet on stand of carved ebony and ebonized wood, late seventeenth century. Ebony, a heavy tropical wood, was also used as a veneer in cabinet-work. Ebonized wood is wood stained black in imitation of ebony.
Right: French marquetry cabinet, c.1690. Pewter and ivory were used in combination with various woods to create a strongly pictorial effect.

lized in a single aspect of furniture-making such as turning, joining, gilding and silvering, and veneering. It is hard to judge to what extent any of these three was involved in the manufacture of a particular piece. Thomas Sheraton in his *Cabinet Dictionary* of 1803 observed that the quality of cabinet work depended on the state of the timber that was used, the ability of the workmen and the directions that were given to them. It was certainly the master himself who discussed with the patron details of the commission – in Chippendale's case no doubt referring him to designs in *The Gentleman and Cabinet-Maker's Director* first published by him in 1754 – and, on acceptance of the estimate for the work, it was he who instructed the craftsmen.

From the seventeenth century onwards pattern books were important as sources of ideas for cabinet-makers. The fact that a piece might resemble a published design by, for example, Boulle or Chippendale, the German Johann Michael Hoppenhaupt or the Italian Giovanni Battista Piranesi certainly does not imply that it was made by the designer, or in his workshop. In the main the books served to illustrate current fashions in the form and decoration of furniture, though in the case of Sheraton's *The Cabinet-Maker and Upholsterer's Drawing Book*, 1791–94, precise instructions were given as to how the pieces were to be constructed. It is, indeed, unlikely that Sheraton practised as a cabinet-maker, and the same is true of Hoppenhaupt and Piranesi.

Left: French ormolu-mounted cabinet by Claude-Charles Saunier inset with panels of Florentine pietre dure, c.1780. Pietre dure was a type of 'mosaic' of hardstones such as lapis lazuli, chalcedony, jasper and porphyry. A workshop employing Milanese and local craftsmen was set up in Florence in the 1580s which continued in production into the nineteenth century. The made-up panels were supplied to cabinet-makers in various European countries.
Above: Roman kingwood-veneered bureau cabinet, mid-eighteenth century. The technique of applying thin sheets of wood to the surface of a piece of furniture is of ancient origin. Revived in the Low Countries in the seventeenth century, it was one of the essential cabinet-making skills.

MAKING THE CARCASE

In cabinet-work, the form of a piece of case furniture was determined by the way in which the 'carcase', or framework to which the veneer would be applied, was constructed. Pine was commonly used for carcasing, and also oak. Oak was the timber most frequently used for drawer linings as it is hard and so able to withstand wear caused by friction.

In constructing the carcase it was important to provide a stable and smooth base for the veneer, with close-fitting joints, and this was dependent on the technique of dovetailing. The dovetail served to join two broad, flat pieces of timber, normally at right angles to each other. It was used to join the front and back to the sides of some solid furniture of the sixteenth century, and from the early seventeenth century it was used in drawer construction and to join the sides to the top and base of a carcase.

The dovetail joint comprises two interlocking parts: 'tails', which resemble in section the fan shape of a dove's tail, and 'pins', the narrower of the two. The taper on both the tails and the pins is described as the 'pitch', 'bevel' or 'rake'. This was varied according to the softness or hardness of the timber and the strength required of the joint. The softer the timber and the greater the required strength, the wider the angle.

On drawer sides, the earliest dovetail joints were arranged two to a side, and they were often pinned for additional stability. Gradually the number was increased, and the space between them decreased. From the simple 'through' dovetail there developed the 'lap' dovetail, the 'double-lap' dovetail and the 'secret' dovetail, and variations of these basic types.

One variation of the lap dovetail was the 'carcase' dovetail, used to give a strong joint when a side rail was joined by mortise and tenon to a table leg and a front rail was to be attached horizontally to the leg for the purpose of inserting a drawer. Because of the difference in thickness, the two tails had to be offset. Another variation was the 'slot', or 'slip', dovetail. This was mainly used to give strength to plinths, frames and cornices, where the joint needed to be hidden from one side.

The through dovetail was the type most commonly used for the backs of drawers, and the lap or double-lap dovetail for drawer fronts. Because a veneer would not adhere permanently to end grain, the double-lap dovetail was the most suitable type of joint where both pieces of timber were to be veneered. The 'secret mitre' dovetail was used only in high-quality work, where the finish was of great importance. Care had to be taken to cut the mitre accurately, so ensuring that no gaps were visible. In the late nineteenth century some designers made use of hand-cut through dovetails as a decorative feature by varying the size of the tails and pins. Machine-cut dovetails of that date are easily recognized because the pins are identical in size to the tails and the pitch at a more acute angle than in hand-cut dovetails.

To make the carcase for bow-fronted (single curve), serpentine-fronted (convex centre and concave ends) and *bombé* (convex on two or more axes) furniture, a type of construction known as 'block building' was common. Small pieces of timber resembling bricks were built up, keeping the grain at a tangent to the curve, then smoothed to the required shape and veneered on the outer surface. This avoided the problems caused by end grain, and was less wasteful of timber than cutting a deep curve from the solid.

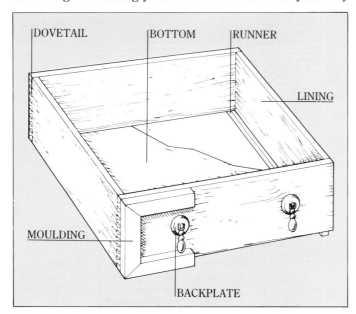

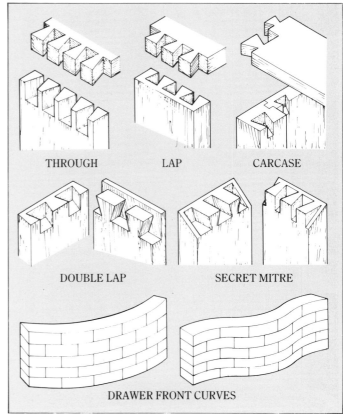

THROUGH   LAP   CARCASE

DOUBLE LAP   SECRET MITRE

DRAWER FRONT CURVES

Above: Typical English drawer construction of c.1790. The front is veneered and has an applied moulding and two brass drop-handles. The sides are joined with lap dovetails to the front and through dovetails to the back. Attached to the bottom is a runner to separate the drawer from the dust board.

Right above: Dovetail joints used in cabinet-making.
Right: Carcase construction for bow- and serpentine-fronted and bombé pieces. An alternative to cutting a curve from solid timber is 'block building', with overlapping rows of small pieces of timber veneered at the front and back.

Left: Through dovetail joining the front to the side of a cypress wood cassone intagliata, *the decoration in penwork with the background cut away, Italian, seventeenth century. The screws are later additions.*
Above: *American semi-circular commode by Thomas Seymour*

(1771–1848), 1809. *The carcase of veneered pieces with a pronounced curve to the front were generally block built. This commode is based on a design by Sheraton.*
Below: *Illustration of a cabinet-maker's workshop from Diderot's* Encyclopédie.

VENEERING

The technique of applying thin sheets of fine wood – in particular ebony – to a ground of coarser wood was known to the Ancient Egyptians, and also to the Greeks and Romans: veneering as a means of using expensive timber sparingly and economically was recommended by Pliny in 77 AD.

In the seventeenth and eighteenth centuries logs were sawn into veneers of $\frac{1}{8}$ to $\frac{1}{16}$ inch (0·3 to 0·6 mm) thickness, some of the timber being lost as sawdust in the process. Jacob-André Roubo in *Art du Menuisier* of 1772 illustrated two veneer cutters at work using a saw in a rectangular frame.

Cutting along the length of the grain in this way produced a 'straight-cut' veneer. A more interesting figure was obtained by cutting across the grain ('cross-cut' veneer), a method which caused greater wastage of timber; or by cutting timber from a fork where the grain divides ('curl' veneer), transversely through a branch or narrow tree trunk ('oyster' veneer) or through an irregular growth or deformity from the trunk or roots of a tree such as walnut, ash, elm, maple or yew ('burr', or 'burl', veneer). The timber for curl, oyster and burr veneers was harder to come by, the sheets had to be cut

Left: English kingwood-veneered chest of drawers, c.1685. The drawers are cross-banded at the edges, and the front of the carcase has an applied 'cushion', or D-shaped, moulding.
Above: Detail from the front of a French mahogany and oyster-veneered fruitwood bureau in the manner of Hache of Grenoble. Pieces of veneer with oval markings resembling oyster shells were cut from the small branches of the tree transversely at an oblique angle.

slightly thicker to make them strong enough to be used and, when cut, they were generally of smaller dimensions than straight and cross-cut veneers. All this contributed to the higher cost of the more decorative veneers. Cabinet-makers would usually use straight-cut veneers on the sides of a piece – or even, in the case of mahogany furniture, solid wood – reserving the more expensive veneers for the front and top.

The differences in the figure on veneers cut in successive sheets from the same piece of timber were very slight and a variety of patterns could be achieved by matching, reversing, pairing and quartering the figure. Veneered table-tops and drawer fronts would often be bordered with a banding. In 'straight' banding the grain of the veneer went the way of the grain; in 'cross' banding the grain went across the grain; in 'feather', or 'herringbone', banding two strips of veneer were laid side by side with the grain of each running diagonally.

Before a sheet of veneer was used it was soaked in water for several hours and then pressed between two boards clamped together with paper protecting each surface. After two or three days the sheet would have dried flat.

The ground was prepared by working the surface with a toothing plane, which smoothed out any serious irregularities and at the same time roughened it. A thin coating of size (a weak solution of animal glue and water) would then be applied, providing a surface to which the glue would readily adhere. The size was left to dry for several hours before hot glue was brushed on.

A method of cutting and joining inconspicuously two sheets of veneer was by overlapping the edges and gluing them together, then cutting through both with a fretsaw in a straight or wavy line. When the excess wood was removed, the sheets

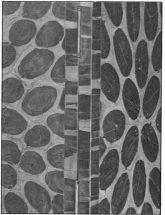

Above: French kingwood- and tulipwood-veneered secrétaire cartonnier, c.1740. This has a roll, or 'tambour', front made up of narrow strips of wood attached to a canvas backing. The carcase is made of oak, and the fall front is quarter veneered.
Left: English rosewood-veneered breakfast table inlaid with brass, c.1820. The circular centre is veneered with four sheets of rosewood cut from the same piece of timber.
Right: English oyster-veneered laburnum wood cabinet on stand, c.1685. The joins between the different pieces of veneer are almost imperceptible.

could be laid flat and side by side on the ground.

To remove all surplus glue and air bubbles from between the ground and the veneer, the surface was worked with a veneering hammer. This had a metal blade at right angles to the handle, and it was pushed across the veneer in a zig-zag motion. Once the glue was completely dry, the edges were trimmed and the surface sanded ready for polishing (see p.50). On curving surfaces sandbags were often used to weigh down the veneer until the glue had dried.

Another method of laying the veneer, employed especially for marquetry, was by 'cauling'. The 'caul', a piece of timber slightly larger than the surface to be veneered, was heated and clamped down. By placing bearers with convex undersides on top of the caul, the greatest pressure was exerted at the centre of the veneer. As the cramps were tightened, the excess glue – liquefied by the heat from the caul – was squeezed outwards towards the edges.

Left: Illustration from Art du Menuisier *by Jacob-André Roubo, 1772.*
Above: English olive wood oyster-veneered cabinet supported on a stand *with turned barley-twist legs, seventeenth century. The design, and then the cutting and assembly of the pieces of veneer involved a considerable amount of time.*

VENEERING

1. The ground was prepared using a toothing plane, which scored the surface. It was then coated with size to seal the pores.
2. Two sheets of veneer were laid so that they overlapped. Animal glue was applied with a brush and spreader to the ground and the veneer.
3. The surface was worked with a veneering hammer, forcing excess glue and air bubbles outwards to the edges.
4. To finish the join, both thicknesses were cut through, with the knife held against a straight edge. The upper and lower waste strips were then removed.
5. In quarter-veneering, four sheets of veneer, cut in sequence and with two of the sheets reversed, were glued and butted together to form a pattern.
6. Elaborate patterns were affixed to the ground by the process of 'cauling'. A heated caul, or flat piece of wood, was laid on top of the veneer and cramped down over bearers. The convex underside of the bearers applied pressure at the centre, and the liquefied glue was forced outwards.

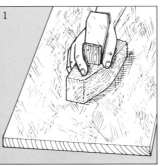

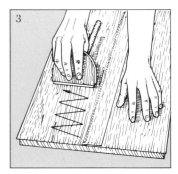

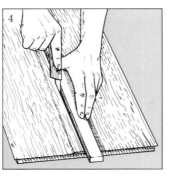

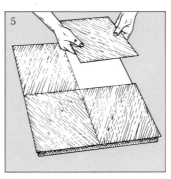

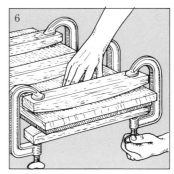

INLAY AND MARQUETRY

Marquetry is a veneer made up of interlocking pieces of wood – and sometimes other materials such as ivory, tortoiseshell and metal – forming a pattern. The effectiveness of the process depends on the selection of veneers to form an interesting contrast of colours when laid down side by side on the ground and the design itself.

The techniques involved in marquetry cutting and laying were entirely different from inlaying, as practised in many European countries in the fifteenth and sixteenth centuries. With this type of decoration, indentations were made in the solid wood by chiselling or gouging with a long-handled shoulder-knife. These were then filled with small pieces of appropriately shaped wood of various colours.

Remarkable effects of perspective and illusion were achieved by this method, notably by the monks of Monte Oliveto, near Siena. Certosina work, executed in Lombardy and in and around Venice, consisted of small pieces of bone inset in geometric patterns. In England, holly, box, yew, sycamore and other native woods were used in inlay on 'Nonsuch' chests – so-named because the designs, of an architectural character, were thought to represent Henry VIII's palace of Nonsuch. The craftsmen are thought to have come from Germany, where a similar type of decoration is found on furniture.

In creating a panel of marquetry one of the first steps was to make copies of the original design. The outlines of the design were pricked on to a sheet of paper beneath or, alternatively, a dark powder was dusted through the pinholes on to the underlying paper. This process was repeated as many times as was necessary to make the required number of copies.

The selected veneers were glued or pinned together, often with a sheet of paper between each so that the layers were easy to separate later. A piece of inexpensive timber might be glued to each side to prevent the saw making ragged cuts on the exposed faces, and a copy of the design was then glued to the top surface.

The 'sandwich' consisting of sheets of veneer, paper and protective timber was held in the 'donkey' (see p. 6). This had a foot-operated clamp, which gripped the sandwich in a vertical position; instead of altering the direction of the saw as he worked, the marquetry-cutter held the saw in a horizontal plane and manoeuvred the sandwich. The donkey replaced the simple sawing-table that was used up until the middle of the eighteenth century. The saw-frame was a modification to the donkey introduced later in the century. It was a frame attached to the side which enabled the saw to be guided more precisely

Far left: Panel inlaid with various woods executed by Fra Raffaelle de Brescia to the design of Giovanni Battista da Imola, Italian, 1521–25. Remarkable effects of illusionism were obtained in intarsia, *or inlay, by Italian craftsmen of the sixteenth century. This panel formed part of the decoration of a choir stall in a church in Bologna.*
Above: English coffer of oak inlaid with bog oak and cherry wood, late sixteenth century. Chests of this type are known as 'Nonsuch' chests because the design of the building with castellations, a high-pitched roof, cupolas and steeples was said to represent Henry VIII's palace of Nonsuch at Ewell in Surrey.
Left: Detail of the inlaid decoration from the chest.

rigid. Setting the saw at a slight angle as it cut along the lines of the pattern reduced the gap between the interlocking parts when they were laid.

When the cutting operation had been completed, the veneers were separated with a thin knife. All but one of the layers would be superfluous for each element of the design. After the pieces had been assembled and coated on the reverse with glue, a sheet of paper was laid over the surface and the veneers fixed firmly to the base wood, generally by the process of cauling.

In marquetry the colour of the veneers was of great importance to the design. Some craftsmen chose woods for their natural colouring, but others augmented the range by bleaching, tinting and shading to emphasize the design. By the mid-eighteenth century in France marquetry panels were described as 'paintings in wood', the remarkable pictorial effects being achieved by the use of dyed materials. The colours were once startlingly bright, but over a period of two centuries they are usually found to have faded and mellowed through exposure to daylight.

In representing in a realistic manner figurative scenes and the appearance of architecture and still-life objects it was essential to understand the rules of perspective and, according to Roubo, it was important to position marquetry furniture in a room so that any shadows that were depicted appeared life-like. When a piece was not destined for a particular position, he recommended that the centre of each panel should be the focus of the light. A final detail was to enrich the surface with hatched lines and stippling. At the same date three-dimensional geometric patterns were reproduced with the same degree of realism. The arrangement of pieces of veneer in a geometric pattern is sometimes referred to as 'parquetry', a term properly used in connection with the laying of floors.

Of an entirely different character was the type of marquetry now known as 'seaweed' marquetry, produced in Holland and England in the late seventeenth century. The design was generally a repeating pattern, executed in only two contrasting woods against a light-coloured background. The effect is comparable to the contrast of materials in Boulle marquetry.

Essentially English was a form of decoration developed at Tunbridge Wells in Kent and used to decorate boxes and other small objects. Pieces of wood of various natural colours were glued together into a solid block so that, in section, they formed a pattern. By slicing across these, sheets of an identical pattern were produced which could be used as a veneer.

Far left: English walnut-veneered bureau *cabinet inset with seaweed marquetry of walnut and sycamore, c.1690.*
Left: Detail of the seaweed marquetry. It was executed entirely in dark and light woods and resembled the intricate designs of Boulle marquetry. It was popular in the Low Countries and in England.
Above: Top of a Tunbridge ware box, English, early nineteenth century. The pattern in Tunbridge ware was made by gluing together small lengths of wood of matchstick thickness and cutting across them transversely. Thirty or so identical designs could be formed by this method.

*Above: Italian marquetry table-top,
c.1850. The design was quartered, so
enabling the four sections to be cut as
a single 'sandwich'. Mother of pearl
and ivory were used as well as
various natural and stained woods.
Left: English marquetry cushion-
frame mirror, c.1680. The veneer
was bonded to the solid wood carcase
using bags of warm sand to weigh it
down until the glue had dried.
Below: Italian marquetry top from
a games table by Luigi Galmelli,*
*c.1808. Since there is no repeating
pattern in the design of the centre, the
pieces of veneer would have been cut
individually.*

BOULLE MARQUETRY

Marquetry composed of brass and tortoiseshell arranged in an intricate pattern, the decorative effect heightened by the contrast in the colour and character of the materials, is associated with André-Charles Boulle, *maître-ébéniste* to Louis XIV. Boulle perfected rather than devised the technique that bears his name: in Paris there were several workshops other than his own where this type of work was undertaken.

In *première-partie* marquetry the background is tortoiseshell and the design in brass; in *contre-partie* marquetry the materials are reversed and the design is in tortoiseshell against a brass background. Pairs of commodes (chests of drawers of French design) and pedestals were veneered with marquetry, one in *première-partie* and the other in *contre-partie*; it was also

possible to combine the two parts in a single piece. Other materials that were used included ebony and pewter.

Two commodes at Versailles with marquetry in brass and dark tortoiseshell are the only documented examples of Boulle's work. No contemporary record survives of the working practices of his workshop, or of any workshop in Paris producing marquetry of a similar kind in the late seventeenth and early eighteenth century. It is generally believed that the sheets of brass and tortoiseshell were cut as a 'sandwich'. One material would have supported the other, and the metal would have helped to prevent bending and cracking of the shell as the complex shapes were cut with a saw. It is possible, though, that the materials were of such different consistency that this

Left: Back of a toilet mirror attributed to André-Charles Boulle (1642–1732), French, early eighteenth century. The mirror is framed and backed with oak and veneered with marquetry of engraved brass and tortoiseshell. This is an example of première-partie *marquetry, with the design of Love beneath a canopy, figures, arabesques and scrolls executed in brass and the background in tortoiseshell.*
Above: Detail from the convex side of an inkstand attributed to Boulle, 1710. The breaks in the brass make clear the size of the pieces of veneer. The engraving on the surface would have been done when the pieces of brass and tortoiseshell had been assembled and glued to the carcase.

BOULLE MARQUETRY

1. The shell was prepared by boiling it, then, while it was supple, pressing it flat.

2. The underside of the shell was scraped. Often it was coated with pigmented glue – brown or black, or more rarely green, red or blue, according to the colour that was required to show through the natural pigmentation of the shell.

3. A 'sandwich' was made with a layer of shell and a layer of brass in the centre; on top was a copy of a section of the design and, underneath, a sheet of paper which would form a bridge between the pigmented glue and the glue bonding the marquetry to the carcase.

4. The sandwich was secured in a 'donkey' and cut with a fretsaw.

5. The layers were separated and the pieces of brass and shell fitted together and glued to the carcase.

6. After any engraving of the brass or shell had been done, the surface was polished with increasingly fine abrasives, the finest being charcoal.

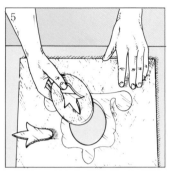
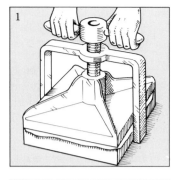

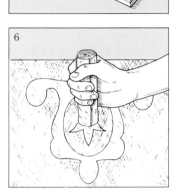
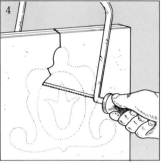

method would have been impracticable until the middle of the eighteenth century, when finer quality tools were developed. The sandwich method was certainly used in the manufacture of later Boulle marquetry.

The 'tortoiseshell' was in fact turtle's shell, and the finest shells came from the island of Coiba in the Pacific. The dry shells would be split into large scales and the pale areas selected for their translucency. These were boiled to make them supple and placed in a press until dry to produce a flat sheet. Joins in the shells were generally concealed in the design, but occasionally a straight or serpentine line is visible where two have been fitted together. The underside was scratched and sometimes painted, the colour showing through the natural pigmentation, particularly of the paler shells. A paper backing was usually added which helped in the bonding of the shell to the carcase.

Once the pieces had been assembled, the narrow gaps between the two materials – the equivalent of a saw's width – were filled with dark shellac. As the eighteenth century proceeded, finer blades were used and the gaps became proportionately narrower. The brass pins which are sometimes to be seen are usually additions by a restorer to hold down lifting brass. Deterioration in the condition of the surface is generally caused by the two materials reacting differently to changes in temperature and humidity.

The finishing process involved filing and scraping the surface flat, and polishing it with increasingly fine abrasives, the finest of all being charcoal. The final decorative detail was often the work of an engraver, who on some pieces incised the outlines of exotic birds, human figures and arabesques in the metal and in the tortoiseshell, though this has often been removed by wear.

Right: Armoire, *or wardrobe, attributed to Boulle, early eighteenth century. The large panels on the doors are in* première-partie *marquetry; above and below them are horizontal panels in* contre-partie.

CARVING

Carving is a simple method of decorating woodwork, a natural development from the basic technique of whittling, or paring and shaping timber with a sharp tool. As practised by Grinling Gibbons in England, Andrea Brustolon in Italy, and carvers working to the drawn and engraved patterns of eighteenth-century designers, it was however a method requiring a high degree of manual dexterity together with the eye and judgement of an artist.

The carver's principal tools were the straight-edged chisel and curved-edged gouge. Technological advances have affected the sharpness and durability of the cutting-edge, but the variety of shapes and the manner in which the tools were used has changed little over the centuries. When carving, it was important for the work to be held firm, either in a vice or between cramps, or with a bench screw. The pointed end of this was driven into the piece of timber to be worked; the other end was passed through a hole in the bench and secured with a wingnut.

He began work with a piece of timber roughly shaped with a fretsaw, an adze or by turning on a lathe. Almost any timber used in furniture-making was suitable for carving, but close grained wood was necessary for finer, more detailed work. Lime, close-grained and yet soft, was considered the best.

Oak, the hard and durable timber of which most furniture was made from the Middle Ages up until the mid-seventeenth century, is open grained and therefore would not take detail. The type of mahogany imported into Europe from San Domingo in the West Indies was exceptionally hard and close-grained, and for carving highly tempered steel tools were required; the result could be as crisp as chased metalwork. For pieces that were to be gilded, pine and beech were often used (see p.52). When chiselling and gouging it was important to work with or across the grain and not against it.

Some carving was executed in the solid timber which formed part of the structure of a piece – the panels of a Medieval chest, for example, or the knee of a cabriole leg (see p.47). Alternatively, the carving might be worked as a separate piece of decoration and applied. Most carved mouldings were applied, their function being to conceal joins.

The technique may be divided into three main types: incised carving, relief carving and carving in the round. With incised work the design was cut into the timber, and simple punched and chip-carved decoration was carried out by a joiner or blacksmith (who made the tools) rather than a specialist carver. With relief carving the ground was cut away, leaving the design standing proud of it. Punches were sometimes used

Left: English carved limewood mirror, c. 1670. Limewood, close grained and at the same time soft, was a timber particularly favoured in England and France by woodcarvers. Below: Detail from the top of the mirror frame showing the crisp carving of the Royal arms and the motto.
Right: English carved mahogany armchair, c. 1760. It has a serpentine top rail, front legs and part of the H-shaped stretchers are carved with blind Chinese fret. The carved ornament on chairs of this date generally derived, wholly or in part, from published designs.

Left: Vase-stand in walnut and ebony
by Andrea Brustolon (1662–1732),
Italian, late seventeenth century. This
is the only signed piece from a set of
highly sculptural furniture in the
Baroque manner carved by Brustolon
for the Venier family and now in the
Ca' Rezzonico, Venice. The figures of
negroes and the classical river gods –
Charon, Cerberus and Hydra – are
exceptional examples of carving in the
round incorporated into a piece of
furniture.
Below: Detail of a walnut cassone,
Italian, fifteenth century. Much
carved ornament throughout the
centuries has been based on
architectural forms. Here, the
decoration is in the form of High
Gothic tracery.

to produce a textured or 'pounced' ground which would contrast with the smooth surfaces of the carved motifs. The size of elements in a repeating pattern – for example, an egg-and-dart moulding with alternating ovals and wedges – would be determined by the width of the tool making the initial, incised outline. Carving in the round was, in effect, sculpting. Supreme examples of the craft are the elaborately carved and gilded cabinet stands and console tables made in the late seventeenth and eighteenth centuries by craftsmen who undertook no other type of work.

Much carved decoration on furniture followed the forms of contemporary architecture, pointed Gothic arches and tracery giving way in the sixteenth century to the columns and round-headed arches of the Renaissance. Carving was an important feature of Rococo furniture and interior decoration, the craftsmen interpreting – and inventing – the asymmetrical, sinuous designs that characterized the style. There was less demand for the carver's skills during the Neoclassical period, though he was responsible for applied details in the form of the anthemion, acanthus, patera, and other motifs derived from the repertoire of Greek and Roman architecture. By 1850 a great deal of carving was being done mechanically.

Above: English carved oak court cupboard, early seventeenth century. Court cupboards were characteristically constructed in two stages, with carved balusters at the front and plain posts at the back, and the friezes decorated with carvings. They were designed for the display of plate.

Left: Flemish oak panel carved in relief, sixteenth century. This is an early example of the use of classical architectural forms; the egg-and-dart ornament, which appears here surmounting the semi-circular arch, was a type of repeat pattern much used as a border by woodcarvers in the eighteenth century. The scene depicted is Christ in the Temple, and an unusual detail is the spectacles worn by one of the figures.

Left: Trophy symbolizing Music carved in limewood by Grinling Gibbons (1648–1721), English, c.1695. Gibbons was the outstanding woodcarver of the Baroque period in England. This example of his work is at Petworth House in West Sussex; such is the intricacy of the carving that even the notes of the music are legible.
Above: English mahogany stool with carved cabriole legs and claw-and-ball feet. The section of seat rail above the shell-ornamented knee was cut from the same block of wood as the rest of the leg and the foot; the other sections of seat rail were made separately and veneered. The cabriole leg was based on a form used by the Greeks for carved marble theatre seats; it first appeared in Europe in the late seventeenth century.

FORMING A CABRIOLE LEG
1. The outline of the knee, leg and foot was marked out on each of the four sides of a block of wood of square section. This was done using a single template and turning it over.
2. The basic shaping of the foot – in this case of the claw-and-ball type – was done by turning on a lathe.
3. The four sides of the block were cut with a bow saw to form the knee and leg, following the marked-out design.
4. Shaping of the leg was done with a spokeshave.
5. Detailed carving of the foot was done with chisels and gouges.
6. The detail on the knee was carved in a similar manner.

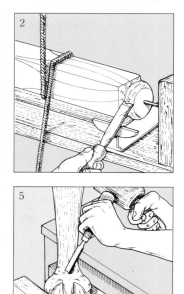
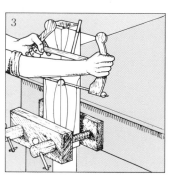
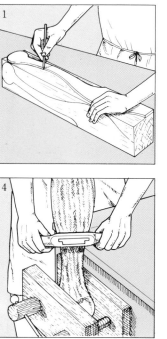
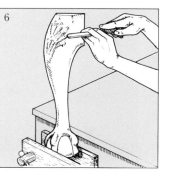

PAINTING AND STENCILLING

The grandest and most expensive pieces of domestic furniture that were made in Italy during the Renaissance were the long chests known as 'cassoni'. In the fourteenth and fifteenth centuries the front, and occasionally the top and sides as well, were ornamented with carving, intarsia work or painting. The painting was carried out in tempera – powdered pigment 'tempered' with size, varnish or egg-white – on gessoed wood. (Gesso was a mixture of whiting and size, and it was applied in several layers.) In both manner of execution and style the panels resembled contemporary easel paintings, and they were often of high quality. Established painters, including Botticelli and Uccello, seem from time to time to have undertaken work of this kind.

Professional painters were sometimes involved, too, in the decoration of the elaborate cabinets made in the sixteenth and seventeenth centuries in northern Europe. The panels were very much smaller and, often within a framework that resembled the façade of a Baroque church, they might be part of a display of works of art that included *pietre dure* plaques, cast metalwork and carvings in materials such as ivory.

Towards the end of the eighteenth century the *maître-ébéniste* Martin Carlin designed pieces inset with painted Sèvres porcelain, and in England a similar pictorial element was introduced in the form of Wedgwood plaques and paintings on copper. At the same period there was a fashion for borders and medallions painted in pale colours and in *grisaille* (tones of grey) on the primed surface of satinwood and harewood veneers. They were painted in oils, and varnished in the same way as an oil painting on canvas.

In the mid-nineteenth century in England there was a return to the idea of furniture as a vehicle for the display of paintings. William Burges, William Morris and Dante Gabriel Rossetti, among others, decorated cabinets and cupboards with paintings of a narrative nature that have something in common with scenes depicted on Italian *cassoni*.

Much painting of furniture was done not in order to produce a unique object but to simulate japanned work (see p.54). In Italy the term '*lacca*' is used to describe japanning and the simpler form of decoration produced by painting on the wood and then applying a coat of varnish. '*Lacca contrafatta*' was a Venetian speciality. Prints, generally of pastoral or Chinoiserie figures (European versions of Oriental figures), were

Left: American rocking chair with painted and stencilled decoration, first half of the nineteenth century. The top splat is decorated with freehand painting of fruit, flowers and foliage; the lower two with a combination of painted and stencilled ornament.
Right: English hall seat of beech painted to imitate white marble with grey veins, 1800. The design was inspired by an illustration of a classical Roman seat published by Charles Heathcote Tatham in 1799.
Below: Florentine cassone with painted decoration, fifteenth century. The wood was prepared for painting in tempera with one or more layers of 'gesso', a mixture of whiting and size.

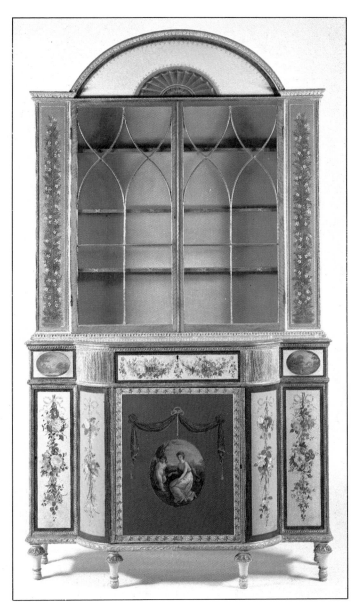

Above: Florentine birthtray with painted decoration of the Triumph of Love by the workshop of Apollonio di Giovanni (1415–65), mid-fifteenth century. The workshop specialized in the manufacture of painted cassoni.
Far left: English painted and gilded bureau cabinet, c.1785. The painted medallion in the centre of the base is in the manner of Angelica Kauffmann (1741–1807), who was employed several times by the Adam brothers. It was Robert Adam who in c.1770 introduced this type of painted ornament on English furniture.
Left: Detail of the painted decoration from the bureau cabinet. It was painted in oil on the primed surface of the satinwood veneer.

hand painted, then cut out and glued to the furniture. A layer of varnish over the whole surface completed the effect.

With timbers such as beech and pine, used for inexpensive furniture in particular, the painting could be done directly on to the wood, but more durable decoration was achieved on a gesso ground. The background colour was generally done in water-colour, and if desired the surface could be burnished with a hardstone such as an agate. Oil paint would be used for the detail, and finally the surface might be waxed.

Graining, to imitate the appearance of wood, was done on a plain painted surface using fine brushes or horn combs, and oil paint or water-colour. For marbling, Stalker and Parker, the authors of a seventeenth-century treatise on lacquering and japanning, recommended that three shades of vine-black (burnt and ground vine cuttings) be obtained by mixing with different quantities of white lead and weak size. On a wet ground, the lightest shade was laid on first with a broad camel-hair brush; the smaller veins were done with the middle

shade and finally the dark shade was used for the wild and irregular veins that occur in natural marble.

A cheap and quick method of decoration, which enabled a pattern to be repeated many times, was stencilling. Paint, used fairly dry, was dabbed through the stencil with a sponge or brush. Different gradations of colour were achieved by increasing or decreasing the strength of touch and amount of pigment used. For a design with several colours, more than one stencil might be used. Stencilling was practised particularly effectively on simple, country-made American furniture.

Frequently, gold leaf or metal powder was used – pure gold, silver, brass, zinc or copper. In this case the surface to be decorated was coated with a thin wash of size mixed with varnish and turpentine. When slightly tacky, after an hour or two, it was ready to receive the metal powder, which was dabbed on through the stencil by means of a soft pad of cotton velvet or chamois leather. A shaded effect could be achieved afterwards by the use of an engraving tool.

STAINING AND POLISHING

At various periods from the seventeenth century, it was fashionable to stain wood. Staining enabled the grain to be seen through a more attractive colour than that of the natural wood, and in particular it was used to give cheap woods the appearance of scarcer, more expensive ones: pine and pearwood was stained to resemble ebony, beech to resemble walnut or mahogany. Sycamore or maple stained greenish-grey is sometimes known as 'harewood'.

There was enormous variety in the ingredients used, and there was a great deal of experimentation in the quest for good, strong colours that did not fade or change with long exposure to light. Various basic dyes were extracted from wood, or from other plants or their roots, generally by boiling them in water, vinegar or alcohol until the liquid was reduced and all the colour had been extracted.

The main dyewoods were logwood (which gave black, reds, yellows, purples, greys and browns), fustic (yellows, browns and purples) and Brazil wood (reds and purples). Dyes were also extracted from madder root (reds and yellows); indigo (blues); 'Yellow', or Avignon berries (yellows and greenish-yellows), and from other substances including verdigris (greens and blue-greens), smalt (blues) and extract from East Asian rattan palm resin known as 'dragon's blood' (reds). Many common chemicals and other additives – potash, alum,

sulphuric acid, sal-ammoniac, iron sulphate among them – could be used to modify the colour.

A stain to imitate a light mahogany was made by preparing a decoction of madder and fustic in water, or by mixing dragon's blood or turmeric root in alcohol. A madder and logwood decoction gave a stain of a darker mahogany colour. Ebonizing, as practised particularly in the nineteenth century, could be done with a mixture of lampblack and size.

A great deal of furniture, whether of solid wood or veneered, was finished by polishing. Not only did the polish seal and help to preserve the wood, but it enhanced its colour and brought out the decorative qualities of the figure and grain. Sometimes the piece was stained before it was polished; sometimes a colouring agent such as lampblack, burnt umber or alkanet was a constituent of the polish.

The patina on furniture is caused by years of use and wear, and polishing, which gives depth of colour and shine. Dust would collect in scratches and blemishes, at the edge of mouldings and in other angles and joins, sticking to the tacky surface of the polish. This accumulation of dirt and polish often appears as a local darkening of the wood, and it is one of the factors which vary the colour and give a desirable mellowness to the surface.

From the sixteenth century wax polishing was one of the

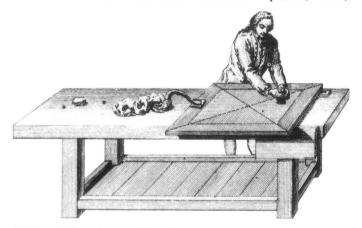

Above: Illustration of a polisher at work from Roubo's Art du Menuisier. *He is shown rubbing wax polish into a quarter-veneered panel using a tightly bound bundle of rushes.*
Right: Herter Brothers ebonized cherrywood wardrobe, American, c.1880. The fashion for dark stained furniture in the 1870s and 1880s in America was inspired by the popularity of Japanese pieces.
Left: Hungarian ash and ebony-bordered secrétaire à abattant in Biedermeier style, second quarter of the nineteenth century. This would have been finished by the process known as 'French polishing' which became popular at the beginning of the nineteenth century. Shellac rather than wax was the principal constituent of the polish.

PREPARING THE SURFACE
1. A smooth and flat surface was achieved by a combination of planing, the use of a cabinet scraper and sanding.
2. Filling of the grain was done with a damp cloth using dry whiting darkened with pigment. A coating of linseed oil might be applied.
3. If the surface was to be water stained, it was first damped down with water to raise the grain and then sanded when dry.

FRENCH POLISHING
1. The polish, made by dissolving flakes of shellac in spirit, was mainly applied with a 'rubber'. The first stage in making a rubber was to fold a piece of wadding in two.
2. The wadding was folded again to form an egg shape. This was used for 'damping in', to seal the timber.
3. A piece of cotton or fine linen was wrapped round the wadding.
4. The polisher twisted and folded back the ends in his hand.
5. 'Bodying up' was done by applying the polish with the rubber by squeezing it through the material, the wadding acting as a reservoir.
6. In bodying up the polisher worked using a variety of movements, including a figure of eight. From time to time the wadding was recharged and a drop of linseed oil added. When a good build up had been reached, the finishing, or 'spiriting out', was done using a solution of shellac with a higher proportion of spirit. This gradually removed the linseed oil and produced a high finish.

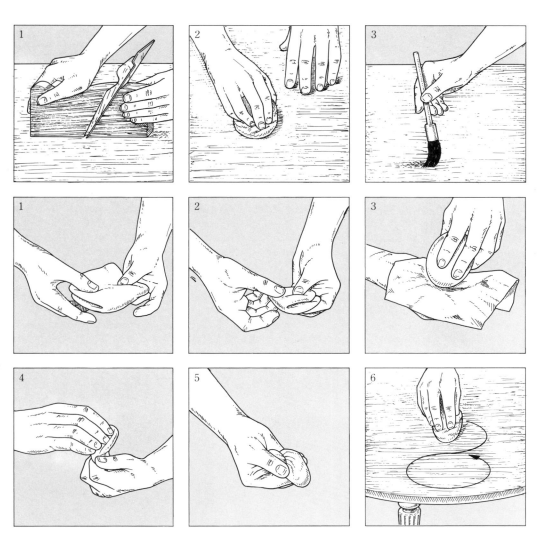

most common finishes. The beeswax was either in a hard state and rubbed into the wood, or dissolved in turpentine and applied as a thin paste. The surface was then burnished by rubbing with a rough cloth or brush. Another kind of finish was effected by treating the wood with resin dissolved in oil or spirit and burnishing it. The ingredients depended partly on the availability of substances such as the resins copal and turpentine, and linseed, olive, walnut, juniper and poppy oil. Tripoli, a fine earth, was used in the burnishing process, and brick dust was used for filling the grain and for removing excess wax.

A process developed in France in the early years of the nineteenth century is known as 'French polishing'. Shellac, the base of French polish, was the principal constituent in a type of varnish that was employed in the japanning process (see p.54) and it had therefore been used on European furniture for more than a century. The polish was made by dissolving flakes of shellac in spirit.

The polish was applied with a 'rubber', made of wadding and a piece of cotton or fine linen. The wadding was folded into an egg shape and the cotton or linen wrapped round it so that there was a smooth base. The ends were twisted round, and the polisher held them firmly in his hand. The wadding formed a reservoir for the polish, the flow of which – through the cloth

on to the surface of the work – was controlled by the tautness of the cloth and the pressure of the polisher's fingers.

The first step was to ensure that the piece had a perfectly smooth and even surface since any irregularity would be emphasized. This was done by careful planing, the use of a cabinet scraper and sanding; sometimes the grain would first have been filled with whiting mixed with linseed oil. If it was to be stained, this would be done next.

The first stage in the application of the polish was known as 'damping in'. Using a cloth, the polish was dabbed on to the wood, which absorbed it at a high rate. 'Bodying up' was done with the rubber, and the polisher worked in a combination of straight, circular and figure-of-eight strokes until a good build up had been achieved. Towards the end a little linseed oil helped to lubricate the rubber and give a good finish. This was removed in the final process of 'spiriting out', which involved rubbing the surface with a solution of 50% shellac and 50% methylated spirit. Another method of removing the linseed oil was to use dilute sulphuric acid. The surface was then brought to a bright shine by burnishing.

In the nineteenth century it was fashionable to strip the polish from earlier furniture and replace it with the hard, glossy finish produced by French polishing.

GILDING

Gold has been used to decorate the surface of wood for at least 4,000 years. From the earliest times it was applied in the form of leaves of beaten gold – 'gold leaf'. The colour varied from a reddish brown to almost white, depending on the source of the precious metal, and the type and quantity of other metals with which it was alloyed (see p.168). The process of rolling and hammering it into sheets of about $1/_{300\,000}$ inch (0·00008 mm) in thickness was delicate and laborious.

In the Middle Ages the craftsman who painted furniture also gilded it. During the seventeenth century, however, when gilding was once again a popular type of finish, the work of the gilder became allied to that of the carver. At that date two quite different methods of gilding were practised: oil gilding and water gilding.

Oil gilding was the cheaper process, and the more durable. It was used on furniture, and on architectural features such as mouldings, cornices and friezes. Water gilding was the superior type of gilding, distinguished by the fact that the surface could be burnished. Parts of the design were brought to a high lustre in this way, contrasting with the matt areas of tooled decoration.

Essential to the water-gilding process was the preparation of a gesso ground similar to that used for *cassoni* panels. It was painted on to the dry, seasoned timber – generally deal, beech or, for the finest work, limewood or pearwood – in several, increasingly thick, layers. Time would be allowed for drying between each coat, and finally the gesso would be sanded to provide a hard, smooth surface.

To facilitate adherence of the gold leaf, the ground was treated with a 'mordant', for which various recipes existed: red clay, or 'bole', mixed with egg white or parchment size and hot water was recommended, while Stalker and Parker in 1688 suggested colouring it with yellow ochre to disguise any gaps that were left after the leaves of gold had been laid on the surface. Some gilders favoured a blue mordant. The inclusion of black lead and white wax was said by some to assist in the burnishing process.

Having prepared the mordanted ground, the gilder would separate a sheet of gold leaf from its folder on a thin, flat sable-hair brush. He stroked the brush against his cheek two or three times and that made it easier to lift the leaf and lay it on his 'cushion'. This was a rectangular piece of wood covered with rough calf-skin, padded out with some layers of cloth to make a slightly domed surface. As the gold leaf would blow away in the gentlest movement of air, the cushion was protected on three sides by a wall of stout parchment. By

Far left: English giltwood pier-glass c.1760. The carved wood was coated with gesso and the gold leaf was applied to this with the help of an adhesive known as a 'mordant'. With water gilding the mordant was pigment mixed with water, egg white or size.
Left: English giltwood armchair, c.1730. The elements of design in high relief were incised in the gesso, then gilded and burnished; flat surfaces could be gilded and then punched to create a matt effect to contrast with the areas of burnishing.
Below: North Italian marble-topped serpentine giltwood commode, mid-eighteenth century.

Left: Venetian giltwood and painted commode, c.1780.
Above: Gilder's workshop from Illustrations of Useful Arts *by Charles Tomlinson, 1867. The gilder lifts the gold leaf from his calf-skin 'cushion' and lays it on the work with a brush.*

blowing lightly on to it, the leaf could be flattened on the cushion, then cut to the required size with a thin, sharp knife. With the same brush it was lifted and laid on the surface to be gilded, this having first been moistened with water – hence 'water' gilding. Some pieces were double gilded with two layers of gold leaf. For a matt effect the surface would be lightly polished or tooled; burnishing produced a high finish. The burnishing-tool might be a dog's tooth set in a wooden handle, or a stone such as an agate.

For oil gilding the mordant was generally linseed oil cooked in the sun until it solidified and became 'fat oil'. This was mixed with ground yellow ochre or raw sienna and, by adding a little linseed oil, a thin, creamy paste was produced. The ground to which it was applied might be of gesso, but a composition of white lead or red ochre ground in oil, or even paint-pot scrapings, could be used. Once the mordant had dried to a tacky consistency, the gold leaf was laid on the surface in the same way as in water gilding, but only as a single layer. Occasionally a piece was oil and water gilded: the matt surfaces were oil gilded and the surfaces to be burnished were water gilded.

The main elements of the design were roughly carved in wood and the detail built up with layer upon layer of gesso, applied with a brush and sharpened up by tooling. Texture was given to the background with stamps and punches, or by sprinkling fine silver sand on the mordant. Some punched work was carried out after the piece had been gilded.

The process of silvering was almost the same as gilding, but the surface was generally varnished to prevent the discoloration caused by oxidization. Silvering was mainly done on the elaborately carved stands of Baroque cabinets.

Right: English walnut bureau cabinet with features picked out in oil gilding, c.1720. Oil gilding was a cheaper process than water gilding, and more durable. The gold leaf was applied as a single layer on an oil-based mordant. Oil gilding could not be burnished.

LACQUERING AND JAPANNING

The brilliant, glossy sheen of Oriental lacquer was greatly admired by Europeans, and a widespread fashion for it was promoted by the blossoming of trade between East and West in the seventeenth century. The panels of screens were used to line the walls of small rooms, or 'cabinets', such as those of Rosenborg in Copenhagen, the Palazzo Reale in Turin and Schloss Brühl in Cologne. Smaller panels, or sections of a panel, were applied as a veneer to furniture. European furniture was even exported to the East in an undecorated state to be lacquered by native craftsmen; the pieces were then brought back to Europe to be sold.

The raw material of Chinese lacquer was the sap of the indigenous tree known then as 'Rhus vernicifera', which was collected and refined. The application of lacquer to an article, even in its most basic form, was a long, complex and painstaking process. The carcase of the piece to be lacquered was prepared by rubbing down until it was perfectly smooth. Then came the coats of lacquer, laid on very thinly. Each coat was allowed to dry completely over several days and rubbed down with pumice before the next coat was applied. The early coats were mixed with clay to ensure a flat, smooth surface; the later layers were mixed with pigment to give the desired colour to the finished piece. Altogether at least 30 thin coats of

lacquer were applied; in the deeply carved pieces it is apparent that up to 200 layers were necessary. A cool, damp atmosphere was essential for the proper, even drying of the lacquer.

The craftsmanship of the Chinese lacquer workers reached a very high standard and many decorative techniques were developed. These included incised designs, inlaid mother of pearl, gold and silver, and intricate small-scale carving.

With the sudden great demand in Europe for Chinese lacquer in the seventeenth century, and consequent hasty production, the quality of Chinese lacquer made for export declined. Good-quality Japanese lacquer was also at this time being made for the European market, however, and confusion arose over the exact origin of the 'real' lacquer. When imitations began to be made, the process was called, in England, 'japanning'.

Cabinet-makers vied with each other to produce a passable imitation of the Oriental wares. Try as they might, they could not discover the identity of the main ingredient, assuming it to be shellac, which was the ingredient of lacquer from India and the Middle East. (Shellac and seed-lac are similar forms of a resin-like substance produced by certain species of insect indigenous to India and South-east Asia). Not until 1720 was the identity of the Chinese tree known in Europe and, when it was known, it was understood that it would not grow in the

Left: English red japanned armchair with cabriole legs, c.1720. The popularity of japanned furniture, which imitated the appearance of Oriental lacquer, was promoted in England by the publication in 1688 of A Treatise on Japanning and Varnishing *by Stalker and Parker.*
Above: Chinese export lacquer cabinet on stand, late eighteenth century. This was made for the European market.
Right: Lacquer panel from the interior of the cabinet.

Left: Leaf from a Chinese black and gold lacquer screen, eighteenth century. Oriental lacquer was made from the sap of the tree known then as 'Rhus vernicifera', which was not obtainable in the West. Shellac and seed-lac were the substitutes generally used by European japanners, the effect they produced lacking the density and gloss of the original. Above: Chinese red lacquer box and cover carved with a camellia design, early fifteenth century. The fine, hard surface of the lacquer made it a suitable medium for intricate carving.

West. Importation of the sap proved impossible because it dried out on the long sea voyage.

Most imitation lacquers were based on shellac or seed-lac. The nature of this material was such that the European process had to be carried out in a warm, dry room – the contrary of the atmosphere necessary for the Oriental process. Recipes and instructions were given in a *A Treatise on Japanning and Varnishing* of 1688 by John Stalker, whose name on all but the first edition was joined by that of George Parker. The treatise was consulted particularly by amateur japanners, of whom there were a great many. Stalker and Parker recommended the use of a smooth, close-grained wood such as pearwood for the base of the piece to be japanned; if coarser woods, such as pine or oak, were used they had to be prepared by applying layers of whiting mixed with dissolved size, well rubbed down with rushes.

These writers suggested that seed-lac rather than shellac should be used. For black japanned work thick seed-lac varnish was poured into a gallipot and to this lampblack was added. Three coats were applied to the surface with thorough drying between each of them. For the next six coats the varnish was thinned with turpentine and the final twelve were just tinged with lampblack. The piece was then left to stand for five or six days before being polished with water and tripoli; after another two days it was polished again, and five to six days elapsed before it was given a final polishing with lampblack and oil.

For white, the basic coats were of isinglass size (isinglass boiled in water and left to form a jelly mixed with whiting); this was covered with coats of white flake and size. Blues of different shades were made by mixing smalt (dark blue glass) with white lead and weak isinglass size; reds by mixing vermilion preferably with seed-lac, otherwise with size; chestnut and olive colours could also be made. All these colours could be varied by adjusting the proportions of additives used.

For decoration they suggested the use of brass-dust, called 'gold-dust', the best quality of which was imported from Germany, or other metal dusts. For raised decoration a solution of gum arabic (derived from species of acacia) mixed with whiting and bole-armeniac (pale red earth from Armenia), ground until it was smooth, could be used. The body was built up by this means, and it could then be carved according to the desired shape.

Tools and equipment included flannel or linen strainers, one for white varnish, the other for lac-varnish; camel-hair

Left: Chinese Coromandel lacquer cabinet on stand, eighteenth century. Coromandel lacquer is characterized by brightly coloured incised decoration. It was made in central and northern China, and exported to Europe by way of the English East India Company trading posts on the Coromandel coast of India.

brushes; Dutch rushes for smoothing the work; tripoli for polishing; and mussel-shells in which to mix the colours.

Eighteenth-century treatises published on the Continent generally agreed with Stalker and Parker on the constituents of the ideal Western japan varnish, but there were some variations. Garlic, absinthe, vinegar and salt were included in French recipes, and gum sandarac were recommended for use as a base. Some of the methods employed by European craftsmen were listed in Filippo Bonanni's treatise of 1720.

The closest imitations of Oriental lacquer were produced in the Low Countries. Spa, near Aix-la-Chapelle, was an important centre of the trade in the late seventeenth century, and it was here that Gerhard Dagly, responsible for some of the finest work carried out in Germany, was born.

England was noted for its red 'lacquer', exported in some quantity to Spain and Portugal. Cabinets were often mounted on silvered stands. In France the work of the Martin brothers was highly regarded, and the term '*vernis Martin*' became widely used to describe its imitations as well as the fine work of the Martins themselves. Although their recipe, a closely guarded secret, was lost, it is known that from 1753 they started to use copal resin from Brazil as a base. This is thought to have been the secret of their success.

Right: Detail of the inside of a door from an English red and gold japanned bureau cabinet, c.1730. Figures and other decorative motifs were sometimes copied from illustrated travel books.

Above: English japanned bureau cabinet in the manner of Giles Grendey (1693–1780), mid-eighteenth century. Grendey was a London furniture-maker. Some of his japanned pieces were exported to the Continent at the time of their manufacture.
Left: Japanese late seventeenth-century lacquer coffer on an English painted stand with a gadrooned edge and bracket feet of c.1750. It was common practice for European craftsmen to make stands for the imported Oriental pieces. Characteristic of Japanese lacquer are the comparatively large areas of unornamented ground.

LATER JAPANNING AND PAPIER MÂCHÉ

The eighteenth-century industrial skill of japanning was quite distinct from the earlier European imitations of Oriental imports described previously. Thick varnishes were applied as both protection and decoration to a variety of materials such as tin, iron, wood, slate, copper and *papier mâché*.

Papier mâché was often made by the japanners themselves. The simple pulp method of making it involved reducing paper to a clay-like consistency suitable for moulding by compression, but it yielded an uneven, brittle surface. Most so-called *'papier mâché'* was really pasteboard, a much stronger, more durable material. It was made by pasting and laminating – spreading in layers – sheets of paper on greased wooden boards backed with sheet iron. On removal from the boards, the panels were as versatile as wood. Complex shapes were made by shaping pasted paper over greased wood or metal moulds. Among the ingenious methods of manufacture that were devised was the making in one piece and subsequent slicing in two of boxes and their lids.

Special rag 'making paper' was employed which had the appearance and texture of thick blotting-paper, but it had the advantage of not disintegrating when wet. The paste was a mixture of flour and glue dissolved and boiled in water. After about every fourth layer of paper, the object was dried in a large oven, or stove, and filed; ten layers provided a substantial panel, although up to 120 might have been needed if the article was to be fluted or gadrooned. The dried, completed object was saturated with oil and heated again to make it hard and water-resistant. The edges were trimmed, the mould removed and the object filed, turned, planed or fluted as required, and polished with chamois leather to prepare it for the japanning process.

Regardless of the basic material, all objects were similarly treated when japanned. The 'blanks' were given preparatory coats of varnish and stove dried. Black, the most common base colour, was generally made from asphaltum or lampblack mixed with turpentine and bound with varnish; alternative ground or base colours were produced by mixing pigments with clear shellac varnish.

Contrary to appearance, pearl was not inlaid but applied at this stage of the decorating process. After 'pouncing' the design on to the blank through a perforated pattern, the parts to be pearled were gold-sized and the shell carefully positioned on the tacky surface and secured by heating. The entire object, including the pearl, was varnished once again, baked and rubbed down with a wet pumice stone until the pearl reappeared. This was repeated until the surface of the varnish was level with that of the pearl. If pearl was not required, the varnish was built up in the same way until sufficiently dense.

Japanned ware was generally decorated with gilding. The earliest gilding was 'bronzing', a technique which involved sprinkling bronze powders over a sticky, sized ground. Later bronzing, introduced in 1845, was achieved with transparent colour washes over metal leaf, and it was used for rich backgrounds.

The most frequent type of gilding used by japanners employed gold leaf (see p. 168). Matt effects were produced by painting the design on to the japanned surface with gold size mixed with colour; the gold leaf was pressed on to the tacky varnish and the excess removed when dry. It was a method that allowed for very fine, lacy work. Bright gold was achieved by using only the purest gold leaf on a wet, polished surface. The gold leaf was applied to the border in sheets before the design was painted with asphaltum; the article was baked or left to dry and the superfluous gold and asphaltum wiped off. A third method combined these two processes to produce rich effects, and sometimes the gold leaf was transfer-printed, a process also used on ceramics (see p. 134).

More quickly produced and less expensive gilt borders were

Left: French silver-mounted vernis Martin nécessaire *bearing the Paris discharge mark for 1756–62.* Vernis Martin *was made by the Martin brothers, whose workshop in Paris* *was one of the most important* papier mâché *centres established in Europe during the eighteenth century.* *Above: English* papier mâché *canterbury, c. 1860.*

Above: English papier mâché *trays with gilded borders, painted with views of Cornwall, nineteenth century.*
Below: English papier mâché *blotter-cover painted by Richard Stubbs and*

gilded by Edwin Stubbs at Henry Loveridge & Co., Wolverhampton, c.1865.
Right: English japanned chair with *the splat and back rail of* papier mâché, *mid-nineteenth century.*

printed with corks. The corks were dipped in a mixture of gold size and lemon yellow and used to stamp repetitive border patterns, over which gold or other metal leaf could be laid.

In conjunction with gilding, japanned ware was often stencilled or painted. The decorators worked with oil colours and the painters used camel-hair brushes and 'pencils', or 'etchers', as the very fine brushes were known, to copy from original designs which hung before them.

When the gilding and painting processes were complete, the object was edged, perhaps with a stripe, and decorated areas protected by copal varnish, which again required heating. The article was polished, first with powdered pumice stone and then with pounce (fine powder), followed by a mixture of rottenstone (decomposed limestone) and oil, and lastly by 'handing' the surface with the heel of the hand and a little fine rottenstone. The japanned article was finished when locks, hinges and any other fittings had been attached.

GLASS

Glass was probably discovered accidentally during metal smelting, when the intense heat melted the furnace wall. The first purpose-made glass objects were coloured beads, made in Syria in about 3000 BC and in Egypt a little later. Another 1,500 years elapsed before the first vessels, also of coloured glass and made by various moulding and casting processes, appeared in these regions. They were highly prized and only persons of rank could afford them. Then, at the beginning of the Roman period, around 64 BC, the invention of the blowpipe revolutionized glassmaking, and colourless glass came into prominence. During the next few centuries the glassblower discovered many of the basic decorative effects used to the present day. Blowing into moulds permitted repeat work of popular decorative lines – an early form of mass production that brought glass into everyday use.

The quality of the best glass of this period was excellent, but its manufacture was empirical and, hence, unreliable. An understanding of the chemistry that was involved dawned in the seventeenth century, when purified ingredients began to be used, but it only came of age with the emergence of the great German glass industry in the nineteenth century. Furnace design was also slow to improve. In 1800 glassmaking at the Baccarat factory in France was so unpredictable that a bell was rung to summon the workers when the glass was ready, and in 1849 Apsley Pellatt, an English master glassmaker with the most sophisticated furnace of his time, still complained that glassmaking was difficult when the wind was in the wrong direction. Gradually new, often easier, manipulative techniques also replaced the old.

Today there is much speculation as to how some of the old processes were carried out. An understanding of the underlying technology not only encourages an appreciation of the master craftsmen who created and decorated glass but also provides practical information about the country of origin and date of a piece.

The major component of glass is silica, as sand or flints. Silica alone melts at about 2000°C – far above the 1200°C or so attainable by glasshouse furnaces. The melting-temperature is lowered by the addition of an alkaline 'flux' – soda (sodium carbonate) or potash (potassium carbonate) – but too much alkali makes the glass become water soluble and unstable. This tendency can be corrected by the addition of calcium, usually as limestone or chalk. The essence of making soda glass is to balance the proportions of sand, soda and lime to form a homogeneous, stable 'metal'.

For many centuries the basic glass had only two ingredients: silica and a source of alkali. The first known source of alkali was crude sodium carbonate, known as 'natron', or 'nitrum', found particularly at Wadi Natrun, an oasis in the Western Desert. It probably contained some lime which, according to Pliny the Elder in the first century AD, could be detected with the tongue.

In ancient Mesopotamia a crude form of soda (which also contained some lime and potash) was obtained from the ashes of a plant appropriately called 'glasswort'. The word 'alkali' comes from the Arabic *'kalati'*, meaning burnt. Plant ash – variously known as 'barilla' or 'Syrian ash' – remained the major source of alkali throughout Europe until the French chemist Nicolas Leblanc discovered the chemical synthesis of soda in the late eighteenth century.

Rock crystal is a natural form of glass used as ornament since Antiquity. Its clarity was the envy of all glassmakers. In about 1460 Angelo Barovier of Murano invented a new, clearer soda glass known as *'cristallo'*. It was the key to Venetian supremacy, and high-quality clear glass has to this

Left: English goblet commemorating the birth of the Prince of Wales, later George IV, in 1762, made in Newcastle-upon-Tyne and decorated with enamelling by William Beilby (1740–1819). Between 1763 and 1769 Beilby decorated eight other such goblets bearing the royal coat of arms. An able painter as well as a remarkable enameller, Beilby came from a talented family of craftsmen. His father was a jeweller and goldsmith, his brother Ralph was a heraldic engraver and Mary, his sister, was also an enameller on glass.

Left: Clichy moss-ground millefiori glass paperweight, French, mid-nineteenth century. Lead glass was developed in England by George Ravenscroft (1632–83) between 1673 and 1683, but it was not copied successfully on the Continent until 1780. In France in the mid-nineteenth century solid glass paperweights made at the St-Louis, Baccarat and Clichy glasshouses exploited the refractive qualities of the lead 'metal'. Millefiori glass was made by embedding sections of coloured 'canes' in molten clear glass.

day been called 'crystal'. *Cristallo* was probably prepared from Syrian ash and – of particular significance – finely crushed pebbles from the river Ticino. The use of pebbles rather than sand gave rise to the name for best crystal of 'flint' glass.

In northern Europe glass was made with ash from wood (usually beech), bracken or straw, and it was called *'Waldglas'* in Germany or *'verre de fougère'* in France. The ashes contained more potash than soda and gave a good-quality glass, though discoloured by metallic impurities.

Attempts to purify the ashes, by boiling with water, filtering off the insoluble residue and evaporating to reclaim the alkali, were only partially successful as the important calcium salts were depleted. This resulted in a less stable glass. At the end of the seventeenth century Continental glassmakers successfully produced a fine, colourless potash glass known as 'chalkglass' by adding both calcium compounds and purified ash to the 'batch' – the mixture of ingredients.

However, even purified ash was contaminated with sodium and potassium chlorides. In making both soda and potash glass they were removed by preheating the batch for up to 48 hours at 700°C in a special furnace called the 'calcar' to form 'frit'. Frit is a crude, granular form of glass. The unwanted chlorides could be leached out with water before it was dried ready for the melting-pot. The development of more efficient furnaces (see p.64) made it possible to transfer the hot frit straight from the calcar into the melting-pot: the chlorides rose to the surface of the molten glass and fused to form a scum, known as 'gall' or 'sandiver', that could be ladled off.

Lead glass was developed between 1673 and 1683 by George Ravenscroft, a London merchant familiar with the Venetian glass industry. His first patent, granted in 1674, produced an unstable glass, the cause of which was too much alkali in the batch. This defect, called 'crizzling', was common to glass at that time. The surface of the vessel developed a fine network of fractures, became 'greasy' to the touch and finally disintegrated. Ravenscroft overcame this problem and affixed

his personal seal to each glass as a guarantee of quality; even so, those that survive often show crizzling. The eventual constituents of the metal were silica, potash, red lead and saltpetre, and the batch, made from purified ingredients, was shovelled straight into the hot melting-pot.

The formula for English full-lead crystal, constituted of 30% lead, has remained substantially unchanged. In 1780 the Cristalleries de St-Louis in France successfully reproduced the English lead metal and thereby secured their future prosperity. In the nineteenth century Continental glassmakers reduced the lead content to 20% to 24%; this 'demicrystal' has less brilliance and an inferior ring when struck.

Glass batch conducts heat very slowly. Melting is greatly accelerated by mixing it with up to 50% of finely broken glass, called 'cullet'. The cullet must be of the same type as the glass being made. Some was bought in, but with hand-worked glass 30% to 50% was wasted and most of this could be recycled.

Ravenscroft's glass was singularly clear and colourless because of its low iron content. Traces of iron (as little as 0.05%) imparted an undesirable blue-green colour, particularly in smoky ('reducing') furnace conditions. This could be corrected by the addition of a 'decolorizer' during the melting which either 'oxidized' the iron to a less obtrusive pale yellow or masked the blue-green by converting it to a neutral grey. Manganese dioxide – a secret component of Barovier's *cristallo* – acted in both ways. Other decolorizers, used later, include nickel, cobalt, arsenic and selenium.

From its origins in Syria and Egypt glassmaking had spread before the third century BC to India, Russia, Spain and, by way of the long-established trade route, to China, where a small indigenous industry already prospered. The rise of the Roman Empire brought glassmaking to Rome, where the arts of cutting and engraving produced fine cameo ware. By the second century AD glassmaking had spread into Gaul and as far north as Cologne, and had penetrated into England before the fall of the Roman Empire in 475 AD.

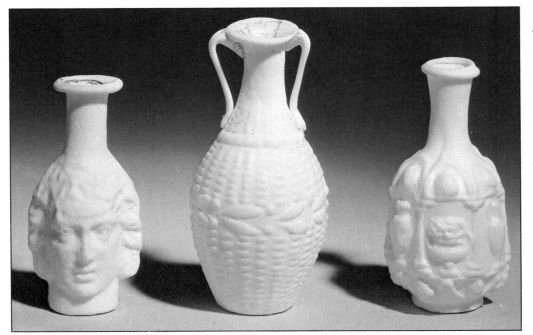

Left: Syrian mould-blown vessels, first or second century AD. Glassblowing is believed to have been invented in Syria. Popular repeat lines, of which these are examples, were made by blowing the glass bulbs into a clay mould in two or three parts, according to the complexity of the design. Moulds for the amphoriskos *in the centre and the double-sided 'Janus' flask – named after the two-headed mythological figure – on the left were made in two parts; the flask on the right in three parts. The handles on the* amphoriskos *were applied afterwards, and the mouth was strengthened by turning the rim inwards.*

Above: Egyptian soda-glass beaker bearing the cartouche of the Emperor Tuthmosis III, c. 1450 BC. This is one of three of the earliest named vessels to survive, perhaps made to honour the Emperor's conquests of Asia, begun in 1481 BC. It was made by 'marvering', or rolling, pale-blue glass on to an earthen core fixed to an iron rod and then trailing on coloured glass decoration.

Right: Eastern Mediterranean core-formed amphoriskos *and* alabastron, *sixth or fifth century BC. The trailed decoration is here more complex, with loops and feathering. The vessels were used for ointments or cosmetics.*

Glassmaking wintered the Dark Ages in Europe with simple but skilfully manipulated *Waldglas*, while Islam, under Persian influence, developed magnificent enamelled ware until the sacking of Damascus by the Mongols under Tamerlane in 1402. Venetian glassmaking now began to flourish and dominated the industry until the end of the seventeenth century. Meanwhile, mid-European glassmakers had developed attractive enamelled ware and emigrant Venetian glassmakers in the Low Countries produced more elaborate styles in the Venetian fashion. The arrival in Britain of glassmakers from France and Venice created an industry that, with the discovery of lead crystal, brought Venetian domination to an end.

In the New World glassmaking naturally followed the paths of emigration. In America attempts were first made at Jamestown, Virginia, in 1608; but it was with Caspar Wistar and H. W. Stiegel that the industry prospered. In Canada early glass styles indicate French involvement, and factories were established in Malorytown, Ontario, in about 1825 and in Quebec in about 1850. Later, styles become confused as American and Canadian workers frequently crossed national borders in the search for work.

Above: German Gothic beaker, c. 1500. The applied 'prunts', or blobs of glass, give the glass the appearance of a cabbage-stalk, or 'Krautstrunk', the name used to describe this type of vessel. The beaker is an example of 'Waldglas', made in a primitive forest glasshouse with wood-ash as the source of the 'flux' which lowered the melting-temperature of the sand.*

THE GLASSMAKING FURNACE

Glassmaking requires a very hot furnace to melt the batch and clay pots of commensurate strength to hold the molten metal. The first furnaces were probably similar to those used for iron-founding and consisted of one small pot heated from beneath. The fire was fuelled with dry wood and continuously blown with primitive bellows. Furnaces of this kind are used in Nigeria today for recycling old bottles as beads and bracelets.

The oldest known account of glassmaking is recorded in cuneiform on clay tablets by the Assyrian king, Assurbanipal. This tells us that by the seventh century BC a major advance had been made with the invention of the reverbatory furnace, the sides of which were continued as a shallow domed roof to direct the heat of the fire down into the pot. The glass was 'gathered', or collected on the end of a solid iron rod known as a 'pontil', through a small aperture called the 'glory hole'. Such furnaces with only minor sophistications, usually for oil burning, may still be seen in operation in Damascus and Hebron. Later came the development of the annealing oven, or 'leer' – a separate chamber, heated more gently by the same

fire, in which the finished articles were cooled slowly to relieve strains produced in the glass during manipulation.

By the fifteenth or sixteenth century larger furnaces, containing four or six open pots, had been developed to meet the increasing demand for glass. The Venetian 'beehive', one of the two later types of furnace, had the leer situated above the pot chamber. The pots were placed on a circular shelf with a hole in the middle providing access to the fire beneath. This arrangement was economical of space – of possible importance for the Venetian glassworkers who had been banished to the small island of Murano in 1292 because of the danger from furnace fires – but the leer was awkwardly placed. The furnace in use in northern Europe, by contrast, was similar to the Arab furnace but elongated to hold more pots and with access to the fire from either end. It was cheap and easy to build, and it was simply abandoned when the glassmaker moved on in search of fresh supplies of wood. This furnace design remained virtually unchanged until well into the eighteenth century.

In England two major developments in furnace design

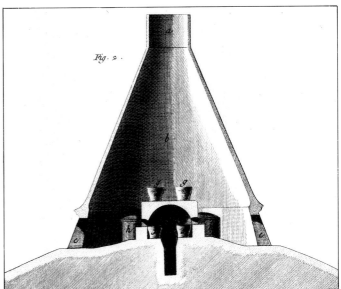

Far left: Illustration from De re metallica *by Georgius Agricola (1494–1555), published posthumously in 1556. It shows a wood-fired 'beehive' furnace of the Venetian type and, on the floor, stone marvers and dip moulds. In the foreground a customer approaches the master glassmaker.*
Left: Constructional details of a beehive furnace from De re metallica *showing the lower fire chamber with a stoke hole for the firewood. The central chamber contains open glass pots, round which the flames would lick; above it is the 'leer' in which the wares were 'annealed' to remove strains in the glass.*
Above: Illustration from Diderot's Encyclopédie, 1751–72. *The 'cone', or conical chimney, was erected over an English furnace to create the draught necessary to burn coal.*

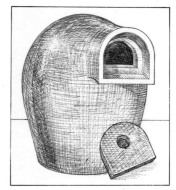

Left: Detail of a painting of the Midlands Technical College Glasshouse, English, c. 1875. The scene in a typical English glasshouse shows glassmakers working in teams round the most skilled workman, who was known as the 'gaffer'. In the foreground the 'servitor' is in the process of marvering a 'paraison', the first blown bulb of glass, ready for the gaffer to complete.
Above: Covered glasshouse pot in which the lead-crystal 'batch', or mixture of ingredients, was melted to avoid contamination by furnace gases.

contributed to the country's pre-eminence in glassmaking in the eighteenth century. Government concern over the competition with the all-important iron industry for wood led, in 1614, to its ban for fuelling glass furnaces. (One glasshouse was obliged to continue wood-burning – at the Savoy, in London, where coal smoke was unacceptable. It was here that Ravenscroft later discovered lead crystal.) Few experiments had been made in coal-firing but this was now the only alternative. Although the quality of the glass at that time was not very good, difficulties with coal supplies and the problem of obtaining a hot fire with the slow-burning, smoky fuel drove many glassmakers out of business. Sir Robert Mansell, who held the monopoly of glass manufacture, experimented with numerous sources of coal. For a while oil shale was used on the Dorset coast with apparent success; this furnace had winged extensions, one of which also formed the leer, a not uncommon feature at that time, and the fuel was now supported on a grid to allow the air access from beneath. Ultimately, Newcastle, for its coal, and Stourbridge, for its clay pots, became the principal centres of glassmaking.

To protect the glass from discoloration by smoke the pots were closed at the top, but difficulty was frequently experienced with creating enough heat to melt the glass. This problem was solved in the late seventeenth century by the second major invention, probably in connection with the even greater heat required for making dark green bottle-glass. A broad, conical chimney was placed over a modified Venetian-style furnace without its leer, which now became a separate oven. Draught was supplied through underground tunnels and regulated by doors in the base of the chimney which also provided access for the workers, who operated in the floor space between furnace and chimney wall. These glass 'cones', 60 to 120 feet (18 to 36 m) tall, became a feature of glassmaking areas in Britain. They remained in use until well into the twentieth century before becoming uneconomical.

The cone, although effective, was inefficient in the use of fuel. Its demise was signalled in 1857 by Friedrich Siemens's discovery of the regenerative process in which the hot waste gases preheated the air coming into the furnace. The twentieth century brought changes to oil or electricity, and the introduction of large tanks for melting the glass for all but the best lead crystal. The advent of cheap bottled gas in the 1950s brought back, first of all in America, small, home-made furnaces run by one or two workers producing 'studio glass'.

To melt the batch and during 'fining', to drive off gas bubbles, the furnace was heated to its maximum for up to 48 hours. The temperature was then reduced to about 900°C, causing the consistency of the glass to become more viscous and ready for working. In the eighteenth century a full pot lasted five days. The glassworkers had two days' rest while the master glassmaker, with his 'tisseur' to fuel the furnace, recharged the pots.

THE GLASSMAKER AND HIS SKILLS

Nothing certain is known about the techniques used before blowing but the investigation of old vessels, combined with laboratory reconstructions, provide a reliable guide to the sort of methods that must have been used.

Simple beads were made by working a blob of glass round a metal rod with a second rod as the glass cooled. The finished bead was placed on a bed of hot ashes to cool slowly. Small items for jewellery and decorative inlays were cast by pouring or pressing the hot glass into clay moulds. Hollow vessels were formed round a core, made of sand and clay with some sort of binding agent, attached to a metal rod. A blob of molten glass was gathered on another rod and 'trailed', snake fashion, as a continuous fine stream on to the core as it was steadily rotated. The surface of the vessel was smoothed by reheating and rolling on a flat surface, made of stone, marble or iron, called the 'marver'. This process, called 'marvering', is one of the basic and most important glassmaking operations. A small foot was fashioned by again reheating the vessel and working the end with metal forceps as the piece was rotated.

Decoration was achieved by trailing glass of a different colour in a pattern over the surface of the vessel, either leaving the decoration proud or marvering it flush. Combing the glass alternately in opposite directions at right angles to the trailed decoration produced a characteristic feather pattern. Such was the glassworker's skill that all these manipulations could be carried out single-handed as he sat or squatted in front of the furnace.

The invention of the blowpipe, properly called the 'blowing-iron', around 64 BC, opened up untold prospects for glass manufacture. In its original form it was 30 to 36 inches (76 to 91 cm) long and about ½ inch (1.3 cm) in diameter, often with wooden insulation around the mouthpiece end; the tip was slightly flared to help hold the hot glass. The worker's other tools were a solid iron pontil of similar length to the blowing-iron; blunt-nosed spring tongs, called 'pucellas', and a variety of wooden paddles and moulds, all used to shape the glass;

large spring forceps to seize glass while working it; shears to cut away any excess glass; and simple measuring devices of various kinds.

The methods used in a small Arab glasshouse today – at the nationally sponsored Abu Ahmad factory in Damascus, for example – differ little from those of 2,000 years ago. There, the glassblower sits on a small stool in front of the furnace, protected from the intense heat from the glory hole by a pivoted clay cover that can be raised by a foot pedal to allow access to the glass pot. A small 'eye' alongside is used to keep the blowing-iron and pontil hot ready for use. The marver forms part of the shelf immediately in front of the glory hole and a little above knee level. The glassblower works single-handed, rolling the blowing-iron on the forceps resting on his right thigh; an assistant was required only to help shape the foot and carry the finished item to the leer.

Working single-handed was a feature of glassmaking probably until the mid-seventeenth century. Then, the development in Europe of larger furnaces with greater glass capacity meant that the glassblower had to work standing up. A lathe, strapped to the right thigh, replaced the forceps used when rolling the blowing-iron.

The development of the glassmaking 'team', which probably centred round the introduction of the glassmaker's 'chair', created a career structure. The apprentice began as 'taker-in' at the age of seven; he carried the finished articles to the leer and did odd jobs. He could progress to 'footmaker', 'servitor' and, if sufficiently skilled, 'gaffer', who was in charge of the team, sat in the chair and carried out the difficult work. The servitor brought glass to the gaffer for various operations such as the making of handles and applied fancy-work; he could perform some operations in the chair if required. The pay of each member of the team was appropriate to the type of work he carried out.

To handle larger masses of glass, and facilitate rolling on the arms of the chair, the blowing-iron and pontil were increased in

Above: Nineteenth-century glassmakers' tools: shears (Figs 1 and 2), blunt-nosed tongs known as 'pucellas' (Figs 3 and 5), forceps (Fig 4), various measuring devices (Figs 6–9 and 11), paddle for flattening and shaping (Fig 10) and footboard for finishing the foot of a wineglass.
Right: Mould-blowing bottles and
marvering, as practised in the nineteenth century. An 'open and shut' mould is being operated by the glassmaker while his assistant marvers a gather ready for the next bottle. The rim would be finished by hand by the glassmaker sitting in the chair.

length to 56 inches (1.4 m). These changes worked well for heavy lead glass. For the lighter soda and potash crystals, often thinly blown and moulded right to the rim, some manipulations – shearing in particular – still had to be carried out standing at the furnace before the glass had time to cool. Today, few gaffers are sufficiently skilled to shear standing up. The reason is that the vessel bowl is blown into a mould and the excess, or 'overblow', is removed by a 'cracking-off machine' which also heat-finishes the rim, thus economizing on the costly time of the gaffer.

Important innovations in the late eighteenth and early nineteenth centuries were the adoption of pucellas with wooden ends which did not leave the unsightly marks made on the glass by the all-metal ones; and the 'gadget', a spring-loaded device that gripped the foot, replacing the pontil for this purpose. The result was that some hand-made glasses of the period have smooth bowls and lack the pontil mark. When the gadget was not used it became common to grind off the pontil mark, even on inexpensive glasses, and, in consequence, the foot became much flatter.

Above: Detail of the frontispiece of the Latin edition of L'Arte Vetraria *by Antonio Neri, 1668. This is the earliest known picture of a glassblower's chair, used mainly by the gaffer. Pots dry on top of the furnace, and on the shelf below are models for the glassmaker to copy. The pontil and blowing-iron are heated in the 'eye' on the right.*
Left: Illustration from Diderot's Encyclopédie *showing glassmakers braving the heat to gather glass from the furnace.*

MAKING A GOBLET
1. With the 'paraison', or gather after it had been blown into a bubble, attached to the blowing-iron, the glassmaker formed a simple stem with tongs, rolling the iron on his knees.
2. To form the foot of the goblet a new gather was collected on the end of the pontil, then a suitable blob cut from it on to the marver.
3. The blob was picked up from the marver on the end of the newly formed stem.
4. Holding with one hand the blowing-iron, to which the partially formed vessel was attached, the glassmaker shaped the foot using tongs and a wooden paddle.
5. After the blowing-iron had been cracked off, the vessel was rested on the marver, then picked up by attaching the pontil to the base of the foot. After this, the rim was reheated and trimmed to size with shears.
6. The final shaping of the bowl was done with tongs. At various stages in the process measurements were taken and compared with those of a model.

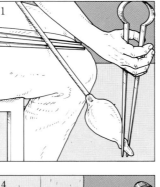
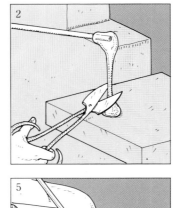
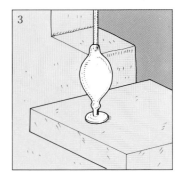

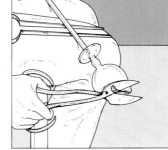
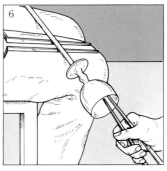

MOULD-BLOWING AND PRESS-MOULDING

Mould-blown glass first appeared in the early decades of the first century AD. The technique that was used combined the new invention of blowing with the older one of fashioning glass in a mould. Elegant mould-blown vessels, mostly of an ornamental nature, appeared in profusion as souvenirs or as items of religious significance. A few Roman makers incorporated the signature or a place of manufacture into the design. Reproductions, made in the Middle East, are usually larger and heavier than the originals and may have been 'aged' with coatings of mud and patches of applied iridescence (see p. 100).

Moulds were originally made of clay; later, wood and then cast iron became the materials of choice. The moulds were valuable possessions which, with the secrets of glassmaking, were passed down through the glassmaker's family. The most versatile type was the one-piece 'dip mould', open at the top and slightly tapered so that the shaped work could be withdrawn easily.

Venetian diamonding was achieved by blowing the glass into a vertically ribbed mould and then nipping the ribs together by hand. This pattern, much favoured in England, became known as 'nipt diamond waies' in the late seventeenth century.

'Font-moulding' involved the use of a small dip mould for shaping a solid 'gather', or blob of molten glass, on the end of the pontil. Typical products were drinking-vessel stems, 'lemon-squeezer' feet and small ornaments.

For more complex shapes the moulds were divided into two, three or even four hinged sections. These were often opened and closed mechanically by foot to leave the hands free. However, tradition is important and some firms, Waterford Crystal, for example, still prefer to employ assistants to operate the moulds used for the manufacture of standard sets of hand-blown drinking-glasses.

In 1828 an American named Deming Jarves patented a

Far left: Syro-Palestinian mould-blown beaker, second half of the first century AD. The technique of mould-blowing was developed in the middle of the first century AD. The moulded decoration on this vessel depicts Gods and Seasons.
Above: French or Belgian covered cup on stand, c. 1830–50. The earliest press-moulding machine was patented in 1828 by the American Deming Jarves (1790–1869). His invention was quickly taken up in European glasshouses for the mass production of cheap glassware.
Left: French press-moulded and overcut candlestick, c. 1830. By using lead crystal, brilliant effects could be achieved with press-moulding, especially when, as here, the surface was enhanced by over-cutting the pressed decoration.

Below: Mount Washington Glass Co. mould-blown castor set, American, c. 1885–95. The Massachusetts glasshouse was founded by Deming Jarves in 1837, and it was here in the 1880s that 'Burmese' glass was developed. The glass vessels which comprise the castor set are Burmese shaded gold-ruby on an opaque

uranium-yellow ground.
Right: Illustration from Curiosities of Glass-Making *by Apsley Pellatt (1791–1863), 1849, showing an early press-moulding machine.*

Left: Hinged two-part mould as used in the manufacture of vases and bottles, foot-operated to permit the glassworker complete freedom with his hands.

machine for pressing glass into a mould and so inaugurated mass production in glass manufacture. The first products were small cup-plates with a fine, lacy pattern moulded on the back. Lead crystal was used and this enhanced the brilliance of the pattern when viewed from the front. Judgement was required to estimate the size of the blob of glass dropped into the mould, but otherwise the work was only semi-skilled. The mould for a cup-plate was quite complex, with separate sections for rim and centre. This enabled the centre section to be changed independently which was convenient for producing a series of commemorative pieces, avoiding the cost of an entirely new set of moulds.

Early press-moulded glass was made of full-lead crystal; in spite of its thickness, the glass will ring when struck. Later, the lead content was reduced and new formulas developed containing, for example, barium. This gave a quicker-setting metal, so speeding up production, and it also helped to produce a bright finish.

Hand-operated press-moulding machines have a long life and are still in use at the Val St-Lambert factory in Belgium – one of the first to introduce this technique into Europe. For better work the pressed item is ground and polished or transferred to a pontil and reheated at the glory hole, either to fire-polish out the mould marks or to give individuality to the shape. A team of three men and two boys could produce 100 fire-polished tumblers an hour.

In the mid-nineteenth century press-moulded designs imitated traditional methods of glass decoration, in particular deeply cut glass, often enhanced by after-treatment with a rotating brush to give a band of matt finish. Later patterns show more independence in design. The nursery rhyme scenes designed by Walter Crane for Sowerby's of Newcastle in the 1780s and used for a variety of coloured pressed ware are particularly noteworthy. By the end of the century, for domestic ware especially, the patterns became shallower, giving the product a smooth and rather dull appearance.

Press-moulded glass can often be identified by manufacturers' marks and pattern registration numbers. Moulds did change hands and reissues were common; modern copies can also confuse. Good indications of mid-nineteenth-century origin are the presence of a pontil mark, shaping that could not possibly have been achieved by the mould alone, or the addition of a hand-made handle, often applied on top of the press-moulded pattern.

BALUSTER-STEM GLASSES

Venetian *cristallo* was a quick-setting glass which could be thinly blown. The delicately drawn curves, which so suited the character of the metal, were possible to achieve because the forms set before they became distorted by gravity. The work demanded a sure eye and deft hand.

Lead crystal had a lower melting-temperature and a greater viscosity than *cristallo*, rendering the metal suitable for thicker, heavier pieces that were shaped in accordance with – rather than in defiance of – gravity. Allowed to flow from the pontil, a gather would spontaneously form an elongated droplet of 'baluster' shape. If the glassmaker indented the gather with his pucellas, an air bubble would become trapped inside the baluster. This, directed on to the upturned bowl of a wineglass, formed the simplest inverted baluster stem, the characteristic feature of the first English glasses to break completely with the Venetian tradition.

Elegant variations in stem design were obtained by adding blobs of glass, called 'knops'; a 'cushion' knop was added just below the bowl and, immediately above the foot, a 'base' knop. Of the various elaborations of the baluster shape the 'acorn' knop, 'angular' knop and 'drop' knop are perhaps the most pleasing. They were made by compressing and tooling the basic baluster shape.

The round-funnel bowl of the glass was made thick towards the base to balance the heaviness in the stem. Its shape was also varied to form a 'thistle', or a straight or flared 'trumpet', beneath which the cushion knop was compressed to a 'blade'. The foot was rarely domed but the rim was nearly always folded under. The lustrous beauty of the glasses owes much to the refractive index of the metal.

Continental glasses of similar style are poor imitations of the English glasses. The most successful were produced at the Lauensteiner glasshouse in Germany in the mid-eighteenth century; some may be identified by a lion rampant or letter 'C' engraved beneath the foot. The metal that was used appeared to have been a potash glass free from lead.

Heavy baluster styles in chalkglass, associated with Potsdam and Silesia, were produced as blanks for the cutters' and engravers' arts (see pp.84–88), and it is on this that their prestige rests today.

A popular stem variation, suited to both chalkglass and lead crystal, emerged in 1714 and became known as the 'Silesian' or 'moulded pedestal' stem. A blob of glass, gathered on the pontil, was pressed into a small dip mould of four, six or eight sides and then drawn into an elegant shape. Stars or other motifs, cut into the base of the mould, appeared in relief on the shoulder of the stem. This form of stem was widely used for half a century or more for sweetmeat glasses, tazzas (ornamental cups with shallow bowls), tapersticks and candlesticks, as well as for wineglasses.

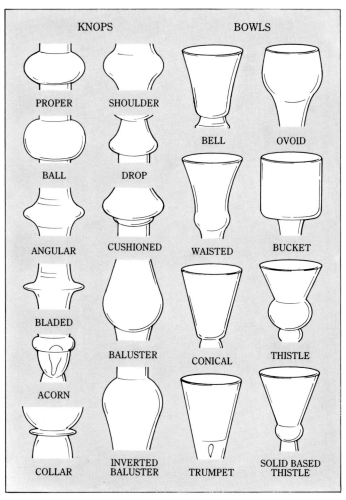

Above: Two Lauensteiner baluster-stem goblets, German, mid-eighteenth century. The Lauensteiner glasshouse was founded in Hanover in 1701. It is said to have employed English workmen, and it was the first to have attempted the manufacture of English lead crystal; many of their pieces show 'crizzling', a fine network of fractures. The goblets illustrated here, made in potash glass with no lead, reflect a fine blend of the English and German traditions, with decorated air beads in the thick base of the bowl and a high domed foot.
Right: Knops and bowl shapes on eighteenth-century wineglasses.

KNOPS BOWLS

PROPER SHOULDER

BALL DROP

BELL OVOID

ANGULAR CUSHIONED WAISTED BUCKET

BLADED

BALUSTER CONICAL THISTLE

ACORN

COLLAR INVERTED BALUSTER TRUMPET SOLID BASED THISTLE

Left: English baluster-stem goblet, 1700–20. The knop is in the form of an acorn pointing downwards, made by manipulating the baluster stem. Above: English pedestal-stem goblet, first quarter of the eighteenth century. The bell bowl, solid at the base, was mounted directly on the stem, an early feature of such goblets. The eight-sided pedestal, or 'Silesian', stem was decorated with stars at the shoulder. The folded, or 'welted' foot, is typical of the period. Similar lead-crystal glasses were made in Norway, although usually with less metal in the base of the bowl. Soda-glass versions, associated with France and the Low Countries, often show crizzling.

AIR TWIST GLASSES

To the early makers of crystal glass, bubbles were a defect, hence the process of fining in glass manufacture. Even Venetian *cristallo* was subject to this trouble. Lead crystal, by contrast, has excellent fining qualities, and the absence of naturally occurring bubbles was one reason why a single, large air bubble could be introduced as a decorative feature. (The presence of many small air bubbles in a glass is a fairly sure indication of a non-lead metal.)

By 1730 the popularity of baluster forms was on the wane. For ordinary domestic use at this time cheap plain-stemmed glasses were made by drawing out the base of the bowl to form the stem, to which a plain or folded foot was attached. The appearance of these 'drawn trumpet' glasses was transformed by indenting a ring of hollows in the base of the bowl so that when the stem was drawn it contained a corresponding series of fine air channels. The initial indentations were made with a simple tool consisting of a short length of dowel, from the end of which protruded a ring of nails. The spiral effect in the stem was produced by twisting the stem during the process of drawing. The technique may have had its origin in the manufacture of light baluster glasses in which one section was decorated with a ring of air bubbles that had become slightly elongated during manipulation of the glass.

Lengths of drawn air twist were prepared which could be cut off, reheated and attached to bowls of various different shapes. An identical technique was later used for Continental and English opaque twist glasses (see p.83).

An uncommon group of glasses, called 'mixed twists', have opaque and air twists combined in the same stem.

The so-called 'mercury twist' was produced by making slit-shaped indentations and drawing the glass to form twisted ribbons of air. Refraction caused the air bubble to look as if it had been filled with mercury, and there was much speculation as to how mercury could have been introduced.

Air twist glasses are characteristically English, although there are in existence a few mid-eighteenth-century soda-glass examples of uncertain origin. The air twist gave way to the opaque twist in about 1745. The type was revived in the middle of the nineteenth century. The air threads were more pronounced, the foot flat and the pontil mark generally absent on these later glasses. In the 1950s Royal Brierley Crystal revived the drawn trumpet air twist under the name of 'Edinburgh', but it is not difficult to distinguish these glasses from their elegant forebears of over 200 years earlier.

The air twist is one of the few glassmaking techniques not anticipated by Roman or Venetian craftsmen, and it was a direct consequence of the invention of lead crystal.

Left: Group of English air twist glasses with engraved bowls, c. 1750–60. On the left and right are two types of glass exhibiting different treatment of the popular hops and barley motif. The decoration was not necessarily related to the drink for which the glass was intended, as illustrated by the presence of the same motif on the two wineglasses second and third from the left. The glass second from the right has a small bowl and was used for cordials; the stem is decorated with a typical double mercury twist.

FORMING AN AIR TWIST STEM
1. A blob of glass was gathered on the pontil, slightly elongated and the end flattened on the marver. Indentations were made in the end of the blob using a ring of nails in a dowel.
2. Meanwhile, the bowl of the glass was blown. Attaching the stem trapped beads of air corresponding to the indentations.
3. As the stem was drawn, and simultaneously rotated, the air beads formed a spiral of silvery air threads.

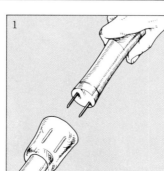

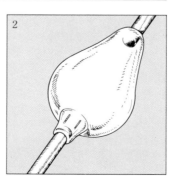

ICE GLASS

The discovery of ice glass (*vetro a ghiaccio*) is attributed to Venetian glassmakers in the Renaissance, and in the sixteenth and seventeenth centuries emigrant glassworkers took the secrets of its manufacture with them to other European centres of glassmaking. According to Apsley Pellatt in *Curiosities of Glass-Making*, published in 1849, the technique had become a lost art, however, 'not since practised by either Bohemian or French glass-makers' until he rediscovered it.

The effect was achieved by plunging the partly expanded vessel, heated to nearly white heat, into cold water. If immediately rewarmed and blown, the glass, which was covered in fine fractures, re-fused. Pellatt described the surface as having 'irregularly veined, marble-like projecting dislocations, with intervening fissures'. He called his creation 'Old Venetian Frosted Glass'; in France it became known, fittingly, as '*craquelle*'. The extent of the frosting seems to have depended on the composition of the glass as well as on the precise manner in which it was treated.

The idea was quickly taken up by other manufacturers and similar effects were obtained by a variety of other means. Another hot method, used by Bacchus of Birmingham and by Bohemian glassmakers, was to spread crushed glass fragments in an even layer on the marver and pick them up by rolling the hot glass bulb over them. Unlike *craquelle*, the decoration is confined to the surface and the glass fragments often retain quite sharp edges. For greater variety, mixtures of coloured glass fragments were often collected on an opaque white or cream base.

Late nineteenth-century frosted finishes carried out on the cold vessel involved the removal of the surface, so that the decoration sat below the original face of the glass. The commonest method, by acid etching with concentrated acid on a lead-crystal base (see p.90), gave a less robust effect than the hot methods, although Jean Daum and Maurice Marinot obtained striking effects by deeply etching thick blanks. Another process involved coating the vessels, which had been matted by etching or sand-blasting (see p.89), with a strong solution of hot glue. As the glue dried, it shrank and in the process tore out fragments from the surface.

For cheaper wares, press-moulding was used, and in the 1930s a simulated frosted finish was achieved by spraying the surface of the glass with enamel, which was baked on.

Below: Ice-glass beaker, goblet and jug, possibly South Netherlandish, second half of the sixteenth century. The vessels, ranging in height from 7½ to 3¾ inches (19.2 to 9.6 cm), were made in the manner of Venetian ice glass by plunging the hot, partially blown glass into cold water and quickly warming it before continuing blowing.

COLOURED GLASS

The earliest known glass beads and vessels were coloured opaque blue, white, turquoise and yellow. In the latter centuries BC, green and red began to be used, indicating an awareness of the importance of furnace conditions. Transparent glass was used more often but, with the discovery of blowing, the use of colour went out of fashion except in the Egyptian mosaic glass industry (see p.78). The colouring agents were probably by-products of the metal industry – as they still were until recently. Scrap bronze would have provided a mixture of copper and tin for making turquoise, while iron scale, from the blacksmith, would have been used for shades of green and amber.

Some colouring agents were used sporadically well before they came into general use. Thus, cobalt was found, uncommonly, in a piece of blue glass from the tomb of Tutankhamun, while the use of gold in the Lycurgus Cup is also exceptional.

The regular manufacture of gold-ruby and cobalt-blue glasses began in the mid-seventeenth century. For ruby, a compound of tin and gold called 'Purple of Cassius' was found to be particularly good for stabilizing the colour. This was necessary because the minute colloidal particles of gold which produced the colour were developed by reheating the metal at the glory hole; if the particles grew too large they reflected a greenish light, as seen in the Lycurgus Cup. Copper behaved in much the same way: the particles could be grown to form glittering spangles. This type of glass, called 'aventurine', was invented by the sixteenth-century Venetian glassmakers. It was a closely guarded secret which did not become generally known until the nineteenth century. Gold-ruby tends towards a warm orange in potash glass but a cool bluish 'plum' colour in lead glass. Copper-ruby has a brownish tinge and is found almost exclusively in non-lead glass; because of its intense colouring power, copper-ruby was sometimes used by Bohemian glassmakers in 'flashing' as a thin overlay over clear crystal (see p.92).

Cobalt came from Saxony in the form of a powdered potash glass called 'smalt', and its export was strictly controlled. In the eighteenth century the distribution of smalt in England was in the charge of William Cookworthy, a Bristol porcelain manufacturer. It is for this reason that cobalt-blue glass is often called 'Bristol blue' rather than because the glass was made in Bristol.

The repeal of the glass tax in England in 1846 made possible the production of coloured glass in competition with the Continental glassmakers. A little earlier, in about 1830, the Bohemian glassmaker Josef Riedel had discovered that uranium, alone or together with copper, could be used to produce dichroic yellow and green glasses which he called 'Annagelb' and 'Annagrün', after his wife Anna. The yellow colour, also called 'canary yellow', is now universally known as 'vaseline'. Uranium, in combination with other minerals, was later used to create a variety of colours and was particularly popular for shaded opal glass (see p.76).

New colours became possible in the mid-nineteenth century with the use of chromium, discovered in Siberia, for the manufacture of lime yellows and brilliant greens. Towards the end of the century a new spectrum of bright colours, ranging through yellow, orange and red, was obtained by combining the sulphides of cadmium and selenium in various proportions. To be able to distinguish these modern colours from the older ones is a great advantage, particularly when assessing the age of Venetian *millefiori* glass (see p.78).

Left: Lycurgus Cup, Roman, c. 400 AD. Seen here in reflected light, the gold-ruby glass is green; by transmitted light it appears wine red. Above left: South German engraved gold-ruby glass flask with silver mounts, early eighteenth century. Above right: Netherlandish copper-blue flask, second half of the seventeenth century. The mould-blown ridges pincered together were known as 'nipt diamond waies'.

Left: Flask, probably Syrian, first century AD. The oldest articles in glass to survive were made of opaque coloured glass; copper (red and blue), tin (white) and iron (blue-green and yellow) were among the earliest colouring agents.

Above: German manganese-purple and clear glass goblet and cover made in Nuremberg, c. 1700. This has a hollow-blown baluster stem and bladed knops. Manganese, when combined with cobalt, produced black glass; in small quantities it was also used as a decolorizer in the making of colourless transparent glass.

OPAL AND OPAQUE GLASS

Many recipes have been devised for making opaque and semi-opaque, or opal, glass. Antimony was used by the Romans, who found that calcium antimonate was an effective opacifier for soda glass. Another, also for soda glass, known to Agricola in the sixteenth century, was the mineral fluorspar; its active ingredient is calcium fluoride. In the nineteenth century England had a lucrative export trade in fluorspar to America until it was discovered there. Feldspar (potassium aluminium silicate), also used in the manufacture of ceramics (see p.103), was first used in the late eighteenth century, while cryolite – a mixed fluoride of sodium and aluminium discovered in Greenland by the Danes – found widespread adoption some 50 years later. Mixtures of these compounds were favoured for the manufacture of the warm, translucent opals used from the nineteenth century for lampshades.

The most easily recognized opacifier for lead crystal is tin oxide, which produced a dense opaque white and a noticeable increase in weight. Arsenic, in sufficient quantity, was equally effective, and it was widely used in the manufacture of 'enamel' for clock dials.

Before 1850, Continental – particularly French – firms were producing fine opaline glass. Popular colours included turquoise, green, yellow and a gold ruby known as 'gorge de pigeon'. At Stourbridge, Grecian-style vases in matt or smooth opal glass were produced by W. H., B. & J. Richardson.

Shaded opals were made by incorporating cryolite in the batch. At the right concentration it gave an initially clear glass;

upon reheating the article at the glory hole opalescence developed, due to the formation of fine crystals of aluminium fluoride. By using a mould to create thick and thin areas in the glass, the opacity formed preferentially where the glass was thick and slow to cool. Against a gold-ruby, uranium-yellow or copper-blue background the result was most attractive and achieved enormous popularity for ornaments – both blown and press-moulded – and for lampshades. Fluorine opacifiers can be identified by the warm 'sunset glow' that comes through the glass when a vessel is held to the light. Today, their use is effectively prevented by factory health regulations.

A common opacifier for all types of glass was calcium phosphate. The usual source was bone ash or, in America, guano (which contains a mixture of calcium phosphate and calcium sulphate). It was often used in conjunction with lime or arsenic.

Coloured opals were obtained by the addition of metallic oxides to opal batch. A popular turquoise colour was obtained with brass filings. Shaded ruby against opaque blue or yellow was achieved with gold salts; the first-formed vessel showed only the opaque blue or yellow base colour but, on reheating at the glory hole, the ruby could be developed to whatever extent was desired. The best-known shaded glass is 'Burmese', patented by the Mount Washington Glass Co. of America in 1885 and manufactured under licence by Thomas Webb & Sons in Stourbridge in the following year. It was much favoured by Queen Victoria and renamed 'Queen's Burmese

Far left: Venetian opaque white glass jug, late sixteenth or early seventeenth century.
Left: Bohemian Lithyalin glass scent flask from the workshop of Friedrich Egermann (1777–1864), c. 1830–40. Egermann was the inventor of Lithyalin, a multi-coloured opaque glass with a polished surface resembling marble.
Below: Bohemian Hyalith beaker and saucer probably from a glasshouse owned by Count Buquoy (1781–1851), c. 1830.

Left: German Milchglas *beaker in opaque white glass, seventeenth century. The cylindrical body of this glassware is decorated overall with combed trails.*

Below: French blue opaline clock case with ormolu mounts, c. 1825. Copper with a trace of manganese in an opaline base glass was probably used to obtain the colour.

Ware' in her honour. Painted decoration looks well on the acidized satin finish that was generally given. Fairy lamps were a popular product as the magnificent colour showed to particular advantage when illumined by candlelight.

A similar shaded glass, ruby on cream opal, was called 'Peach Blow'. It was inspired by the crushed strawberry hue of an old Chinese vase that achieved fame by virtue of the $18,000 paid for it at auction in 1886. Individual firms produced their own versions, each trying to circumvent the patent rights of the others. In England, Stourbridge firms also experimented with Peach Blow colours, while the Bohemian glasshouses skilfully undercut the luxury market with cheaper versions.

A multicoloured opaque glass that has virtually defied imitation is 'Lithyalin', created by Friedrich Egermann in 1830 and manufactured only by the few Bohemian glasshouses that discovered his secret at the time. This magnificent metal is said to have been made in a single batch. The effect is of a vessel formed of layer after layer of deep red, brown and yellow-orange glass blown exceedingly thick. Deep-cut panels in the glass reveal its beauty in depth in a series of marble-like contours. Other shaded colours were also produced.

Towards the end of the nineteenth century beautiful textured opals were produced – forerunners of today's 'Art Glass'. Best known is 'Clutha', produced by James Couper & Sons of Glasgow. Clear pale-coloured glass was rolled over the marver strewn with chemicals, powdered glass and mica fragments. These were picked up to form random shadowy patterns of coloured flecks and bubbles of different sizes. Another fine, textured glass was 'Moss Agate' produced by the Stourbridge firm of Stevens & Williams.

MOSAIC AND MILLEFIORI GLASS

A feature of very hot glass is its ductility; the long thin rod obtained by drawing a gather is called 'cane'. As far back as 1500 BC short sections of cane, cut in cross-section, were built up round a clay core and then fused to form a vessel. The name 'mosaic glass' aptly describes the method of construction.

The next development was the manufacture of cane with a pattern in the cross-section. By the first century AD cast mosaic bowls were being made from patterned cane. The sliced cane was arranged in a clay mould, either closely packed or widely spaced, and infilled with plain glass, purple and green being favourite colours. After being fired to fuse the canes together, the bowl was reheated and pressed into its final shape before the surface was ground and polished.

Although Roman glassworkers grouped canes into patterns, the term 'millefiori' (meaning 'a thousand flowers') originated in Venice in the fifteenth century. Marcantonio Sabellico, Librarian of St Mark's, referred to millefiori glass made by the artisans of Murano as including 'in a little ball all the sorts of flowers that clothe the meadow in spring'.

Venetian millefiori was built up on the pontil by marvering and tooling successive gathers of coloured glass. To make more complex patterns the hot mass, with the pattern already partly formed, was shaped so that it would pick up a ring of coloured cane arranged round the interior of a dip mould. The final design, fused at the glory hole, was often nearly as wide as it was long before the cane was drawn. The skill lay in creating the millefiori patterns and in having ready simultaneously glass of all the colours to be used, for which purpose small 'piling' pots were employed. In due course specialist canemakers emerged who supplied the glassworks with pre-formed canes.

The word 'millefiori' is closely associated with glass paperweights. These were first produced at Murano, but the craft was revived and reached its zenith of artistic achievement in the French glasshouses of Baccarat, Clichy and St-Louis in the mid-nineteenth century. Fashioned from lustrous lead crystal, rather than the cristallo used by the Venetians for their millefiori, they are distinguished by the cane patterns, which may include the initials of the firm, and by the pattern of facets cut on the face of the paperweight. Some bear the year of manufacture, the earliest date being 1845.

Millefiori paperweights of lesser quality were produced in Bohemia, England and America. William T. Gillander, a talented English glassmaker, learned the art at Bacchus & Sons, in Birmingham. In 1853 he took his skills to the New England Glass Co., in America, and eventually founded his own firm. Another Englishman, who founded the Steuben

Left: Eastern Mediterranean mosaic glass patella cup, first century BC or AD. The bowl was cast in a mould by setting short lengths of amethyst cane with opaque white centres and green cane with opaque yellow centres in translucent glass.
Above: Fragment of a Roman mosaic glass tile, first century BC or AD. Lengths of opaque coloured glass cane were assembled, fused and then sliced transversely to make tiles.

FORMING A MILLEFIORI GLASS CANE
To form a cane incorporating a star-shaped pattern, the glassmaker applied successive overlays of glass to the initial gather on the pontil, tooling and marvering them into shape.
1. The first gather was marvered to a cylindrical shape, overlaid and then tooled to form a star shape.
2. The process was repeated with a gather of a different colour.
3. The star shape was transformed into a cylinder with a fourth gather.
4. A concentric ring was applied by the same method.

5. Cylindrical canes set in a mould were picked up by inserting the mass in the mould.
6. The final gather was marvered to enclose the design. The rod, which at this stage was almost as wide as it was long, was then ready to be drawn. An assistant charged his pontil with hot glass and attached it to the end of the mass, which had in the meantime been reheated and cooled to the right temperature. The assistant walked rapidly backwards, so drawing the cane. A slatted wooden track prevented the cane from touching the ground.

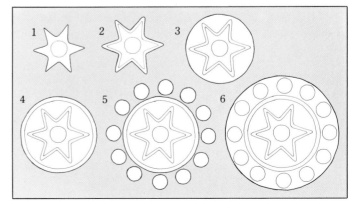

CORE-FORMING A MOSAIC GLASS VESSEL

1. Short lengths of opaque coloured-glass cane were built up in a pattern round a clay core and fixed in position with a temporary adhesive. The cane was made by drawing a gather into a rod of glass.

2. An outer layer of clay kept the canes in position during firing.

3. After firing and annealing, the core and outer layer were chipped away and the surface ground and polished.

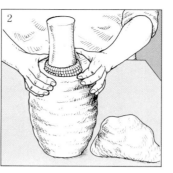

Left: Bohemian millefiori glass scent bottle, mid-nineteenth century. Scent bottles characteristically had a narrow neck and small opening to help control the flow of the liquid. 'Millefiori' was the term adopted in Venice in the fifteenth century for the flower-like designs embedded in clear glass. Millefiori glass scent bottles were made in Bohemia, France, Italy, England and America in the mid-nineteenth century.

Glassworks at Corning, New York, in 1903, was Frederick Carder. He made *millefiori* cane by a simplified method. Short lengths of coloured cane were arranged cold to form the design and bound together with iron wire. One end was heated and a pontil attached to the loosely fused bundle. The wire was then removed and the bundle further heated and marvered ready for drawing into patterned cane.

After World War II Baccarat took some seven years to rediscover the old skills which had been lost. Each top-quality weight contains about 200 *millefiori* canes and reflects seven hours of labour.

Doyen of the new Scottish paperweight industry was Paul Ysart, a Spanish immigrant who was apprenticed to the Edinburgh & Leith Flint Glass Co. (now Edinburgh Crystal) at the age of eleven. The Ysart family moved to Perth and began making paperweights as well as opal 'Monart' glass. The firm foundered in the 1950s but from its ashes emerged Perthshire

Paperweights. Challenging the skills of the French glass-makers, it prospers to this day.

Blown *millefiori* glass was a Venetian invention: in the Roman world the blown glass of Syria and the mosaic glass of Egypt were widely separated industries. Short lengths of *millefiori* cane were scattered on the marver, picked up on a gather of hot glass, melted in and the vessel blown so that the coloured pieces were incorporated into the vessel wall. Although simple in concept, the problems of finding glasses which were compatible in working, and could be annealed without producing stress cracks as they cooled, were considerable. Sixteenth-century examples are rare, but nineteenth-century lamps, vases and cups are common. Modern pieces of indifferent quality often include bright cadmium red and chrome yellow in the cane, although fine modern Muranese *millefiori* glassware testifies to a long tradition of craftsmanship.

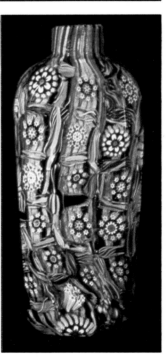

Left: Venetian millefiori *glass miniature ewer, sixteenth century. The vessel, measuring 5 inches (12.6 cm) in height, has a flattened globular body with heavy ribbing and silver-gilt mounts.*
Above: Clichy millefiori *paperweight in the form of a basket, c. 1845–55. More complex in design than the paperweight from the same glasshouse illustrated on page 61, it incorporates the characteristic Clichy motif of an open rose.*
Right: Bohemian millefiori *glass bottle, mid-nineteenth century. Without its stopper, the bottle measures 2³⁄4 inches (7.1 cm) in height.*

Left: Baccarat millefiori *glass paperweight, 1853. The diameter is 3 inches (7.8 cm). The dome of transparent glass, shaped with a wooden mould, serves to magnify the design formed by the cross-sections of coloured and patterned cane.*
Above: Baccarat millefiori *glass triple paperweight, French, c. 1845–55. The Compagnie des Cristalleries de Baccarat was one of the three main manufacturers of* millefiori *glass in France.*

MAKING A MILLEFIORI PAPERWEIGHT

1. Short lengths of millefiori *cane were arranged in a pattern on a cast-iron former and held in position by a detachable collar.*

2. The assembled canes, heated to just below melting-point, were picked up by a gather of clear glass. This formed the base of the paperweight.

3. The exposed faces of the canes, the other ends of which were embedded in the gather, were reheated and rendered plane. A 'neck' was formed close to the end of the pontil.

4. The glassmaker guided a gather of clear glass on to the exposed canes to form the dome of the paperweight and then cut it from the pontil.

5. The dome was shaped and polished with a wet wooden block.

6. The weight was allowed to cool, then cracked off at the neck with a cold iron rod. Cutting or gilding of the surface was done after the paperweight had been annealed and polished.

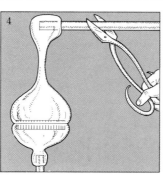

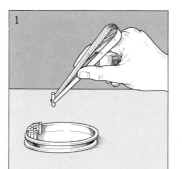

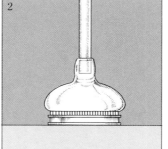

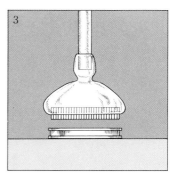

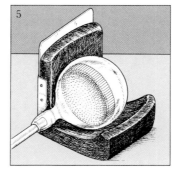

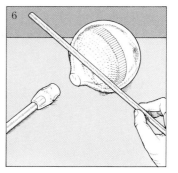

FILIGREE GLASS

In about 1525 Venetian glassmakers discovered that white 'enamel' cane had many decorative applications for blown glassware. 'Filigree', or *'vetro a filigrana'*, is the general term for this type of work.

'Vetro a fili' describes vessels in which simple *lattimo* (opaque white) stripes have been introduced into the glass by arranging short lengths of thin cane, also called 'threads', in a row on the marver. These were then picked up by rolling a bulb of hot glass over them. After reheating, the threads were marvered into the surface and the vessel was completed in the usual way.

To obtain an even distribution of many fine threads around the hot bulb, *lattimo* and clear canes were arranged in an alternating pattern around the interior edge of a dip mould. For variation, the canes could be made to curve in the vessel wall by rotating the blowing-iron as the hot mass was withdrawn from the mould. Italian glassmakers who settled in Castile and Catalonia in the sixteenth and seventeenth centuries produced a characteristically Spanish form of closed jug and drinking-vessel – known respectively as a *cántaro* and a *porron* – decorated in this way.

A further development was *'vetro a reticello'*, also called *'vetro di trina'* and, in Germany, *'Netzglas'*. Two bulbs were prepared with the curved pattern of canes running in opposite directions. One bulb was then opened up and cupped over the other to produce a pattern of crossed threads. Because the threads protruded slightly above the surface of the glass, a small air bubble was trapped in each cell of the network so produced. The remarkable feature of this work was the way in which the two bulbs were united to produce patterns with almost perfect geometrical precision.

Equally impressive was the use of canes of complex design – though less complex than those used for *millefiori* work. They were twisted during drawing to enhance the pattern and for this reason the glass is described as *'vetro a retorti'* (or *'retortoli'*). Working was the same as for *vetro a fili*. Some vessels were constructed entirely from cane. With one method of manufacture a number of short lengths of cane were arranged, side by side and as close together as possible, on the marver. Next a disc of hot plain glass was prepared on the blowing-iron and rolled along one end of the row of canes so that they were picked up to form a cylinder with a plain glass base. By further heating and marvering the cylinder of canes was fused together. The end was then pinched off with the pucellas to give a bulb that could be worked into a vessel composed of a series of, by now flattened, vertical rods, each of which displayed the original pattern of the cane.

In the sixteenth and seventeenth centuries *lattimo* canes were particularly favoured; in these early pieces there is a distinctive greyish tinge to the glass. The Venetians carried their skills to other parts of Europe, in particular the Netherlands and Liège in Belgium. Because the country of origin of a piece with filigree decoration is often impossible to determine, the description *'façon de Venise'* ('in the Venetian manner') is used. Later pieces tend to be much whiter and, from the nineteenth century, lead glass was often used. Shades of blue, pink and yellow, as well as gold, became commonplace in accordance with nineteenth-century taste. The best modern work is still carried out at Murano. Less expert pieces with irregular wavy rims occur; this is due, in part, to the uneven annealing properties of the canes used.

A recent development of *vetro a retorti* in studio glassmaking is to coil that hot cane round a former so that the pattern runs horizontally around the piece.

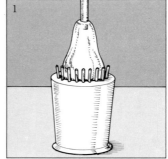
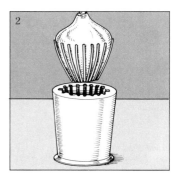

MAKING FILIGREE GLASS
1. *The paraison, or partially blown bulb of hot glass, was lowered into a dip mould lined with opaque white canes.*
2. *The canes adhered to the hot paraison, and they were fused by reheating and marvering. The vessel was then formed by the processes of blowing and tooling. For making an opaque twist stem (see opposite), a solid gather, rather than the paraison, would be used to pick up the canes.*

Left: Venetian cristallo *bucket in* vetro a retorti *with additional mould-blown decoration and turnover rim, seventeenth century. Alternate canes of twisted blue and white and twisted white gauze are separated by canes of plain white. The handle, made from a twisted cane with one thick and three thin white threads, is supported on applied clear glass loops. The height of the bucket, with the handle raised, is 4¹/₄ inches (11 cm).*

OPAQUE TWIST GLASSES

The Venetians developed a type of drinking-glass with elaborately shaped stems formed from patterned cane. In northern Europe – in England in particular – from about 1750 to 1780, canes were used for the so-called 'opaque twist' stems. These were relatively short and straight, manipulative variation being limited to up to four knops or, rarely, an applied collar half way up the stem. Considerable variation was introduced into the pattern of the cane; sometimes two or three canes were combined to give the double or triple series twist. The stem might be made from pre-cut cane, but more often it was drawn hot from the first-prepared mass of glass containing the pattern which was known, because of its shape, as a 'carrot'.

'Mixed twists', which have stems with entwined threads of air and enamel, are less common than opaque twists; rarer still are twists with coloured enamels. English twists invariably have the twist going clockwise up the stem, whereas Continental twists may rotate in either direction. Norwegian glasshouses, under English masters, produced some English-style opaque twists; the country of origin may only be determined by their provenance or additional decorative features such as engraving.

In about the middle of the eighteenth century English glasshouses produced drinking-glasses with a variety of 'compound' stems. In these, short lengths of opaque twist were combined with sections of plain glass decorated with knops or air beads. The knop might additionally be decorated with cut facets (see p.84) extending on to the bowl.

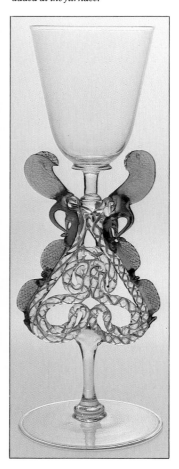

Below: Façon de Venise *serpent-stem goblet, seventeenth century. Winged glasses in the style of Venetian pieces were made in Germany and the Netherlands, often by emigrant Italian glassworkers; their exact place of manufacture is frequently not known. The elaborate stem of this example was first formed at the lamp (an oil lamp with air blown into the flame with bellows) from cane with twisted white threads; trailed-on and pincered cresting on the outer edge in copper-blue glass, and the bowl and foot, were then added at the furnace.*

Above: Group of English lead-crystal wineglasses with coloured opaque twist stems, c. 1765. The difficulty and expense of producing coloured twists meant that such glasses were not made in great numbers. In the two on the left the twist is a single tape; in the third from the left the tape is intertwined with a single thread, and in the one on the right of the group the tape is intertwined with two threads, white and pink; the glass in the centre has a stem composed of a white tape bordered in red and green intertwined with a white rope twist; to the right of it is a glass with a blue, red, green and white 'tartan' twist stem.
Right: English lead-crystal cordial glasses with coloured opaque twist stems and bowls decorated in the manner of the Beilby family, c. 1765.

CUTTING

The term 'cut glass' is something of a misnomer as the technique actually involves grinding away the surface of the glass by means of an abrasive wheel. Cutting dates back to pre-Roman times, when stone wheels were used. By the nineteenth century steam power had made possible the use of iron wheels fed with a continuous stream of fine, sharp sand; nowadays, synthetic carborundum or diamond-faced wheels are used. According to the design, the size of the wheel was varied up to 25 inches (63 cm) in diameter and 2 inches (5 cm) thick; they were always used wet. Stone wheels were delivered to the cutter 'in the rough', and his first job was to true them and shape the edge according to the type of cut that was required.

Cutting workshops were initially small and independent of the glasshouse that provided the 'blanks' for cutting. The wheel was turned either by a foot treadle operated by the cutter, by hand with an assistant, or, more rarely, by water power. The cutting tended to be shallow and slightly uneven.

With the advent of steam power in the early nineteenth century cutting workshops were developed as an adjunct to glasshouses. The blanks were blown thicker to accommodate the new deep cutting that now became possible, and the original line of the vessel disappeared under a profusion of ornament. A contemporary account described the workshop as being long and spacious, with skylights under which the men worked at their 'frames'. Each frame carried between its two main side supports the removable spindles, to which the wheels were fixed with large nuts. The spindles were driven by a leather belt from an overhead shaft. However, the most immediate impression given by a large cutting shop at work was noise.

Cut glass is characterized by more or less geometric patterns of prisms and facets of generally four, six or eight sides, and a minimum use of curves which, with large cutting wheels, were difficult to achieve. The cutter held the vessel between himself and the wheel so that he had to look through the vessel to direct his cut. He worked freehand with only the outline of the design, marked in waterproof paint, on the glass. After this 'roughing out', the design was gone over with a fairly smooth stone wheel, and it was then ready for polishing with cork or wooden wheels lubricated with pumice or a mixture of white lead and putty powder. The polishing frequently took longer than the cutting and gave a satisfying crisp edge to the cut. A final polish was often given with a rotating brush dressed with wet ground pumice mixed with rottenstone (decayed sandstone) powder; this may explain the faint haze that frequently occurs round the cut of early examples.

Wheel polishing is still used for the best work at Waterford Crystal. Most modern factories, however, use acid polishing with a mixture of hydrofluoric and sulphuric acids. This technique, discovered about the turn of the century, actually dissolves the surface of the glass; it both 'softens' the edges of the cutting and largely removes the wheel marks that characterize earlier work.

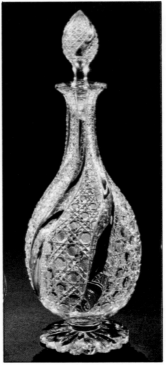

Left: Nineteenth-century steam-powered cutting workshop with a glassworker 'roughing out' a bowl. On the wall behind him are various wheels for cutting and polishing.
Above Left: Stevens & Williams full lead-crystal port decanter, English

c. 1880. Rolled pillars separate the swirling diagonal panels of laced-cane cutting.
Above right: C. Dorflinger & Sons lead-crystal drawn trumpet vase, cased in green glass and through cut, American, c. 1886–90.

Britain's pre-eminence in the production of soft, highly refractive lead crystal, ideally suited to cutting, made her the leader in the cut-glass industry in the second half of the eighteenth century. In the nineteenth century fierce competition came from the Continent – particularly for the popular market – whilst America, towards the end of the century, developed her own style of deep, highly polished 'brilliant' cutting on very thick blanks. The popularity of English cut glass declined in the late nineteenth century due to the protest of John Ruskin against the artistic barbarism of smothering a vessel with cut decoration. In the twentieth century more restrained designs have brought cut glass back into favour. Many patterns in production today are based on the successful designs of a century or more ago.

Today, cheaper cut glass, usually of Continental origin, is commonly made by overcutting a pattern that has been press-moulded into the glass. The mould marks may have been polished out, but close inspection will reveal a change in the angle of the glass at the edge of the cutting that could not possibly have come from the cutting itself; part of the moulded decoration may even be left uncut. Square whisky decanters are often made in this way.

Top: J. Hoare & Co. lead-crystal punch bowl and ladle decorated with brilliant cutting in 'Kohinoor' pattern, American, c. 1900–10. Considerable skill and strength were required to manipulate a piece such as this bowl against the cutting wheel, features of particular note here being the cutting of the rim and foot. Brilliant cutting, a type of highly polished cutting on thick blanks, was developed in America in the late

nineteenth century.
Above: Irish lead-crystal oval preserve bowl and dish, c. 1825. Both the bowl and the dish have denticulated rims. The bowl has oval panels of strawberry diamonds separated by cut flutes; the dish has plain diamonds between cut flutes.

ENGRAVING

Engraving is easier to describe than to define, for it embraces the decoration of glass by a wide variety of abrasive techniques. These include the use of diamond or steel points operated by hand or mechanically driven, as well as rotating wheels of copper, stone or some other material either fixed on a lathe or hand held and driven by a flexible shaft from an electric motor. It also embraces sand-blasting (see p.89) and acid etching (see p.90).

Although the hardness of the diamond was recognized in Antiquity, its use for scratching patterns on glass was not discovered until the mid-sixteenth century, almost certainly in Venice. In England it is first found on glasses made by Jacopo Verzelini, who in 1574 was granted a monopoly to produce *cristallo*. A small number of Verzelini glasses survive, their diamond-point decoration attributed to an immigrant Frenchman, Antony de Lysle.

In the eighteenth century the Dutchman Frans Greenwood discovered the art of stipple engraving. This involved pecking at the glass with a diamond flake mounted in a simple handle. He achieved remarkable pictorial effects by spacing dots close together to form highlights or further apart and more lightly struck to produce shading, the glass itself acting as a black 'canvas'. In Holland, stipple engraving on the soft English lead crystal achieved an outstanding degree of perfection in the hands of amateurs such as David Wolff and Anna Roemers Vischer. Calligraphy on glass, executed in diamond point, was the speciality of William Jacob van Heemskerk. In this century Laurence Whistler has been an outstanding exponent of the diamond point.

Steel point, a coarser form of engraving associated with Newcastle in north-east England and Alloa in Scotland, became a popular way of decorating bottles and cheap soda glass souvenirs in the mid-nineteenth century. The crude, robust, but nonetheless attractive, manner of execution contrasts with the sophisticated delicacy of the diamond point.

Engraving glass by means of small rotating abrasive wheels goes back, perhaps 3,000 years, to the manufacture of Assyrian cylinder seals. In the late sixteenth century, the Emperor Rudolph II founded a workshop in Prague for cutting and engraving precious stones, and it was here, in 1609, that

Right: Cristallo *goblet made in London by the Venetian Jacopo Verzelini (1522–1616), decorated with diamond-point engraving by the Frenchman Antony de Lysle, dated 1586. In 1574 Verzelini was granted a monopoly to make* cristallo *in England, and his glasshouse was the first in the country to decorate glass with diamond-point engraving.*
Left: Illustration from Pellatt's Curiosities of Glass-Making *showing a nineteenth-century engraver using a treadle-operated lathe.*
Below: Detail of an English lead-crystal facet-stemmed Friendship wineglass made in Newcastle and decorated with wheel engraving by Jacob Sang (died 1783), 1761. The glass was exported from England to Amsterdam, where Sang worked.

Left: English lead-crystal goblet decorated with stipple engraving by Frans Greenwood (1680–1761), c. 1744.
Right: Bohemian chalkglass goblet and cover decorated with wheel engraving by August Böhm (1812–90), 1840. The pictorial engraving was based on a painting by Lebrun.
Above: Detail of the goblet. Greenwood, who worked in Rotterdam, was the first to execute designs on glass in 'stipple', or small dots, using a diamond flake.

Caspar Lehmann received the earliest known patent for wheel engraving glass. Nuremberg became a flourishing centre of engraving in the seventeenth century, recognized as one of the great periods for engraved glass. At first the decoration was superficial but, as the quality and annealing of the metal improved, deep-cut 'relief' and 'intaglio' engraving were developed.

Copper-wheel engraving was carried out on a lathe driven by foot pedal or, latterly, an electric motor. In the course of engraving a single vessel many sizes of wheel were used, varying in thickness, diameter and profile. Interchangeability was achieved by mounting each wheel on to a tapered shaft that fitted, by means of a keyway, into a correspondingly tapered socket on the main shaft of the lathe. The engraver made his own set of about 40 wheels, the ability to true and shape each wheel according to the particular need being a prerequisite of the art. In use, a continuous film of fine oil was fed to the wheel from a leather tongue fixed above it. The engraver held the vessel behind the wheel, guiding it with both hands, but every few seconds he used one finger to apply a smear of carborundum paste to the edge of the wheel in order to maintain its abrasive action. Skilled engravers worked entirely freehand. Pictorial effects were built up progressively, considerable expertise being exercised to minimize the number of wheel changes required.

For relief engraving a thicker blank was used so that the design could be exposed by grinding away the surrounding glass. Intaglio engraving is the reverse of this process: the design was like a negative and cut deep in the glass. A three-dimensional positive effect was created when the engraving was seen from the other side. For this work, small stone wheels were used in addition to copper wheels. The invention of the stouter, intaglio lathe in the later nineteenth century is attributed to the outstanding Stourbridge glassworker John Northwood.

In the second half of the nineteenth century a method was discovered in France of giving a high polish to the whole engraved design. The technique was developed in Britain, particularly in conjunction with a preliminary sculpturing of the glass. This was sometimes achieved by blowing the blank into a mould so that a three-dimensional effect was obtained over the entire surface of the vessel. For obvious reasons, this form of decoration was known as 'rock crystal engraving', and it reached its peak during the last two decades of the nineteenth century. After this, the cost of production was greater than the market could stand and, although high-class engraving was often given a rock crystal polish, the expensive preliminary sculpturing was discontinued.

Above left: English ewer decorated in Stourbridge with rock crystal engraving by William Fritsche, completed 1886. With rock crystal engraving a high polish was given to the entire surface of the vessel; the sculptural effect was often achieved by blowing the blank into a mould. This type of decoration was developed in Britain by the Stourbridge firm of Thomas Webb. Webb's and Stevens & Williams were its principal exponents. The ewer, 15 inches (38.5 cm) in height, took Fritsche 2½ years to complete, working part time. On the neck is the mask of a river god in high relief; the body is engraved with dolphins and the foot with shells; the flowing lines indicate waves, and streams and rivers running down to the sea.

Above: Rock crystal goblet in the form of a cornucopia, possibly from the Miseroni workshop, Prague, c. 1660, with nineteenth-century mounts. In the early decades of the seventeenth century glass was already being decorated on lathes used for carving rock crystal. The search for a substitute for rock crystal probably contributed to the development of the lime-based potash glass known as 'chalkglass'.

Left: Thomas Webb & Sons lead-crystal goblets decorated with rock-crystal engraving, English. The gold-ruby cased glass on the left was decorated by the Bohemian glass engraver F. E. Kny in 1884; the one in the centre has floral ornament; the one on the right of 1906, decorated with bees and flowers, has heavy spiral sculpturing to the stem and foot.

SAND-BLASTING

Sand-blasting dates from 1870, when Benjamin Tilghman patented in America a machine for directing a fine stream of sand on to a glass plate at high velocity, initially by means of compressed air. Steam and other propellants could also be used. He exhibited his machine at the Vienna exhibition in 1873 and caused astonishment at the speed with which a variety of decorative effects was achieved.

Because the equipment was large and expensive, G. F. Morse, another American, devised a machine for home use. With this, the abrasive fell from a hopper down a tube 8 feet (2.4 m) long with a restricted orifice at the bottom, beneath which the glass was moved in the sand spray. The dust from both machines was a considerable health hazard and led to the development of enclosed cabinets within which the vessel and sand could be manipulated in safety. As with etching, templates or resist paints were used to define the decoration and protect areas to be kept clear; for one-off pieces, stiff paper, pasted on, was adequate.

Towards the end of the nineteenth century quantities of crudely decorated wares were produced for the various 'Trade and Industry' exhibitions. For a small extra fee these could be personalized to order and given as presents or kept as mementos of the occasion.

In order to keep down costs many firms now prefer sand-blasting – or 'sand-etching', as it is sometimes called – to wheel engraving for the longer runs of commemorative ware. The rather flat result may be greatly improved by touching in highlights with the engraver's wheel. An attractive decorative treatment employed at the Val St-Lambert factory involves fired-on gilding over a sand-blasted pattern to give the effect of embossing. Such work is considerably more difficult and time-consuming than flat sand-blasting and is, in consequence, expensive.

Its most sophisticated application has been in the hands of David and Chris Smith of Stourbridge, who have created delightful shaded 'cameo' ware (see p.92) using coloured overlay blanks from the Webb-Corbett (now Royal Doulton) factory.

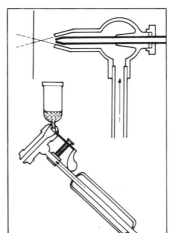

Far left: English press-moulded tumbler with sand-blasted decoration of oak leaves surrounding a cartouche of Queen Victoria, 1887. The patriotic decoration commemorates the jubilee of the Queen's accession.
Below: Detail from an English press-moulded tumbler with sand-blasted decoration commemorating the Bristol Industrial and Fine Arts Exhibition of 1893.
Left: Two types of gun used in sand-blasting: vacuum fed (above) and gravity fed (below).

ACID ETCHING

Alchemists were familiar with the fact that certain minerals, when heated with vitriol (sulphuric acid), gave off fumes that attacked glass. Rare examples of sixteenth-century decorative etching have survived.

Hydrofluoric-acid etching became widely known before the end of the eighteenth century, but its commercial exploitation was a nineteenth-century development; even so, pieces from the first half of that century are hard to find. By 1835 the Dudley firm of Thomas Hawkes was producing acid-etched presentation ware. John Northwood had seen experiments in acid etching at the Richardson factory and formed a partnership with T. Guest to exploit the new decorative process. This split in the early 1860s to form two important Stourbridge firms specializing in etching, J. & J. Northwood and Guest Brothers. At the same time, in France, acid etching was adopted at the Cristalleries de St-Louis. Technical knowledge was important; so, too, was financial backing, as the outlay for plant to make the sulphuric and hydrofluoric acids was considerable. This almost certainly explains the absence at an earlier date of the widespread practice of acid etching.

The glass to be etched was coated with a 'resist', initially a mixture of rosin and beeswax. (Resist inks and bituminous paints, for transfer-printing, were developed later.) The pattern was drawn through the resist with a boxwood stylus, but it proved to be both difficult and time-consuming to get good results, and to speed up production Northwood invented the template etching machine. Cutting the templates which automatically guided the stylus was itself a highly skilled process. The difficulties were overcome in 1865 with Northwood's invention of the geometric etching machine, by means of which both vessel and stylus were moved by adjustable gear wheels. This ushered in the application of etching to the cheaper sort of tableware, two of the earlier popular patterns being 'Key' and 'Circle'. Similar developments were taking place in other European glassmaking centres, particularly in France and Bohemia. Etching found particular use in the production of cameo glass (see p. 92).

The etching process itself was carried out by immersing the vessel in the acid at an appropriate dilution – as found by trial – for long enough to give the desired depth of cut. The stronger the acid, the deeper and rougher the cut. For very deep cuts, repeated immersion in acid was necessary, the walls of the cut being protected by further resist painting between each immersion. Hydrofluoric acid alone, or sulphuric acid-hydrofluoric acid mixtures, left a transparent surface; by contrast, 'white acid', made by neutralizing hydrofluoric acid with soda or ammonia, gave a dense white, matt finish. After treatment, the acid was washed off and the resist removed to reveal the decoration.

Although W. H. and B. Richardson had patented the use of a mixture of hydrofluoric and sulphuric acids for obtaining a bright finish in 1857, its application to polishing cut glass, instead of using cork wheels and putty powder, was only developed towards the end of the nineteenth century. Similar mixtures are nowadays used to remove stains and deposits from old glassware. Both acids are dangerous and the fumes extremely toxic.

Etching was widely used for decorating and obscuring flat glass panels and windows in commercial premises – a technique known in the trade as 'embossing'. For simple embossing the pattern was etched to a depth of about $\frac{1}{10}$ inch (2mm) and then matted by abrading with flour-emery and water. The embossed side of a window was always mounted facing inwards to protect it from the weather. In its most sophisticated form, called 'French embossing', multiple shading of the pattern was obtained by treatment of the glass with a series of acids of increasing strength; sections of the pattern were progressively protected with the resist as the work proceeded. French embossing was often combined with cut decoration.

ACID ETCHING
1. Using a magnifying glass, the glass decorator etched the copper plate with the pattern and it was then coated with resist ink.
2. An impression of the pattern was taken on a sheet of paper.
3. The pattern was then transferred to the bowl of a goblet.
4. Parts of the goblet which were not to be decorated were painted with resist to protect them when the vessel was immersed in the acid.
5. When the goblet was immersed, the acid attacked the exposed parts of the pattern. The depth of the cut depended on the strength of the solution and the length of time it was left in the acid.
6. After immersion, the goblet was washed in water and gently warmed so that the resist could be rubbed off.

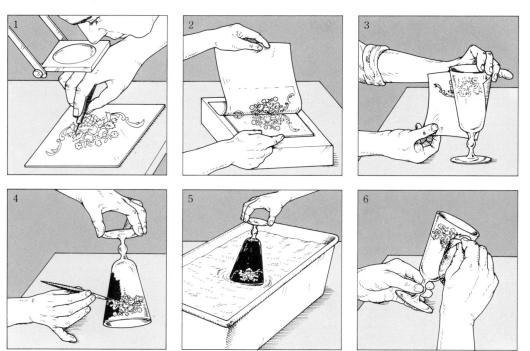

Left: Stevens & Williams cased-glass vase decorated with acid etching and gilding probably by William Northwood (1858–1937), English, late nineteenth century. The decoration is of exotic birds and blossom in Oriental style.
Below: Stevens & Williams claret jug decorated with acid etching. In this Grecian scene matt relief decoration is combined with bright etching in dots.

OVERLAYING AND CAMEO CUTTING

Gold, cobalt and tin produce intense colours in glass; for this reason they were often used to provide a thin casing of coloured glass over a base glass of contrasting colour. Attractive decorative patterns were produced by cutting through the overlay, and for elaborate work a series of overlays of different colours was used. The technique originated in Bohemia.

The problem to be overcome was achieving compatibility of expansion between the different glasses. In 1874 the Stourbridge firm of Pargeter had great trouble preparing the blank of white overlaying blue for John Northwood to attempt his famous copy of the Portland Vase. During the carving, Northwood frequently took it to the British Museum to compare with the original, made in Greece in the fourth century AD. After two years' work, disaster struck one cold day when the glass spontaneously cracked as he took it from its case. It was too late to start again and the scar of inadequate technology is there for ever.

English cameo glass followed the Greek tradition, with the overlay finely carved to create shaded effects against the base glass beneath. The blank was first matted by abrasion or with acid to allow the small steel chisels used for carving the pattern to bite into the surface of the overlay. The vessel was rested on a velvet cushion, and the chisels had to be sharpened every few cuts. Execution was slow, painstaking and unforgiving of mistakes. It took Northwood three years to carve his copy of the Portland Vase, regularly working long hours each day.

Cameo cutting was subsequently accelerated by roughly

Below: Thomas Webb & Sons cameo glass vase decorated with carving by George Woodall (1850–1925), English, late nineteenth century. The clear glass vase was cased in white glass on the outside. This was carved away to show the decoration against a gold-ruby glass flashed on to the inside.

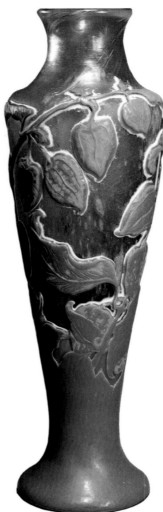

CAMEO CUTTING
1. The cased vase was first matted with acid, then the pattern roughly protected with resist so that unwanted parts of the overlay could be eaten away with acid to reduce the work of the engraver.
2. The vase, with the resist removed, was laid on a velvet cushion and the pattern executed by fine chiselling of the surface with steel tools that required frequent sharpening.

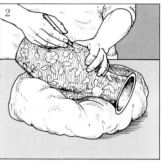

Above: Triple overlay vase by Emile Gallé (1846–1904), French, late nineteenth century. Layers of green, blue and grey glass with foil inclusions were wheel engraved and carved to depict sturgeons rising from turbulent waters and waving water weed. Vessel form, colour and carving here combine to express an aquatic theme.
Right: Quadruple overlay vase by Gallé late nineteenth century. The thick opaque overlays in cream and shades of coral were wheel engraved to depict a floral pattern, which forms a striking contrast with the translucent turquoise ground, streaked, mottled and flecked, with inclusions.

outlining the design with hydrofluoric acid. Even so, production was limited and, in consequence, extremely expensive. Much English cameo glass was produced by a team of artists under the direction of the brothers Thomas and George Woodall, working for Thomas Webb & Sons. Their innovative glass blanks included one for polychrome cameo, with applied patches of coloured glass relating to the cameo design. Another talented cameo engraver was Joseph Locke, who made a second copy of the Portland Vase before taking his skills to the New England Glass Co. of Cambridge, Massachusetts. Other American cameo glass producers were Tiffany, Corning and the Mount Washington Glass Co.

At Nancy, in France, Gallé and Daum had large workshops producing acid-etched cameo glass. The Art Nouveau designs were sometimes heightened with wheel engraving. Gallé's outstanding technical and artistic ability is reflected in the way he incorporated overlay and vessel into exaggerated three-dimensional designs. Up until the early years of the twentieth century many European workshops responded to the challenge of making cameo glass. The Orrefors factory, in Sweden, reheated thinly cut cameo glass and overlaid it with clear crystal; this variant, giving greater fluidity in the design, was called 'Graal' glass.

Chinese glassmakers independently discovered cameo glass after the Imperial Palace Glass Works was established in Peking in 1680. Production was prolific in the following century, particularly of snuff bottles. Both vessels and overlay were made in bright opaque colours; sealing-wax red on Imperial yellow was one favourite combination.

The coloured glass used for overlay work was made in small quantities in piling pots placed in the main furnace. Today, the casing colour may be obtained from a specialist firm as a short thick carrot that can be heated at the glory hole and a piece transferred to the blowing-iron.

An extremely thin copper-ruby overlay over clear crystal, invented by Friedrich Egermann, is almost the hallmark of Bohemian glassmakers. This 'flashing' was easily cut through by wheel engraving to reveal the design in clear glass against the ruby background.

A cheaper substitute for flashing was copper staining, obtained by applying the oxide as a paste to the finished glass. After firing, the paste was washed away to reveal a deep ruby stain permanently fixed in the glass. Silver nitrate gave a yellow stain. This treatment was particularly suitable for light, wheel-engraved pieces and was widely used to decorate spa-town souvenirs.

ENAMELLING ON GLASS

Enamelling is the technique of fusing a vitreous substance (enamel) in opaque or transparent colours on to a metal base (see p. 195). This process, with slight modifications to the composition of the enamel, was also used for fired-on painting on ceramics (see p. 132), and glass.

Enamelled glass goes back to Roman times but it first came into popular use in thirteenth-century Islam. Aleppo, Raqqah and Damascus, in Syria, were major centres of manufacture. Large lamps, cups and flasks were elaborately decorated with animals or scenes in red, blue, yellow, green and white enamels. These were ornamented with scrolls and Arabic writing in fired-on powder gilding (see p. 97), often outlined in red enamel. Souvenir trophies and presentation pieces found their way to Europe and the Far East.

As with other aspects of glassmaking, the sacking of Damascus in 1402 shifted the centre of glass enamelling to Venice, where new decorative styles developed.

Theophilus recorded that enamelling on glass was practised in central Europe in the early twelfth century. In the second half of the sixteenth century the tall tankards used for drinking beer, known as 'Humpen', were frequently decorated. The large flat surface of the tankard was ideal for the heraldic motifs which were favoured in southern Germany; in Bohemia historical, biblical and allegorical scenes were particularly popular. On Spanish glass colourful enamelling served to distract the eye from the crude glass beneath. The practice of enamelling glass declined towards the end of the seventeenth century, when the quality of the glass improved, styles changed and engraving became the new form of decoration.

'Schwarzlot', painting in black lead enamel, originated in the Netherlands, and in about 1660 a Nuremberg painter, Johann Schaper, applied the technique to glass vessels. He was probably the first to use transparent enamels – as distinct from opaque enamels – on glass.

In Bohemia and Silesia a tradition of working independently at home developed and many artists are known from the late seventeenth and early eighteenth centuries. Particularly notable 'Hausmalerei' (painters at home) were Daniel Preissler and his son Ignatius.

Painting in transparent polychrome enamels, much favoured on spa glass souvenirs, reached a high standard in the first half of the nineteenth century due to Samuel Mohn and Anton Kothgasser.

In eighteenth-century England enamelling on glass was associated with Newcastle, and William and Mary Beilby. William Beilby's polychrome enamelling on commemorative pieces is particularly remarkable (see p. 60). Other English decorators of the period, on both glass and porcelain, were James Giles, in London, and Michael Edkins in Bristol. The decorators of much English enamelled glass of this period – which was often ornamented with flowers on an opaque white ground – are unknown but were part of a thriving industry in the Staffordshire area.

Perhaps the most technically proficient glass enameller of all was Emile Gallé, in the late nineteenth century. His father owned a glass and a porcelain factory, and Emile designed and practised decorative enamelling for both. After his father's death he took charge of the glass factory and developed new ways to involve enamelling techniques in his own art creations. Enamel was no longer used as surface decoration but was

Above: German tumbler with Schwarzlot *decoration by Johann Schaper (1621–70), mid-seventeenth century. The technique of painting on glass in transparent black lead enamel was brought to Nuremberg by Schaper from the Netherlands, later spreading to Bohemia and Silesia.*

Left: German Humpen *and cover decorated with coloured enamelling, 1656. Made of green-tinted* Waldglas, *the tankard with its double-ogee cover is 14 inches (35.5 cm) in height. Below: Detail of the* Humpen *showing the figure of the Holy Roman Emperor enthroned executed in painted enamels. The decoration probably derives from a woodcut.*

incorporated in the overall design of the piece. His inventiveness is revealed in notes submitted to the Jury of the Paris Universal Exposition of 1889 where he describes new translucent enamels that remained effective under all lighting conditions. His '*Emaux-Bijoux*' (Jewelled Enamels) were a new series of translucent enamels which produced a remarkable effect when fired over metallic foil – for the winged back of a scarab or the eye of a dragonfly, for example. This was an extension of the early fifteenth-century enamelling known as '*émail en résille sur verre*' in which coloured enamels were inlaid in grooves cut into the glass.

Left: Viennese beaker decorated with transparent enamelling by Anton Kothgasser (1769–1851), 1812. Kothgasser was a miniature painter as well as a decorator of porcelain and glass. His decorations on glass were of flowers, often, as here, with inscriptions in French, and also of landscapes and allegories.
Below: Vase decorated with moths engraved and enamelled by Gallé, c. 1885–90. Gallé, who took over the family glassmaking and ceramic business in 1874, was one of the creators of the French Art Nouveau style.

Above: German Humpen decorated with portraits of the Dobrich family in coloured enamelling. The tankard was made in the second half of the nineteenth century, two centuries later than is suggested by the inscription and the style of decoration.

GILDING

For those in search of luxury, the combination of gold with glass must have appeared the ultimate indulgence. The Romans knew how to beat gold into sheets so thin that 300,000 were required to make 1 inch (2.5 cm) in thickness (see p. 168). Adhesion of this 'gold leaf' to a clean glass surface was mediated by a 'mordant'. F.S. Mitchell in 1915 recommended a solution of Russian isinglass shreds – one small teaspoonful dissolved in a pint of boiling water, filtered and applied warm. Alternatively, weak solutions of gelatine, gum tragacanth, gum arabic, egg white or even diluted whisky or gin might be used. Once dried, the gilding was washed with hot water to 'settle' the gold leaf on the mordant and gently polished with cotton wool. The best commercial work was doubly gilded by applying another layer of leaf over the first in the same way. With commercial gilding of, for example, a shop fascia, the edge of the gilding was protected by a thin layer of lacquer lipping the edge of the glass.

This description differs little in principle from a 1697 account of gilding by Haudicquer de Blancourt, who advocated a gum-water mordant, fixed by firing – a treatment readily applicable

Left: English loving cup made at Stourbridge and decorated with gilding by Jules Barbe, late nineteenth century. Barbe, an outstanding exponent of fired-on thick gilding and enamelling, was a Frenchman. He was employed as a glass decorator in England in the 1880s.
Below: English scent bottle in cobalt-blue glass with gilding attributed to the workshop of James Giles (1718–80), c. 1765. Giles ran a workshop in London for decorating glass and porcelain.

Above: English cruet bottle in cobalt-blue glass decorated with faceting and gilding attributed to Giles, c. 1770. Various pieces are attributed to Giles, though no signed examples of his work are known.

Far left: German goblet and cover, eighteenth century.
Left: Detail of the goblet showing the gilded decoration. The design was first engraved, then painted with powder gilding and fired.
Below: Nineteenth-century illustration of a gilding furnace. Gilded buttons were fired in a perforated steel drum, which was rotated.

to small vessels. Before firing, the leaf could be cut with a hardwood stylus to form patterns or pictures. Fired gilding was usually burnished, traditionally with a dog's tooth, bone or agate. For greater permanence the gilding could be washed over with borax solution (an enamel flux), dusted with finely powdered glass and then fired. This protected the gold with a thin film of glassy enamel.

An essentially similar method of protection is described in the earliest known description of gilding. It was written by Theophilus in the twelfth century and appears in his *De Diversis Artibus*. Gilded glasses from his time still survive. In earlier, Roman, pieces the gilding is usually protected by a second layer of glass, sometimes of a different colour, to form a 'sandwich'. The technique of making gilded sandwich glass, or *Zwischengoldglas*, has found decorative and practical applications right up to the present day; one of the more common uses was for protecting the gilded labels on pharmacy drug jars.

These methods of gilding are ideal for a fire-polished glass surface but less so for embellishing the rough surface left by the wheel engraver. This fact may explain the introduction of mordants variously compounded from linseed oil, chalk, red and white lead oxides, and turpentine, as used for gilding other materials. Cold 'oil gilding' was typically English and not very durable. On eighteenth-century glasses a darkness in the engraving generally provides the only evidence that such

gilding ever existed. Gilding was, however, used with conspicuous success in the eighteenth and nineteenth centuries to decorate so-called 'Bristol blue' – decanters, cruet bottles and other wares. The work of James Giles, Michael Edkins and Isaac and Lazarus Jacobs is notable in this connection.

On the Continent, powder gilding, using chemically precipitated gold, was favoured, and a valuable description is preserved in a manuscript from the Nöstetangen factory, in Norway, which started gilding in 1760. For application, the powdered gold was mixed with oil of spike (lavender) and all unduly large grains removed. 'The laying on', it was stated, 'should be undertaken by one who has a light hand and good eyes, and understands drawing'. Three coatings were given, followed by firing, and finally the cooled glass was burnished.

Other forms of powder gilding in which gold was mixed with powdered glass and borax so as to stand out in relief from the glass surface may be considered as a variant of enamelling.

In the late nineteenth century English gold leaf, which was supplied in books of 25 leaves, $3\frac{1}{4}$ inches (80 mm) square, became pre-eminent for commercial work, which accounted for the bulk of all glass gilding. Mirrors in public places and elaborate shop fascias – few of which survive – were often embossed and counter-gilded with silver or platinum. The gold was graded in colour from white to red and of specially selected thickness for glass work. For powder gilding, however, the Continental product remained supreme.

SILVERING

In early times mirrors were made from polished metal, but the knowledge that glass backed with metal would give a reflecting surface has a long history. The problem to be overcome was the uneven surface and variable thickness of the glass. By the sixteenth century both Islam and Venice had flourishing looking-glass industries. In England, in 1621, Sir Robert Mansell was able to claim in a petition to Parliament that he was the first in the country to manufacture looking-glasses; his workers were, however, Venetian. At that time Venetian looking-glasses were banned, and the battle over imports was to rage for the rest of the century. The imports might be in the form of blown sheets – called 'rough plates' – ready for polishing, polished but 'unfoiled' (not silvered) plates, or the finished article.

By the mid-1660s the Duke of Buckingham had taken over the monopoly. His glasshouse at Vauxhall, on the south bank of the Thames, became famous for the manufacture of plates up to 72 inches (175 cm) long. In 1691 the Bear Gardens Glass House advertised blown plates up to 90 inches (220 cm) long.

Blown glass was used for the mirrors in the Galerie des Glaces at Versailles, created in 1678–84. However, the French were also experimenting with 'cast plate', patented by Bernard Perrot in 1688. The famous St-Gobain plate-glass factory first lit its massive wood-fired furnaces in 1695, and to watch the casting was one of the spectacles of the age. The glass itself, based initially on Venetian *cristallo*, was a pure soda glass that was particularly free from bubbles and other blemishes. By 1760 a potash crystal, containing purified pearl-ashes

Right: Illustration of casting and running plate glass in a French factory from A New and Complete Dictionary of Arts and Sciences, *1754. The molten glass was ladled into the iron box, from which it was run at a controlled rate on to the casting table and rolled flat with a polished cast-iron roller. The cooled sheet was then annealed.*
Far right: Grinding and polishing plate glass by rubbing one against the other with an abrasive between them. Top pressure was provided by sprung poles, the wheel facilitating movement of the upper sheet.
Below: Foiling plate glass. The table had a lip to catch the mercury squeezed out by the weights, which are shown beneath it. An earlier stage in the process is to be seen on the left.

Right: Cutting plate glass. For decorative cutting of large sheets and for 'bevelling' – cutting the edges at an angle – the weight of the glass was supported by an arrangement of ropes and pulleys, and counter-balanced so that it could be manipulated against the cutting wheel.

(potassium carbonate), saltpetre and borax, was also used.

In 1773 the commercial potential of manufacturing cast plate led to the construction of the British Cast Plate Glass Company's factory at Ravenhead, near St Helens. Its casting hall became the largest building in the country, and the manager was appointed from St-Gobain. Initial problems, due to coal-firing affecting the colour of the glass, were overcome by changing to closed pots. The industry prospered, and the Napoleonic wars eliminated the competition from France.

At first the plates were ground flat and polished by hand. Essentially, this consisted of rotating one sheet of glass against another. The bottom sheet was embedded in putty and the top sheet fastened to a wooden block. A springy pressure was continuously applied to the top sheet by a bent hardwood 'bow' levering against an overhead beam; the operative had only to apply the rotating motion and feed in the abrasive or polishing powder, lubricated with water.

The actual silvering was known as 'foiling', or 'foliating'. A flat table, covered with thin blotting-paper, was sprinkled with chalk. A fine sheet of tinfoil was spread on this and rubbed all over with a thick film of mercury using a hare's foot. A sheet of paper was laid gently on the newly formed tin-mercury amalgam and, on top, the plate glass. By withdrawing the paper carefully, the amalgam was brought into close contact with the glass without air bubbles being introduced. Excess mercury was 'dried' out by loading the plate with heavy weights (bags of sand or shot) and tilting the table.

Tinfoil amalgam could be used only for flat sheets; a different process was necessary for convex mirrors and for hollow vessels such as the globes known as 'witches' balls'. Bismuth, lead and tin, in the ratio 2:1:1, were melted together and when nearly cool 4 parts of mercury were added. This amalgam became fluid with very gentle heat and could be poured into a convex glass supported by a plaster mould.

As the foiling industry grew, the extreme toxicity of mercury fumes became apparent and was commented upon by nineteenth-century writers. This may have promoted the introduction of silvering with real silver, a technique discovered in 1835 by Justus von Liebig, a German chemist, but probably first practised on a commercial scale in France.

Silvering was much more rapid than foiling; it could be applied to any shape of vessel and to those of very large size; and it was more durable, particularly when protected by a coat of lead-oxide varnish. Initially, it was difficult to eliminate blemishes, and it gave a darker reflected image and was more expensive. Consequently, for flat mirrors foiling was only slowly replaced in spite of the health hazard.

The decorative potential of silvering for hollow-ware was quickly exploited in an invention patented in December 1849 by F. Hale Thomson & Edward Varnish of Berners Street, London. The patent covered double-walled vessels, silvered on the internal faces by way of an orifice in the base which could be sealed to prevent tarnishing. Inkstands, salts, candlesticks and other useful articles could be produced by this means, as well as ornamental cups and vases. Silvered overlay glass with decoration cut or engraved through the outer, coloured, layer has a special brilliance.

The Bohemian glass industry produced a quantity of thinly blown wares, often used as fairground prizes; their best pieces were attractively acid etched, lightly engraved or hand painted, and sometimes stained internally to give a gold effect. In America the New England Glass Co. had registered a patent for silvered door knobs by 1855 and numerous other firms took up production, although the vogue was short lived.

IRIDESCENT GLASS

Externally metallized glass, often called 'lustre ware', was usually made at the furnace. While still red hot, the article was rotated in an iron oven in which metallic salts were sprayed or volatilized; reheating at the furnace in a smoky, reducing, flame may have been required to develop the metallic finish, which was fairly durable. Thomas Webb & Sons registered the first English patent for iridescent glass in 1877. Their iridescence should not be confused with that seen in old Roman glass which is due to decay of the glass surface.

Early Islamic lustre, on both pottery and glass, was obtained by painting the cold vessel with metallic salts and refiring. Its revival, in about 1875, almost certainly began in Bohemia, probably at the Lobmeyer factory, where a pleasant pearl effect was often given to clear glass. A typical mixture employed for this contained 90 parts of tin chloride, 5 parts of strontium nitrate and 3 parts of barium chloride. Replacing the barium with iron chloride gave orange, typified by the peculiarly American press-moulded 'Carnival' glass, the actual colour of which varied with the colour of the base glass. As the lustre was opaque, different patterns could be pressed on the inner and outer faces of the vessel.

For the luxury market, the most exquisite results were said to have been obtained with gold, silver and platinum salts, first calcined (reduced to a powder by burning) with sulphur and oil of turpentine or rosin. The ash was finely ground, suspended in oil of lavender, rosemary or fennel, applied to the vessel and refired to develop the gleaming metallic finish. Arthur J. Nash, of Tiffany Studios, was a master of this art and made the firm world famous with his fabulous 'Peacock' iridescence. In Stourbridge many of the factories produced iridized pieces. Of particular note are Webb's 'Bronze' and Richardson's lustred alabaster ware.

In about 1905 Frederick Carder, at Steuben, brought out 'Verre de Soie' which, with its pale, silky iridescence, had an immediate appeal. Carder's 'Aurene' glass is said to have contained silver salts that were reduced to give a shining metallic surface, over which iron chloride was sprayed to produce the iridescent finish. In spite of its golden appearance, Aurene does not contain metallic gold.

In France an outstanding painted and fired iridescence was developed by Amédée de Caranza, while Gallé used iridescence as yet another of the diverse components of his complex creations. The Loetz factory, in Austria, was also notable for its iridescent glass.

Far left: Tiffany Cypriote glass vase, American, 1898. Cypriote glass, developed by Arthur J. Nash (1849–1934), imitates the appearance of ancient glass and the effects of natural decay and corrosion on its surface. It was made by melting crushed glass, picked up on the marver, into the vessel followed by the application of iridescence.
Left: Tiffany double gourd-shaped vase, 1900. The threads were trailed on to the globe, then combed. After blowing the vessel to its final shape, the iridescence was applied.
Below: Fenton Art Glass Co. bon-bon dish in pressed Carnival glass, with orange iridescence over a green base glass, American, c. 1915.

Left: Austrian iridescent glass vase made at the Johann Loetz-Witwe glassworks, c. 1900. Iridescent glass from this glassworks was exhibited at the 1893 World's Columbian Exhibition in Chicago and became extremely popular.
Above: Eastern Mediterranean mould-blown head flask, fourth or fifth century AD. Natural iridescence in ancient glass was produced by the leaching out of salts over a long period of time. The colours result from the diffraction of light by the thin multi-layers of decayed glass, analogous to the way colours are produced in a butterfly's wing. Glass such as this was probably the inspiration for Cypriote glass.

CERAMICS

The material composition of pots – the 'body' – is almost as varied as the shapes into which it can be formed. A large part of the earth's surface can be used to make pots, and the ancient belief that mankind was formed out of clay perhaps acknowledged this. Two of the most commonly occurring compounds, formed when the earth was cooling, were the oxides of silicon and aluminium, known as 'silica' and 'alumina'. Pure clay is formed of these two compounds in a fine mix with water. The presence of water provides plasticity and enables the clay to be shaped. The most important alumino-silicate is feldspar, present in granite and other primary rocks.

Clays are divided into two main types: primary and secondary. Primary clays are those which are in the position where they were formed, not removed from their parent rocks by wind, water or glacial action. They tend to be free of contaminating materials and are comparatively pure, though not easy to mould. Typical of them are the kaolins, the whitest and purest clays, which fire into a white colour. Secondary clays are those which are moved from their original position. They are composed of smaller particles as a result of having been ground down by the movement and are more malleable, or 'plastic'; having contaminations of minerals such as iron, they fire to a buff, brown or red.

Kaolin, or china clay, is the essential ingredient of hard porcelain and of bone china, and fine deposits occur in Europe at Limoges in France and in Cornwall in England; in North and South Carolina and Ohio in North America; and in Asia. The Chinese discovered its use in making porcelain at least a thousand years before the West. At first the Chinese used kaolin to make a softish earthenware but, with the development of higher-firing temperatures, they were able to produce true porcelain. Kaolins lie in pockets, mixed with quartz and feldspar, and powerful hoses are used to wash the clay and impurities through sluices into settling ponds to remove the quartz and feldspar. This method is very old.

Ball clays, which are secondary clays, are more plastic than kaolins, but they cannot be used by themselves since they shrink considerably during firing. They are mined from the ground in solid form and some parts of the world have considerable quantities. Ball clay can be added to kaolin to improve plasticity but, the greater the amount of ball clay used, the poorer the whiteness and translucence of the body.

Other main types of secondary clays are stoneware clays, earthenware clays, fire clays, saggar clays and terra cotta clays. Stoneware clays are very plastic, and they mature, or vitrify, at temperatures of between 1200° and 1300°C. Among the most adaptable of clays, they can be used as saggar clays or, without being mixed with any other clays, they can be thrown on a wheel to make fine pots. They can be left unglazed or glazed with salt or slip (liquid clay). Earthenware clays are the most common clays and fire at between 950° and 1100°C. The natural colour varies from red, brown, green to grey, depending on the quantity of iron oxide present, and they fire from buff to red, brown or black. This 'common clay', as it is sometimes called, is the very stuff of local pottery, and everything from bricks and tiles to fine pots are made from it. In general it is much too plastic and sticky to be used by itself and needs to be tempered with sand or other clays. Fire clays are used for refractory purposes, such as fire bricks, parts for kilns, furnaces and melting-pots. They can be fired at high temperatures (up to 1500°C) and are ideal for withstanding great heat. Saggar clays are used for making 'saggars', the boxes in which pots are fired to protect them from the flame and direct heat of the kiln.

Left: Chinese Tz'u-chow ware vase, Sung dynasty (960–1279). This superb vase was thrown on a wheel. The sprays and butterflies were painted in bold brushstrokes with great freedom, the decoration enhancing the splendid and vigorous form of the pottery vessel.

Left: Dish from William de Morgan's studio pottery at Merton Abbey, near London, late nineteenth century. The design, in a Moorish style and painted in ruby lustre, was possibly influenced by the work of William Morris, with whom de Morgan was associated.

EARTHENWARE

Earthenware is a name usually given to clay bodies that are not translucent when fired. Early pots were entirely made by hand, and this is the method used in many parts of the world today. In countries such as Mexico, and in many areas of Central and South America and Africa, potters still make their pots in the time-honoured way of coiling (see p.114). In these cultures the pottery used to be produced by the women, whereas in other parts of the world the men were traditionally the potters. In the present century this distinction has disappeared and there are as many fine European and North American women potters as there are male potters in the more primitive parts of the world.

In Africa pots were mainly functional, although some were produced with such feeling for the material and for form that they can be regarded as artistic creations. In the Pre-Columbian cultures of Central and South America some of the finest pottery that the world has ever seen was produced by the simplest means, by potters who could neither read nor write and were without the use of the wheel. These pots were all produced by hand and frequently burnished by polishing the surface with a smooth stone before firing in a bonfire kiln. They

are remarkable for being light in weight and well balanced; they served the purpose for which they were made admirably.

In the civilized world potters have been at work for many thousands of years. Pottery articles were made to be used, or as ornamental objects of religious significance, or for burial with the dead. Some countries produced superb pots as long ago as 6000 BC, notably around the Mediterranean – in Cyprus, Greece, Egypt and Anatolia – and in China. Pots were decorated in slips with geometric or naturalistic patterns. In Greece black and red figure painting developed in the sixth and fifth centuries BC with pots being used as if they were canvases for finely detailed paintings, some of them executed by painters whose names are known from their signatures.

In the Far East the great potters of China produced vessels during the Neolithic period, several thousand years BC, which can rival anything produced since and have greatly influenced craftsmen potters of the present day. In the dynastic periods that followed, particularly in the Han (206 BC–220 AD), T'ang (618–906) and Sung (960–1276) dynasties, the craft of making pottery was brought to a high standard as exemplified by the

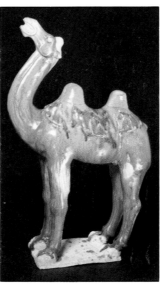

Above: Peruvian hand-built pot, Nazca culture, c. 600 AD. Earthenware clay is the most common type of clay, used throughout the world for functional as well as decorative vessels. It fires buff, red, brown or black, and this Pre-Columbian pot from Peru, with a double-bridge spout-handle, was painted in polychrome clays with birds and fish.

Right: Chinese model of a camel, T'ang dynasty (618–906 AD). The craft of the potter was brought to a particularly high standard in China at this period. Tomb horses and camels were covered in rich amber, yellow and green glazes.

Above: Wedgwood creamware teapot, English, 1760s. Creamware, or cream-coloured earthenware, was developed in England by Josiah Wedgwood (1730–95) in c. 1760, and by 1775 manufacture had spread to the Continent. Whitish clay mixed with calcined flint was used as the body. Creamware was invented at a time when the production of porcelain was beginning seriously to affect the popularity and sales of earthenware. The teapot has decoration boldly painted in metallic oxides.

*Left: Cretan black-figure hydria,
second half of the sixth century BC.
The painting is of Herakles in combat
with the Hydra and Iolaus searing the
heads. A hydria was used by the
Greeks for carrying and storing
water, and characteristically it has
handles by which to lift the vessel.
Below: Peruvian hand-built stirrup-
handled portrait vessel, Mochica
culture, c. 300 AD. The practice of
modelling or moulding jugs, mugs
and various other vessels in the form
of a human head has been common
to many different civilizations.
Bottom: Egyptian bowl, c. 4000 BC.
The potter formed this bowl by the
simple method of coiling, building up
the sides with rolls of clay; it would
have been fired upside down in a
wood fire.*

T'ang tomb horses or camels, so full of vigour and movement, with running green, amber and yellow glazes. They are just as beautiful as the pieces produced in the Sung dynasty in stoneware and porcelain – the supreme invention of the period and of the history of ceramics.

The invention of porcelain (see p.110) led to the need for competitive pottery, and in the third quarter of the eighteenth century the invention of creamware (cream-coloured earthenware) and pearlware (earthenware made with calcined flint and cobalt which had a white body resembling porcelain) in England brought about the decline of other forms of earthenware bodies for table wares. Heavier earthenwares continued to be made in the form of ornamental wares, such as the chimney ornaments made in Staffordshire, and William de Morgan encouraged a renewed interest in lustre wares (see p.129). In this century the pioneer work of Bernard Leach has contributed to the worldwide revival of interest in craft pottery.

STONEWARE

Stoneware is a high-fired ceramic body which even when unglazed is impervious to liquids. Salt glazing of stoneware (see p.129) was developed towards the end of the fourteenth century in the Rhineland. The shapes were similar to Medieval earthenwares: large beakers, tall tankards and jugs, squat jugs with curious human faces known from the eighteenth century as 'bellarmines'. The deposits of stoneware clay on the slopes of the Westerwald started a thriving industry and the wares were exported throughout Europe, including England.

Trace elements in the clays and sand of the different regions caused variations in the colour of the bodies. Stonewares from Cologne and Frechen were dull grey in colour and fired yellow to brown when a wash of slip was applied. Siegburg wares had a natural white-firing body. The wares from Raeren are characteristically a dark brown; Jan Mennicken's workshop there was in 1587 the first to apply the cobalt-blue glazes which were to become associated with Westerwald or Rhenish types of wares. Salt-glaze stoneware manufacture spread from there to other parts of Germany, to Beauvais in France and then to England.

In 1671 John Dwight of Fulham in London was granted a patent for 'The Mistery of Transparent Earthenware, commonly knowne by the names of Porcelain or China and Persian Ware, as alsoe the Misterie of the Stone Ware vulgarly called Cologne Ware'. He certainly produced salt-glaze stoneware, especially bellarmines and other jugs and bottles of a German type, and also figures and finely potted stonewares which may have been attempts at making porcelain.

Left: Stoneware vase by Bernard Leach (1887–1979), 1931. Leach learned the craft of the potter in Japan. In 1920 he settled at St Ives in Cornwall, England, where the raw materials were close to hand. He believed that the craftsman should be involved at every stage in the creation of a pot, from digging the clay to the final firing, and he brought about a revival of interest in traditional methods.
Below: Staffordshire salt-glaze stoneware cat, c.1745. Brown and white clay was used for this press-moulded figure of a cat, a type of ware known as 'agate' because of its resemblance to the stone.

By the end of the seventeenth century a number of other potters had started up in England and in 1693–94 Dwight took legal action against a number of these: James Morley of The Pot House, Nottingham, the Wedgwood family from Burslem in Staffordshire, and John and David Elers of Fulham. Morley was producing fine mugs (which he called 'moggs') and teapots in red stoneware, often delightfully carved. The thin redware was an attempt to imitate the Yi-hsing stonewares from China. These were brought to England in East India Company boats to satisfy a demand caused by the fashion for drinking tea. The Elers brothers moved to Bradwell Wood in Staffordshire and continued to produce unglazed red stoneware, often with applied clay shapes known as 'sprigs'. Lady Celia Fiennes noted in her diary in 1698: 'I went to this Newcastle in Staffordshire to see the makeing of the fine teapotts, cups and saucers of the fine red earth in imitation and as curious as that which comes from China, but was defeated in my design, they comeing to an end of their clay they made use of for that sort of ware, and therefore was remov'd to some other place'.

The Elers brothers were said to guard their secrets carefully, only employing dull-witted assistants. Two young potters, Astbury and Twyford, are reputed to have worked for the Elers for two years pretending to be idiots while learning to make stoneware, and they then set up on their own.

The making of stonewares spread through the Potteries – the 'Five Towns' which together formed the centre of pottery manufacture and are now all part of Stoke-on-Trent. As well as unglazed redware, a fine white body was perfected by adding calcined flint to a light-coloured clay. Incised patterns in the clay might have cobalt rubbed into them, producing 'scratch blue'. Intricately moulded teawares and the development of sprigging added to the success of white stoneware. Among the most interesting pieces are the rare figure subjects, particularly the so called 'pew groups' of figures on a church bench.

From about 1750 coloured enamels (oxides of metals) were fired over the glaze and reacted chemically with it to produce splendid effects. Equally fine are the 'agate' wares, made from blended clays and simulating agate, but the rapid success of creamwares changed the whole development of the Potteries and salt-glaze stoneware declined. Manufacture continued for a while in centres such as Nottingham, where the pots were washed with ferruginous clay, giving a shiny, iridescent, metallic-brown sheen to the surface. Potters in North America continued to make salt glaze into the twentieth century, and in England there was renewed interest in the second half of the nineteenth century at Doulton's Lambeth factory in London, where fine vases and tankards were made with incised or applied details.

Perhaps the most extraordinary work in salt-glaze stoneware was produced by Robert Wallace Martin and his brothers Walter, Edwin and Charles in the late nineteenth century. Their most famous pieces are probably the covered jars in the shape of strange birds and other vegetable and anthropomorphic forms. These creations kept the idea of stoneware alive and are still an inspiration to craftsmen potters of the present day.

Left: Wedgwood Portland Vase, nineteenth century. A type of fine-grained unglazed stoneware known as 'jasper' was used for this reproduction of the famous Roman glass vase in the British Museum. Above: Elers redware teapot, English, c.1700. Thin, unglazed red stoneware was made by John and David Elers in imitation of Chinese Yi-hsing stoneware. The applied shapes, made from moulds, were known as 'sprigs'.

ORIENTAL PORCELAIN

The Chinese were not only the inventors of porcelain but it might fairly be said that they were also the greatest makers the world has known. The West so admired the magnificent white, hard and translucent material that they gave their attempts to imitate it the title of 'china'.

Hard-paste, or true, porcelain was made by the Chinese from the two fusible materials kaolin and petunse, known in the West as 'china clay' and 'china stone'. Kaolin, the refractory white clay, kept the pot in shape during the firing and petunse, the feldspathic rock, produced the natural glaze. Thus it was possible in the one high firing to produce a fully glazed piece, although a low 'biscuit firing', which hardened and vitrified the body, could be carried out first if required. The earliest porcelain was undecorated, except for incised patterns on some examples, the potters delighting in the pure form of the pieces. By the start of the Ming dynasty (1368–1644) the pots were being decorated with elaborate cobalt-oxide paintings, and blue and white wares became enormously popular in the West. The cobalt had originally been obtained from Persia and taken to the city of Ching-tê-chên, the great centre of porcelain manufacture. The painting was done on the raw clay and the pot was then glazed and fired in the one high firing,

which vitrified the piece and protected the decoration under the glaze. In the fifteenth century the custom began of putting six-character reign marks on the bases, but these marks should be treated with caution as later generations of Chinese imitated both the style of Ming porcelain and the marks.

Contemporaneously with the famous blue and white, porcelain was also produced with underglaze copper-red decoration and numerous overglaze colours, achieved with metallic oxides which were fused on to the glaze in subsequent firings. Sometimes delicate onglaze colours were added to underglaze blue patterns. Towards the end of the Ming dynasty there was a growing trade in porcelain to markets in the Far East; also in the West through the Dutch East India Company. Countrywide upheavals accompanied the collapse of the Ming dynasty, and in the early years of the Ch'ing dynasty (1644–1912) the Dutch had to procure most of their porcelain from Japan. However, during the reigns of K'ang Hsi (1662–1722), Yung Cheng (1723–35) and Ch'ien Lung (1736–95) the difficulties were overcome, and production at Ching-tê-chên reached new heights both in quantity and in quality. The porcelain city is said to have had a million people working in the industry, and white ware or underglaze-blue decorated

Above: Chinese porcelain bowl, sixteenth century. Hard-paste, or true, porcelain was developed by the Chinese in the seventh or eighth century. It was made from the white clay kaolin and the rock petunse, which produced the natural glaze. The pieces were formed either by throwing on the wheel or by moulding or modelling. Early Chinese porcelain was generally undecorated; underglaze blue decoration in cobalt-oxide colours became popular at the beginning of the Ming dynasty (1368–1644), and the early work was superbly painted.

Left: Chinese porcelain mug, Chi'en Lung (1736–95). The mug was painted in famille rose *colours, with rose-pink enamel predominating. This was a type of decoration popular in Europe. The tobacco-leaf pattern was a design much used during the reign of Chi'en Lung.*

Above: Chinese blanc-de-Chine *porcelain figure of Buddha, 1662–1722. The translucent undecorated porcelain with a thick glaze was first made in the later years of the Ming dynasty. It was copied at St Cloud and Mennecy in France, and at Bow and Chelsea in England.*

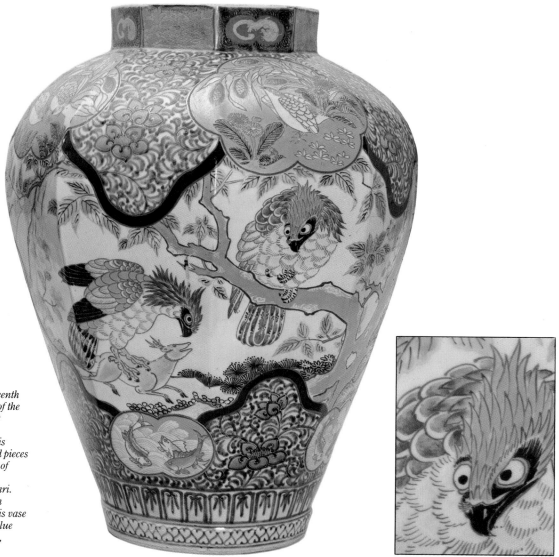

Right: Arita porcelain vase, Japanese, seventeenth or eighteenth century, and detail (far right) of the decoration. Porcelain was first manufactured in Japan in the seventeenth century. The vase is typical of the richly ornamented pieces made at the porcelain factories of Arita for export to Europe and despatched from the port of Imari. This gave rise to the description 'Imari pattern'. The sides of this vase were decorated in underglaze blue and overglaze coral, aubergine, brown, green and turquoise.

pieces were sent from there to Canton to await purchase by ships' captains from the West. In Canton a great number of painters were employed to decorate the pieces with coats of arms and mottoes, or special ornament in colours. The porcelain was then fired and loaded on to the boats, together with other such rare commodities as tea, spices and silks.

The K'ang Hsi reign produced the characteristic *famille verte*, or 'green family', colour scheme comprising a strong green and thin red, yellow, violet and a translucent blue. Other 'families' with French names attached to them are *famille noire*, which has a glowing black ground, and *famille jaune* with a yellow ground. Also produced for the home market were superb monochrome glazed wares such as the high-fired copper-based *sang-de-bœuf*, or 'ox blood', and *flambé*. This was produced by a high-temperature firing in a reducing atmosphere (see p.122) using copper to produce predominantly red colours. Other wonderful glaze colours were turquoise, yellow and aubergine. In the short reign of Yung Cheng some early Sung effects were re-introduced and the beautiful new colours of 'tea dust', 'iron dust' and 'robin's-egg

blue' appeared. A characteristic colour family in this and the subsequent reign of Ch'ien Lung was *famille rose*, a type of decoration which included a predominantly rose-pink enamel and was very popular in Europe. By the end of the reign of the Emperor Ch'ien Lung the wares had become derivative and were mass produced, and the nineteenth century saw a decline in quality, epitomized by porcelain in the over-elaborate Cantonese style.

The Japanese were also successful manufacturers of porcelain, and their wares were at one time as popular in Europe as Chinese wares. Porcelain manufacture began at Arita in the seventeenth century, and the superbly decorated vases associated with the Kakiemon family, with a typical palette of red, turquoise, yellow and blue, are justly famous. Kakiemon designs are particularly impressive when large areas of the porcelain are left undecorated, and it was this type of ornament that made a great impact upon German, French and English factories in the eighteenth century. The so-called 'Imari' patterns, or 'Japans', with underglaze blue and onglaze reds, greens and gold continued into the early nineteenth century.

EUROPEAN SOFT-PASTE PORCELAIN

Chinese blue and white porcelain made a tremendous stir when it gradually began to reach Europe in the fifteenth and sixteenth centuries. So unlike the home-produced earthenwares, it must have seemed miraculous, and it is understandable that monarchs and rulers vied with each other for pieces. Elizabeth I is said to have been so pleased with a vase that she had it mounted in gold. The Italian princes were especially delighted by it and one of them – the Florentine grand duke Francesco I de' Medici – succeeded, in about 1575, in producing the first European porcelain.

Medici porcelain, like other early European porcelain, was a soft-paste, or artificial, body. The manufacture of hard-paste porcelain was not discovered until about 1708 at Meissen (see p. 112). Before then, ignorant of the correct raw materials that were needed for hard paste, the experimenters were rather like alchemists searching for the magic stone – adding a bit of this and a bit of that into the mix in the hope that it would produce porcelain. Between 1575 and about 1613 a number of pieces were produced in Florence, but only a few dozen of them survive; all are decorated in underglaze blue.

Other Italian cities, such as Pisa and Padua, tried to make soft-paste porcelain but did not persevere. Half a century later an attempt was made in France, probably because of the growing craze for tea and coffee, which were drunk from Chinese porcelain. It is perhaps not surprising that experiments were conducted at existing faience factories to make a translucent white porcelain. A licence was granted to Louis Poterat of Rouen in 1673 permitting him to make porcelain as well as faience but, as he worked alone and in great secrecy, very little about his production is known. At St Cloud, near Paris, the faience potter Pierre Chicaneau passed on a formula to his son and his widow. The factory was on the estate and under the patronage of the duc d'Orléans, Louis XIV's brother, and it owed much of its success to his support. Decoration was in the blue and white style of Rouen or in soft

colours with gilding in the style of Japanese Kakiemon; they also made white porcelain. Production continued until 1766.

Other soft-paste porcelain factories were established in France, mostly under the patronage of a nobleman. To own a porcelain factory and be seen to be contributing to scientific discovery, and to manufacture objects of beauty, were causes for esteem in France. The prince de Condé established a factory at Chantilly in about 1726, directed by Ciquaire Cirou. The body was similar to that of St Cloud, but the glaze had tin in it which gave it a very special quality. The decoration was usually based on Chinese and Japanese porcelain from the Prince's superb collection, but later they were based on European flowers. At Mennecy, near the *château* of the duc de Villeroy, a small faience factory produced porcelain very much in the style of Chantilly from 1748. After 1768 Mennecy was united with the nearby factory of Sceaux. A successful factory was established at Tournai – alternately French and Flemish – in 1751.

All these factories paled into insignificance when the royal manufactory was established at Sèvres. The experimental work for Sèvres was done in 1738 at Vincennes by the Dubois brothers from Chantilly. In 1741 François Cravant took over, and four years later it was granted a special licence. Losses were heavy, and in 1753 Louis XV became the principal shareholder of the 'Manufacture royale de porcelaine'. Thereafter the mark of two interlaced 'L's' was used with a consecutive letter for each year in the centre of the mark, beginning with 'A'.

The factory was moved to Sèvres, strategically placed near Madame de Pompadour's château de Bellevue. She had a great influence on production, much of the work being made for her, notably a large number of beautiful porcelain flowers. The quality of the painting at Sèvres has never been exceeded; outstanding artists such as Oudry and Boucher inspired hundreds of other painters, who were allowed to use marks to

Left: Group of Chelsea soft-paste porcelain pieces, English, c. 1748. These all date from the first phase of production at the Chelsea factory when the pieces were marked with an incised triangle. The pair of crayfish salts and the coffee-pot were inspired by silver shapes, a style favoured by Nicolas Sprimont (c. 1716–71), an owner of the factory who was also a silversmith. Many of the early Chelsea pieces were left in the white.

identify their work and were kept busy painting specialist subjects. The later move into hard paste, and then the Revolution, brought to an end the first great days of Sèvres.

In England the manufactories were not of royal foundation and had to survive independently. Chelsea, from 1745, used a difficult, vitreous body for its many delightful pieces, based on silver forms, which were often left white. The factory was sold in 1769 and run in combination with Derby. Bow, also in London, was a more pedestrian factory in the main. It used a bone-ash formula, as did Lowestoft, the wares tending to stain brown and craze. Worcester was established in 1751 following experiments at Limehouse and Bristol using Cornish soapstone, ball clay and sand. (Worcester, of all the early English soft-paste porcelain factories, survives today.) A number of factories in Liverpool used the soapstone formula, and so too did Caughley in Shropshire. By the end of the eighteenth century England had developed a special bone-china body. This modernized soft-paste formula was constituted of 50% animal bone, 25% china clay and 25% china stone, and it is still produced to this day by many famous factories.

Above: Mennecy soft-paste porcelain Chinoiserie figure set in a bronze d'oré mantel clock, with hand-made soft-paste porcelain flowers made at Vincennes, French, 1740–50. The royal porcelain manufactory was at Vincennes before it was moved to Sèvres. Chinoiserie was a style of decoration that imitated Chinese art and was popular during the seventeenth and eighteenth centuries. Right: Worcester soft-paste porcelain coffee-pot, English, c. 1758. The moulded form was painted with underglaze blue floral sprigs. Soft-paste procelain is still made at Worcester, one of the early porcelain factories to be founded in England.

Above: Chelsea soft-paste porcelain figure of an owl, c. 1750. The design for this humorous piece was probably taken from an engraving. It dates from the raised anchor period (1750–52).

EUROPEAN HARD-PASTE PORCELAIN

The discovery of European true, or hard-paste, porcelain was made at Meissen in Saxony in about 1708. The fact that many centuries had passed since the Chinese first made this magical material attests to the care with which the secret had been kept. At the time many European monarchs were losing interest in the quest to be the first to discover how to create gold from base metal, an interest replaced by the desire to make porcelain in the Chinese manner.

In 1701 a young apothecary, Johann Friedrich Böttger, was persuaded to work for Augustus the Strong, elector of Saxony and king of Poland, and he was installed in the castle at Albrechtsburg to try to produce gold. Three years of failure led to the abandonment of this idea and, together with a celebrated physicist, Ehrenfried Walther von Tschirnhaus, he moved into other experimental fields, trying, for instance, to produce gemstones from various minerals.

Almost by chance, while working on refractory clays, they produced a superb, hard, red stoneware body which was not unlike the Chinese and English red stoneware. This was called 'Jasper' when it was exhibited at the Leipzig Fair in 1710, perhaps in the hope that it would be recognized as a gemstone,

and it was polished and cut as if it were a genuine gem. Another experimental success was a dark-brown glaze which enabled gold and lacquer decoration to be applied to pieces.

In 1708, by substituting for red clay the white clay from Meissen, Böttger produced the first European hard paste, and Augustus founded the Meissen manufactory. Over the entrance of the laboratory Böttger had inscribed, in German, 'God the Creator has made a potter out of an alchemist'. The work was kept very secret, and the production of superb and exotic porcelain objects – vases decorated in the style of Chinese and Japanese porcelain, white figures in the style of *blanc-de-Chine* and curiosities of a European nature such as dwarfs – were the marvel of Europe. Many pieces were gilded in the Augsburg workshops, starting a vogue for decorating Meissen blanks outside the factory by independent artists, known as '*Hausmalerei*', a practice that was also followed in Germany for decorating glass.

Although the secret was carefully guarded, it could not be kept for long. In 1719, the year in which Böttger died, two workmen – a gilder named Hunger and the kiln-master Samuel Stölzel – defected to Vienna and helped the Court official

Left: Meissen hard-paste porcelain group of Shepherd Lovers modelled by Johann Joachim Kändler (1706–75), German, 1740. From 1736 Kändler modelled many of the small figures and groups that were manufactured at Meissen as table ornaments.
Above: Meissen coffee-pot, 1725–30. European hard-paste porcelain was invented in about 1708 by Johann Friedrich Böttger (1682–1719), who in 1710 was appointed the first director of the Meissen factory. Böttger's patron was Augustus the Strong, elector of Saxony and king of Poland, and it was he who founded the Meissen factory near Dresden, the first in Europe to produce hard-paste porcelain.

Claudius Innocentius du Paquier to set up a rival manufactory. Stölzel returned to Meissen the following year, accompanied by the gifted artist Johann Gregor Höroldt and the superb modeller Johann Joachim Kändler.

The new team enabled Augustus to raise production at Meissen to a very high standard. Chinoiseries (Western decoration inspired by Chinese art), Oriental flowers and German flowers were painted on vases and tea- and chocolate-services by the growing number of fine painters, by 1731 numbering 40. Kändler and the chief modeller Johann Gottlieb Kirchner produced ornamental figures that were of increasing quality, either small in size and intended as table decorations or full-size models of birds to stand in Augustus's Japanese Palace. An attempt to make a life-size porcelain model of Augustus himself failed as the material was not suited to such things, fire-cracking being a serious problem. Perhaps Kändler's most famous pieces are his figures from the *Commedia dell'arte*, or Italian Comedy – Harlequin, Columbine and others – but equally remarkable are the great services with a unifying theme, among them the Swan Service made for Count Brühl. This comprised more than 1,400 pieces, decorated in relief with swans, dolphins and other motifs associated with water.

At the outbreak of the Seven Years' War in 1756 the Baroque style of Meissen was overtaken by the many factories starting up in Europe making hard paste in the new Rococo style. In the second half of the eighteenth century there were 23 manufacturers in Germany as well as many in Italy and France that were capable of making hard paste, notably Nymphenburg, Berlin, Doccia, Capodimonte and Sèvres. In France the town of Limoges developed a hard-paste porcelain industry rivalling in scale the English Five Towns' dominance in the field of earthenware and bone china. The earliest English porcelain factories were Chelsea and Bow, and in America the fine china clay of the Carolinas was used experimentally by André Duché. In Denmark, manufacture at the Royal Copenhagen Manufactory has been continuous since 1775.

Above: Meissen hard-paste porcelain tankard with a silver-gilt cover, c.1735. The forms of early Meissen pieces were dependent on those used by metalworkers, and by silversmiths in particular.
Below: Meissen hard-paste porcelain from a monochrome tea-service, 1725–28, and from a polychrome tea-service, c.1730. Early porcelain tea-services included a small cup without a handle, based on the Far Eastern model.

MAKING BY HAND

The basic methods used by an individual craftsman or studio potter to make a pot have changed little over the last two thousand years. The clay bodies can be bought ready made, the wheel can be driven by electricity, new electric kilns can take a lot of the hard labour and guesswork out of firing, but essentially it involves one man taking a lump of raw earth and turning it into a pot. The fashioning process can be divided into two main types: hand building and throwing.

Many people imagine that a fine pot can only be produced by the technique of throwing on a wheel, but many of the world's masterpieces in pottery have been hand built. All the great vessels made in Pre-Columbian Mexico and Peru were produced without the benefit of the wheel, itself an ancient practice. Methods include pinching and coiling, pressing and slab building, or combinations of all of them.

Pinched pots were produced by hollowing out a ball of clay and then pinching and squeezing to raise and gradually reduce the thickness of the wall of the pot. The potter turned it round in the hand rather in the manner of a very slow form of throwing. A pot made in this way has a particular directness, with the hand of the potter still almost discernible. Many of the ancient Japanese bowls for the traditional tea ceremony, which are generally regarded as great works of art, were produced in this way.

A pinched pot could be used as the base on which coils, or 'sausages', of clay were added to extend the size and height. The potter squeezed these extra coils on, sealing the joins between them and perhaps smoothing or scraping the sides to give an even surface. With skill and patience very large and complicated forms could be produced, African water-pots and some modern pieces providing evidence of how fine such work can be. The process was inevitably much slower than the more complex one of throwing on a wheel.

Below: Wrotham tyg, English, 1649. A tyg is a large drinking-mug with several handles. The body of the mug, made from local red clay, was thrown on a wheel; the handles were made by hand and attached with slip.

Far left: Gallo-Roman earthenware vase with overlapping scales, second half of the first century AD. Measuring only 4½ inches (11.4 cm) in height the vase was probably thrown in two parts. The scales would have been made by thumbing and pressing with a spatula and applied from the top of the vase downwards.
Left: Terracotta pot from Azande, North Congo, c.1880–1920. The traditional method of forming a pot in Africa was by coiling. The decoration was incised while the clay was damp.

MAKING A PINCHED POT

1. A lump of clay was kneaded and worked into a ball.
2. Using the thumb, a hollow was made in the centre of the ball.
3. By pinching and squeezing, the sides of the pot were gradually raised and reduced in thickness as it was turned in the potter's hand. Revolving the pot was similar to the action of a wheel. Only small pieces could be made by this method unless coils were added to heighten the sides.

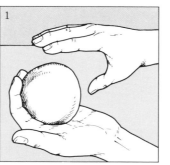
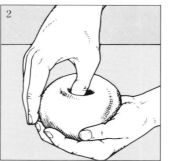

MAKING A COILED POT

1. A lump of clay was rolled out into a thin 'sausage'.
2. The base of the pot was formed either by pinching the clay into shape or with coils of clay laid flat.
3. Moistened with liquid clay, or 'slip', to seal the joins, the clay was coiled around the base.
4. Using a modelling tool, the coils were smoothed into the base and flattened on the inside and outside while still damp.
5. Further coils were added to build up the sides, the previous one having been allowed to dry and become firm enough to bear the weight of the new clay. To increase the diameter of the pot, each coil was slightly larger in circumference than the last; reducing the circumference caused the sides of the pot to curve inwards.
6. When the completed pot was 'leather' hard, the sides were scraped smooth and the surface was then ready to be decorated.

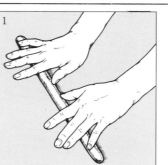
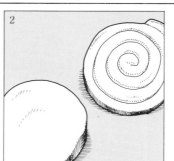
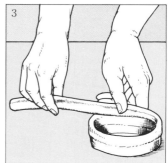

With the slab-building and press-moulding processes sheets of clay were rolled, flattened or cut. For slab building the clay needed to stiffen to a 'leather' or 'cheese' hardness before the edges could be cut to a chamfered angle, and scored and joined together with thick slip. Press moulding involved pressing sheets of clay which were still in the 'green' stage, with some moisture still in them, into or over shaped moulds, gently coaxing with fingers or sponge until the slab took the shape of the mould. The edges were trimmed or the surplus cut away, and when dry the pot could be tipped from its mould. This method was ideal for making round, oval or rectangular dishes; with more complex moulds – in two or more parts – simple figure subjects could be made as well as complicated vessels. The seam marks produced by the moulds were scraped away once the clay had dried. Casting using slip, done at a factory, was a logical development from the technique of press moulding (see p.120).

Throwing on a wheel produced symmetrical pots much more quickly than hand building. The process was dependent on three factors: the rhythm of the wheel, the plasticity of the clay and the skill of the hands. The clay was centred on the wheelhead and, by opening up the centre and squeezing on the sides while the wheel was spinning, the pot rose. Forms natural to the process were the bowl, cylinder and sphere.

The finished shape was cut off the wheelhead and left to dry into a leather-hard state, and it could then be worked on. Sides were sometimes thinned down or the foot turned with metal turning-tools; ornamental details were added or clay cut out; handles and spouts were stuck on to the vessel with slip; sprigs which were made in moulds were added on when the clay was leather hard; and incised details were made with metal or wooden tools. After the pot was finished and fully dry, it was ready for kiln firing. It might require just one firing, or separate biscuit and glost firings, the latter to fire the glaze on to the body (see p.128).

Triple lamp from Bida, Nupe tribe, Nigeria. The middle, box-like, section would have been *made of slabs of clay joined together at the corners and along the edges with slip.*

MAKING A SLAB POT
1. The clay was rolled out to an even thickness.
2. When 'leather' hard, the clay was cut to a slab of the required shape.
3. The edges were straight cut or chamfered, depending on how the slabs were to be joined.
4. The edges were roughened with cross-hatching and moistened with slip to facilitate joining.
5. With the slabs held upright, the edges were pressed together.
6. The join was strengthened on the inside with a strip or 'sausage' of clay.

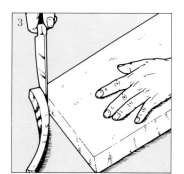
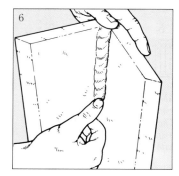

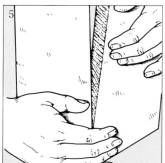

THROWING A POT

1. A ball of clay was slapped down on to the centre of the wheelhead.
2. With the wheelhead turning, the clay was centred.
3. Using both hands, the clay was drawn up into a cone and pressed down again, a process that was repeated until the clay was smooth.
4. The thumb was pressed into the centre and drawn outwards to form the base of the pot and to start forming the sides, a small amount of water being used used as a lubricant.
5. Supported from the outside with one hand, the walls were raised from the inside, again a small amount of water being used.
6. The sides were raised to the required height and width.
7. Curves were formed by applying pressure from the knuckles on the outside of the pot.
8. With the wheelhead still revolving, the neck was formed with the fingers.
9. With the wheelhead still, the pot was cut off with a wire and left to dry.

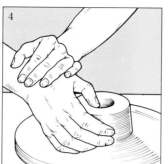
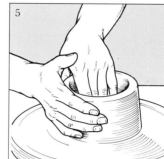

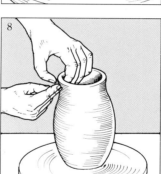

Above: Chinese potter at his wheel, from a woodcut illustration. The potter is helped by an assistant to rotate the wheel with his foot.

Left: Chinese celadon bowl, Sung dynasty (960–1279). The shallow bowl was formed by throwing on a wheel, a technique thought to have been practised as early as 3500 BC. The short footrim would probably have been shaped with a tool, rather than the potter's hands, and would have been one of the last operations performed while the wheelhead was still revolving. Celadon was a type of Chinese stoneware with a greenish glaze derived from iron oxide.

THE CRAFT OF THE MODELLER

The modeller was of key importance in the production of a factory piece as it was he who made the model from which the finished shapes derived. In a small, one- or two-man business, pots were generally made entirely by hand, without moulds, so they were direct, individual objects: each one was a little different from the last, each made from start to finish by the one potter. In a factory, specialists worked on their own particular sequence and it was necessary to have a model.

The modeller usually made the original model in clay, wax or, in more recent times, plasticine, scaling up the size of the model to take account of the fact that the fired piece would shrink considerably – by about a sixth in height, width and breadth – during the firing. This shrinkage meant that an animal – a bird, for example – that was to appear life size after firing had to be modelled at almost twice that size. As a result of the shrinkage complicated details could become so small as to be meaningless. Due account had to be given to the problems of the firing: it was no use modelling something that could not be produced. The modeller also had to take account of the cost of making the item, since the greater the number of moulds needed, and the more complications in production, the higher the expense of the piece and perhaps the fewer sold.

Among the greatest modellers were those who worked for the eighteenth-century German and Austrian factories. Meissen had a succession of superb modellers, all individualists, who modelled in the style of the Baroque. First was Kirchner, who produced some splendid large models for Augustus the Strong's Japanese Palace at Dresden, and he was succeeded by Kändler. Kändler produced some extraordinary pieces, including, in 1731, a life-size heron, which were an important influence on the rest of Europe. When he could, Kändler modelled from the life, and his work has great accuracy allied with a sculptural quality reminiscent of a fine Chinese bronze or an Italian marble statue.

Skilled modellers emerged at other German factories, too: Simon Feilner at Fürstenberg, Johann Peter Melchior at Höchst, the Lück brothers at Frankenthal and Wilhelm Beyer at Ludwigsburg. Perhaps the greatest of the mid-eighteenth-century modellers was Franz Anton Bustelli, who worked at Nymphenburg. If Kändler's figures were the epitome of the Baroque, Bustelli's models breathed the new freedom and movement of the Rococo.

England produced no factory modellers to compare with these until the second half of the nineteenth century, when artists such as James Hadley of Worcester came forward. Hadley's work is characterized by infinite attention to details such as hair, fingers and toes. In the twentieth century the same attention to detail is evident in the models of horses and bulls by Doris Lindner and birds in foliage by Dorothy Doughty. Both these modellers studied their subjects with great care, not only knowing the underlying structure of the animal but also spending a long time observing the individual qualities of the particular creature. Some of these models had to be cut up into dozens of small pieces, and from these were made the moulds (see p.120). The cast pieces from these moulds were then fitted together to make the complete figure.

Left: Group of Frankenthal porcelain figures depicting Astrology from a set of the Liberal Arts, German, c. 1770–75. The modeller was Karl Gottlieb von Lück (died 1775), who produced the models for some of Frankenthal's most popular figures in the *Rococo style. The Frankenthal factory was founded in 1755 and closed in 1799, when some of the moulds were taken over by other German factories. Above: Photograph of a modeller at work at the Spode factory, Stoke-on-Trent, Staffordshire, c. 1905.*

Left: Pair of Royal Worcester models of a Japanese lady and gentleman modelled by James Hadley (1837–1903). They were produced from a large number of pieces cast from moulds and then fitted up. After firing and glazing, the metallic oxides and gold were fused on in further separate firings. Hadley, one of the most talented modellers at work in England in the late nineteenth century, was meticulous in his observation of detail. The Worcester factory has been known as the Worcester Royal Porcelain Company since 1862.

Above: Höchst figure of a boy representing Autumn, German, c. 1775. The model was made by Johann Peter Melchior (1747–1825), chief modeller at the factory from 1767 to 1779. He is noted as the creator of a series of charming pastoral figures.

FACTORY PROCESSES

The processes used in a factory were in many ways like elaborate versions of the hand-craft methods. The major difference was that each craftsman did work at which he was particularly skilled before passing the piece on to the next craftsman. So, a factory-made pot was the work of a number of specialists, not of just one potter. Most good factories employed an overseer – an art director, perhaps, or a designer – whose job it was to co-ordinate the various operations and make sure that the finished object had unity.

The craft of the mouldmaker was one of the most skilled in the factory. Most moulds are made nowadays from plaster of Paris, the absorbency of which abstracts the moisture from the ceramic body, allowing the piece to be taken out of the mould. Another advantage of using plaster is that good, clear casts can be made; however, the material is not as long lasting as pitcher (fired clay, not fully vitrified and still porous), which was used previously. The original model was cut up into as many parts as was necessary to permit the pieces to be removed from the mould without causing distortion. The moulds were produced in sequences of a negative and then a positive. Working moulds were made from the positive. From the mouldmakers the mould was passed to the makers, who either used solid body or liquid clay.

Flatware was mainly made by 'jiggering' – hand pressing on a wheel – and the craftsman was known as a 'jiggerer'. He flattened out a piece of body into what was called a 'bat' (nowadays this is usually done by a machine) and placed it upon the mould which was to form the upper part of the piece. The mould was placed on a revolving head and the jiggerer pressed the bat with his hand. Then he brought down a template which bore the profile of the underside of the object – including, in some instances, the foot – set so that the space between corresponded to the thickness required. After the whole piece had been formed, the mould was put aside to dry until the piece could be lifted from the mould. A more perfect object could be manufactured by this process than one made entirely by hand, but of course it lacked the individuality of a hand-made piece. Dishes or plates could be made by hand by pressing out the bat upon the mould with a sponge and trimming the edges with a sharp knife, the craftsman being called a 'dishmaker'.

The process for making hollow-ware was called 'jolleying' and the craftsman a 'jolleyer'. It was a mirror image of jiggering and involved opening up a ball of clay inside a hollow mould while it was spinning round on a wheel. Later the top was trimmed and, when the mould had dried, the pot could be tipped out. The foot required 'turning' by the 'turner', who placed the pot on a horizontal chum and cut away the surplus clay around the foot with a metal turning-tool, also trimming the sides and rim if necessary.

Many of these traditional crafts are now being superseded by machine manufacture. The disadvantage of making pots by fully mechanized methods is that the shapes have to be adapted to suit the machine and consequently the piece usually has less grace and quality than a hand-made one.

In slip casting, liquid clay was used instead of solid body. This was poured into the mould and left for a critical length of time during which the moisture was absorbed, leaving a skin of body building up on the inside of the mould. When sufficient thickness had built up, the surplus slip was poured out, the mould was allowed to dry and the item could then be removed. A great deal of ordinary domestic hollow-ware such as teapots and bowls was – and is – made in this way, but the process really came into its own when complex figure models were to be made. A complicated figure subject might have had dozens of separate parts – hands, arms, legs, bodies – which, when cast and removed from the moulds by the caster, were cleaned and tidied up, the seam marks scraped away and the pieces 'stuck up'. This involved putting thick liquid slip on to all the pieces and sticking them together, and building up the complete figure like a three-dimensional jig-saw puzzle. The caster who assembled these figures was the descendant of the craftsman who was called a 'repairer' in the eighteenth century and it was his job to build the arrangements of supports, made of the same material that they were supporting, which held the figure straight in the kiln firing.

Below: View of the Wedgwood Etruria factory in Stoke-on-Trent. Opened in 1769, it was built by the canal for easy movement of raw materials and finished pieces. Two bottle kilns are shown on the right.

Left and above: Making a mould involved pouring plaster of Paris over a prepared model to produce a solid block. From the block a hollow working mould was made, and it was from this that the piece would be produced. It was sometimes necessary to divide the original model into several parts so that the cast pieces could be removed from the mould without damaging them.

SLIPCASTING

1. Slip, or liquid clay, was poured into a porous mould, either of pitcher (fired but not fully vitrified clay) or plaster of Paris.
2. After the required thickness had built up inside, the surplus slip was poured out.
3. Once dried, the parts of the mould were separated and the cast piece removed. The complete object was then assembled by sticking together the pieces with thick slip.

JOLLEYING

1. The template, which would form the interior of the pot, was set in the correct position above the hollow mould, which would form the exterior, and the mould dampened.
2. A ball of clay was placed in the middle of the mould and the mould rotated on the wheelhead.
3. The template was lowered on to the spinning clay and the process of jolleying begun.
4. The jolley arm, to which the template was attached, was raised, revealing the clay formed into a pot.
5. The surplus clay at the top edge of the pot was trimmed flush with the mould.
6. The mould was removed from the wheelhead and the pot left in it to dry and shrink so that it could be lifted out. The pot was then ready for kiln firing. Jolleying was the reverse of the process known as 'jiggering' in which the template bore the profile of the underside of the pot. Flatware was made by jiggering and hollow-ware by jolleying.

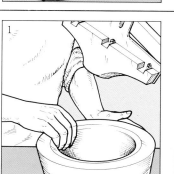

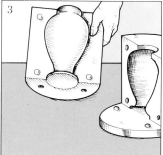

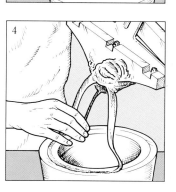

FIRING

All pots have to be subjected to heat to transmute the raw body of clay or stone into a hard ceramic body. The earliest and simplest kilns in which pots were fired were of the bonfire type: the pots were piled in a pit and combustible material was placed on top and set on fire. When the pots were raked out of the hot embers, the potter discovered how many had survived.

This method, as violent in practice as it sounds in the telling, is the way in which early pots were produced in Europe, Africa and America. It is hard to realize that some of the world's greatest pieces were fired in this way. A specially prepared body was necessary to withstand such a firing, the addition of grit or sand helping the pot to stand. With an oxidized firing, where the fire burned clear, the pots would emerge buff coloured or brown; with a reduction firing, induced by smothering the oxygen and producing a smoky fire, the ware would be grey or black. Much variation could, of course, occur and this provides some of the interest of pots thus produced.

More sophisticated kilns, using special constructions of clay or brick, have been in use for several thousands of years. These are less wasteful of fuel and can produce higher temperatures than the 800° or 900°C that was the maximum for the bonfire kiln. A great number of different types developed, with the heat conducted in through a variety of channels, or 'firemouths'. The most elaborate were developed in the Far East, where climbing kilns were constructed up the side of a hill. They had 20 or so chambers, through which the heat was progressively drawn. In England the characteristic shape of the bottle kiln dominated the skyline of Stoke-on-Trent, the huge bottle being only the outer shell concealing the main structure of the kiln, which was inside. These kilns were originally fired with wood or coal, but in recent years a change

Left: View of the nineteenth-century pot bank in Stoke-on-Trent, with the various factory buildings clustered round the bottle kilns in which the ware was fired. The main structure of the kilns was concealed beneath the outer, bottle-shaped shell.
Above: The Furnace, an illustration from Li Tre Libri Dell Arte Del Vasaio by Cipriano Piccolpasso (1524–79), 1556–57. Two stokers tend the fire, directed by the kiln foreman who sits in front of the kiln with an hour glass. He is said to have been able to tell that the kiln had been heated to the correct temperature when his eyebrows started to singe.

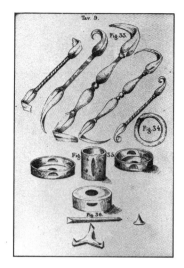

Above: Potters' tools, saggars – the boxes in which pots were fired to protect them from the flame – and kiln furniture, an illustration from Piccolpasso's sixteenth-century treatise on the art of the potter.
Right: Placing the unfired pots in the fireproof saggars. The stacks of saggars were known as 'bungs'. Some saggars had holes in the sides for pins, and the pieces rested on these during firing.

Right: Taking the saggars into the kiln for placing in bungs, an illustration of 1884.

has been made to gas or electricity. Today the kilns are often of the tunnel type, the pots progressing through the kiln on 'cars' the name given to the trucks of ware.

Modern kilns are, of course, much cleaner in use and do less damage to the environment than the older type. In the ceramic centres such as Stoke-on-Trent a century or so ago the smoke pollution was so great that even on a fine day the town was not visible from the hill above, and the gutters of houses had to be made of wood because fumes from the salt-glaze kilns quickly rotted metal.

There were serious hazards in working in the kilns themselves, especially in the removal of the pots after the firing, an operation known as 'drawing'. Unscrupulous owners of pot banks sent young boys in to bring out the pots before the kiln had cooled down so that it could be loaded up and fired again as quickly as possible. This caused great damage to their health: their hair and nails fell out, and their voices became hoarse. It was one of the perils of working life commented on by Samuel Scrivens, Her Majesty's Commissioner, in a report to the Houses of Parliament in 1843 which led to the alleviation of some of the dreadful conditions of work.

The firing of a kiln at a factory, large or small, was supervised by the kiln foreman. This was one of the most important positions in the factory – perhaps the most important, as so much depended on a good kiln firing. The foreman would supervise the loading of the kiln, ensuring that the pots were correctly placed in their saggars, if needed, and

the huge stacks of saggars, or 'bungs', were positioned properly. Then the entrance would be blocked with clay and the fire-boxes lit, the heat raised to the correct temperature and held for the necessary length of time before the kiln was allowed to cool down.

In the days before the temperature could be measured, the kiln foreman had to judge progress from the colour of the fire or by drawing out small test pieces. It was said that the foreman could tell that the kiln was right when his eyebrows started to singe. A good foreman would stay by the kiln day and night during the firing, which could take several days. He had his food and snatched a brief rest by the fire-boxes in case a sudden storm or change of atmosphere affected the kiln firing.

For pots requiring separate firings at different temperatures, or sequences of biscuit, glost (in which the glaze was fired on to the body), decorating and gold firing, they could go through the kiln anything up to ten times, although many pieces required only two firings, and some just one. For the craftsman, taking a good and perfectly fired piece out of the kiln never ceases to give pleasure.

Perhaps a lot of the fascination has been taken out of factory ceramic making by the abandonment of the huge bottle ovens in favour of tunnel kilns fuelled by oil or gas; it has, however, meant that the factories are now cleaner and healthier to work in. There are people who look back at the old method of kiln firing with nostalgia, and when the last firing of a bottle was done in Stoke-on-Trent, thousands turned out to watch.

RETICULATING

The process of reticulation is the cutting out of small holes from the ceramic body during the clay stage. The name derived from 'reticule', an openwork bag resembling a net, and the craftsman was called a 'reticulator'.

Reticulation was practised by the Chinese and Japanese in a type of piercing known as 'rice grain'. Cut-out holes the shape and size of rice grain were allowed to fill with glaze, creating small windows which were much more translucent than the rest of the piece. Hirado of Japan produced fine examples of incense-burners and ornamental pieces, as also did Sèvres in France. Meissen made plates with finely pierced borders, and these later declined in Germany into the 'ribbon plates' with rectangular cut-out shapes from which the plates would be hung on the wall with a ribbon. In England pierced baskets for fruit were made in a porcelain body by such factories as Derby, Worcester, Caughley and Lowestoft; at Leeds the earthenware body of creamware, which was easier to work on, was cut into intricate shapes.

In the late nineteenth century the process reached its height of popularity at Worcester. Fine vases, baskets and pot-pourri and other receptacles were produced, either by cutting out the pieces from vessels which had moulded patterns impressed into them or by the much more difficult method of reticulating by eye and hand alone. In both methods the small pieces of clay were cut with a sharp, pointed knife, usually just dipped into water. The body had to be in the green stage and, if the work were going to take a long time, moisture had to be kept in the piece by either covering it with damp cloths or putting it into a wet-box – a metal-lined box with damp cloths or a bowl of water inside. If the clay dried out beyond a certain point it would crumble when touched. After the reticulation was finished the pot was allowed to dry, and then it was biscuit fired. If the piece was to be glazed, the glazer had to ensure that the holes did not fill up with glaze, unless the 'rice grain' effect were required; a glost firing followed.

The technique of reticulating was brought to a peak of perfection by George Owen, who worked all his life at Worcester until he died in 1917. After many years of working on moulded shapes he evolved his own methods of cutting by eye and hand, regrettably never allowing anyone into his room to see him working nor telling anyone his secrets. (This was not unusual in the ceramic crafts, where secrecy has always been important.) His pots are unique, no sequence of holes and shapes being like any other. Some of the pots have thousands of intricate shapes cut out of them – diamonds, hexagons, vase-like forms – and they must have taken several weeks to complete. The problem of drying out was ever present and necessitated the constant use of a wet-box. The work was delicate and required of him an enormous degree of concentration since there was always the danger of two holes becoming one by a slip of the knife. To put a broken-out piece back in the raw clay stage was almost always unsatisfactory as it was likely to come out again in the kiln firing: 'clay never forgets', as the saying is. During the biscuit firing faults sometimes became apparent for the first time: a fire-crack might cause the minutely separated holes to merge into each other, and stresses that could have come from jarring or vibration in the clay stage caused damage that could mar the piece and days or weeks of work could be ruined. The true potter accepted such things with calmness.

Above: Worcester porcelain fruit basket, c. 1770. The reticulation process was carried out with a sharp, pointed knife while the body was still in the green stage, and it was important to retain the moisture until the work had been completed. Once the piercing – in this case in the form of diamond-shaped holes – had been done, the piece was allowed to dry; it was then given a preliminary biscuit firing.
Right: Sèvres porcelain pot-pourri vase, French, 1761. This piece is more elaborately reticulated, and the decoration would have required the skills of several different craftsmen.

Left: Royal Worcester vase reticulated by George Owen (1847–1917), 1907. Each small shape was individually hand cut without a pattern or mould to work from. Owen would start at the top of the piece and work down. One of the particular difficulties of the technique was ensuring that the cut sections did not fall inside the pot, from where they could not be retrieved. Concentration, great skill and calm patience were required.
Below: Dutch delftware puzzle jug, probably from the de Grieksche factory, 1724. Puzzle jugs caught the unwary drinker and drowned him in beer unless he knew the secret of how to drink from that particular model. This example has reticulation in simple shapes around the neck.

SLIP DECORATING

Slip – liquid clay – has long been used for decorating pots. The ancient Peruvians were highly skilled at painting in clay of one colour on clay of another, and they sometimes used four or five colours in their decorations. The Greeks and Romans produced a large number of wares painted by brush with geometric and other, more complicated, patterns.

The heyday of slipware was in the seventeenth and eighteenth centuries, when the finest trailed-slip decoration was done at Wrotham in Kent and in Staffordshire. The potters of Wrotham specialized in the making of jugs, dishes, cups, pots for drinking the beverage posset and the multi-handled cups known as 'tygs', which had studs in white slip stuck on to the basic red clay pot, or white dots, trailed patterns, initials and dates squeezed on from a bag, the process resembling that of icing a cake. The slips could be stained with metallic oxides and then covered with a clear lead glaze to produce a rich honey-coloured effect.

The finest pieces of all were made in Staffordshire by the Toft family and potters such as Wright and Malkin, who occasionally signed their work. Particularly impressive are the large dishes with a border of criss-cross lines and elaborate centres depicting the royal coat of arms, Adam and Eve, Charles I in an oak tree or the Pelican in her Piety. The best work of Thomas Toft is boisterous and naïve, with the slip, stained dark brown, red or green, contrasting with the red clay under a yellowish lead glaze. These wares were presumably intended for decoration rather than use, and they were popular then as they are now.

The most complicated decoration could be done with the use of a trailing-box or a hollowed quill. Large dishes might have different coloured slips joggled together to make splashes of colour; trailed lines could be 'feathered' by drawing a thin point across them to drag the pattern into feathers, as in a Battenburg cake; wiggles and snake-like patterns could be

Above: Egyptian bowl discovered at Koptos, probably first century AD. The pot was decorated in white and pink slip – clay and water mixed to a creamy consistency and stained with metallic oxides.

Left: Staffordshire slipware owl, the head forming a cup, c. 1700. Staffordshire and Wrotham, where the tyg illustrated on page 114 was made, were the main two areas of slipware production in England in the seventeenth and eighteenth centuries.
Below: Staffordshire earthenware dish decorated with trailed slip by Thomas Toft (died 1689), late seventeenth century.
Right: Minton porcelain vase decorated in pâte-sur-pâte *by Marc-Louis Solon (1835–1913), English, nineteenth century. With the technique of* pâte-sur-pâte *the pattern was built up with layers of slip, in this instance to form a continuous band of children bathing. Drying time was allowed between each application, and the final layer could be finely sculpted.*

trailed on; pots could be dipped into slip and when the slip was dry a pattern scratched through it with a point or incised in it to reveal the original colour of the body beneath – a process called '*sgraffito*'.

Slipware was made in many centres in England, in Derbyshire, Yorkshire, North Devon, Somerset and Sussex, and many of the eastern and southern states of America produced ware which reflected the influence of England. Slipware was still being made in the late nineteenth century on both sides of the Atlantic and has recently had a great revival through the work of modern craftsmen potters.

All the work so far described was on simple earthenware, but the most superb form of slip decoration was to be found on porcelain. The process was called '*pâte-sur-pâte*', or 'body on body'. *Pâte-sur-pâte* involved a slow build-up of the pattern in white slip on a tinted biscuit body, layer after layer being applied by brush to thicken certain areas, which could then be carved. The thinner layers appeared almost diaphanous when covered by a translucent glaze.

The technique was first used in eighteenth-century China and was introduced at Sèvres in the mid-nineteenth century, and shortly afterwards it was employed at Meissen. Undoubtedly the finest work was done by Marc-Louis Solon, who went to Minton's factory from Sèvres in 1870. The process was enormously time-consuming, and it was one of the most technically difficult forms of ceramic decoration, though at the same time it could be considered one of the purest forms comprising simply the application of clay on clay. Solon generally chose to decorate his pieces with classical subjects, building up the figures in a pale colour against a dark ground. Like Toft, his work was highly acclaimed at the time and commanded high prices. Comparing *pâte-sur-pâte* with the boisterous simplicity of some forms of slip decoration shows what a versatile medium slip can be.

GLAZING

Glaze is a fusible material which is fired on to the surface of pottery and porcelain to make it watertight and to facilitate cleaning. With artificial, or soft-paste, porcelain the glaze is put on to the once-fired biscuit body and fused in the glost kiln at a lower temperature so that the glaze is a surface skin. It can be likened to a sandwich with the body as the filling and the glaze as the bread on either side. Soft-paste glaze is fairly soft and this allows subsequently fired colours to fuse much more deeply into the glaze. True, or hard-paste, porcelain has a feldspathic glaze which is fired at a high temperature (about 1400°C) and fuses with the body, which can have had a low biscuit firing first. Earthenware glazes are much more varied than those that can be used on porcelain.

The earliest glazes on pottery were developed by the Egyptians, who used soda compounds mixed with copper to produce lovely blue and turquoise glazes on beads and figurines. These alkaline glazes had drawbacks in that they tended to craze and flake off. An improvement came with the discovery that lead in the form of galena (lead sulphide), when powdered and then dusted or painted on to the pot, fused to a shiny glaze which could not be erased. Early Syrian and Babylonian lead-glazed vessels are very beautiful, especially those where metallic oxides such a copper, iron and manganese were used to make the coloured glazes.

The Chinese used lead glazes from about 500 BC, and the English Medieval potters followed. With some English Medieval pots the galena was dusted on to the damp pots in places, producing attractive particles of glaze of a green, speckled yellow or brown colour. Lead oxide mixed with sand and red clay produced a fine, rich glaze that became the staple of most country potters in England and America. Until the mid-nineteenth century the dangers of lead poisoning caused by working with lead or using the vessels were not realized.

Alkaline and lead glazes are relatively low fired (up to 1050°C). The development of higher-firing kilns in China enabled different glazes that fused at higher temperatures to

Left: Chinese porcelain jar, Dao Quang (1821–50). The vibrant flambé glaze was achieved by coating the surface with a copper-oxide glaze and firing it in a reducing atmosphere. The glaze was developed in China during the Sung dynasty. Above: Hispano-Moresque earthenware plate, 1469–79. The plate was tin glazed and decorated in lustre with the arms of Ferdinand and Isabella.

POURING AND DIPPING GLAZE
1. To glaze hollow-ware, the pot was filled with the liquid glaze and the excess poured away.
2. The pot was dipped into a tub of glaze to coat the exterior.
3. After the pot had been removed from the tub, it was shaken and swivelled to spread the glaze evenly.

Left: Earthenware dish by Bernard Palissy (c. 1510–90), French, c. 1550. Similar lead-glazed pottery is still produced in western Europe, the decoration in relief and with boldly contrasting colours.
Above: Raeren stoneware covered jug, c. 1600. Salt glazing was developed in Germany in the fourteenth century. During the firing salt was thrown into the kiln, where it vaporized and combined with the silica in the pottery to form a thin glaze. It produced a characteristic pitted surface that resembled the skin of an orange.

be used. One type was ash glaze – wood ash contains potash, soda, silica and alumina – and this produced some beautiful effects. The Chinese also developed glazes made of clay itself, especially red clays which had impurities, and they were spread over pots made of a more refractory body.

Salt glaze was developed by the Germans in the fourteenth century. The process involved firing the pots in a normal kiln and, when they had reached the maturing temperature, throwing salt into the fire-boxes. The salt vaporized in the kiln and combined with the silica in the pots to form a thin glaze which had a characteristic 'orange peel' appearance. Different kinds of clay produced different colours, ranging from a dull brown if there were little iron oxide in it to a heavy brown if there were a lot. Other colours included the blue that resulted from the use of cobalt. The process spread to England and later became a favourite of many of the craftsmen potters such as the Martin brothers.

Tin glazes were developed in the Near East and spread to Persia, Spain, Italy (where it is called 'maiolica'), France and Germany ('faience'), Holland and England ('delft'). Tin oxide is an opacifier, producing a white glaze that does not allow the crude earthenware body to show through, so, although it was not translucent and the glaze had a tendency to crumble away

from the rims, the piece looked enough like Chinese porcelain to make it attractive. Cobalt oxide to produce blue and a small range of metallic oxides to produce yellow, brown, red, green and purple were fired with the glaze to make delightful decorations imitating the Chinese.

The problem with painting was that it had to be done on the raw glaze, which was a little like trying to draw in ink on blotting-paper – a mistake could not be rubbed out without removing the glaze as well – so the painting was done boldly and quickly. It lacked, perhaps, the care and refinement of porcelain painting, but it was strong and direct. Some maiolica was lustred, a difficult process developed with great skill in Persia and later re-discovered by William de Morgan in England in the nineteenth century. It involved painting metallic pigments over an opaque-white tin glaze, then firing again in a reducing atmosphere.

In present-day factories most glazing is done by aerograph (an atomizer also used for applying ground colours, see p.131), or by spraying. Glazing by hand is still done by craftsmen potters and in small factories. The glazer dips the piece into the tub of glaze, shaking and spinning it round to spread the glaze while ensuring that he touches as little of the surface as possible to avoid leaving finger marks.

COLOURED GROUNDS

Grounds are panels or bands of one colour which either form or frame the main decoration of a piece. The area left free of any ground colour but surrounded by it is known as the 'reserve'. Appearing mainly on porcelain, the colour is composed of cobalt oxide applied to the biscuit under the glaze or of one of a range of onglaze metallic oxides. They have a long history, having been introduced by the Chinese during the Ming dynasty. In Europe coloured grounds were first used at Meissen in the 1720s and were later taken up by all the great factories.

At first the colours were put on by brush and, where there was a large area to be covered, the effect was sometimes rather blotchy and uneven. Some of the Meissen ground colours were superb, however, particularly the lilac, lime green, puce, gold and iron reds. Technically the yellow was the most remarkable. Having a very narrow tolerance to firing temperatures, it was a most difficult colour to control in the kiln; for this reason the yellow could vary a great deal.

The finest ground colours of all were those produced in the 1750s at Vincennes and Sèvres, where the colours were fused on to the soft-paste porcelain to create a gorgeously deep effect. Wonderful blues were produced, lapis lazuli and royal blue making their appearance in 1753; and in 1755 a sky-blue ground was used on a service made for Louis XV. After daffodil yellow and apple green had been introduced came the pink which is associated with Madame de Pompadour, who bought items decorated with the colour in 1757 and 1758. Perhaps the most admired ground colour of all was developed at Sèvres: *bleu celeste*, or celestial blue, a superb turquoise which has a glowing translucent quality.

All these ground colours were imitated by other factories, in England notably by Chelsea and Worcester. They were never as fine as the originals, although Worcester did produce by a long and slow process a characteristic scale-blue ground. The dark overlapping scales and blobs were painted on the once-fired biscuit over a pale wash of cobalt in the areas between shaped panels. These were left reserved so that birds and flowers could be painted in after the glazing. The blue needed to be hardened on to the biscuit in a further firing before the glaze was applied to drive out the oils and prevent the glaze from running in the glost firing. The extra firing that was required to produce scale blue naturally added to the cost of a piece, and they were expensive items in their day.

As well as painting in the centres or reserves of the scale-decorated pieces, elaborate gilded patterns could be put on top of the grounds which had names as evocative as '*œil de perdrix*' (resembling a partridge's eye), 'vermicelli' (small wriggles like vermicelli) and '*caioutte*' (different-sized circles). An elaborate

ground-laid piece with painted subjects and gilding could have taken up to 400 or so hours to complete.

The process of ground-laying was the main method of putting on ground colours in the nineteenth century. By this method the area which did not need the ground colour was protected with a resist. The ground-layer painted the remaining part with a drying oil, which he then bossed by buffing it with a thick pad to remove the brushmarks. The special powdered colour was dusted on with a pad of cotton wool and the excess shaken off. After drying, the resist was removed in warm water. It was a difficult process and has nowadays been dropped in favour of coloured lithographic prints, which are easy and quick to apply.

One of the most complicated ground-laid colours was powdered blue. The cobalt was blown through a gauze-ended tube so that it speckled into the oiled panels, the panels intended for painting having been protected by shaped-paper cut-outs. In the eighteenth century there was an interesting complication in that copper green (usually termed 'apple green' nowadays) would not take gold over the top; in the nineteenth century the problem was overcome by using a chrome-green ground-lay which it was possible to gild (see p. 136). On early greens, and several other grounds, the gold could only be used to outline the panels.

Above: Meissen porcelain dish, 1760s. The dish has a mosaic ground, the centre painted with flower sprays.
Left: Meissen porcelain tea-caddy, c. 1745. It has a rare tomato-red ground reserving panels painted with figures in a landscape. The first use of coloured grounds on European porcelain was at Meissen in the 1720s, and the practice spread from there to other European factories.

Left: Sèvres porcelain ewer and basin, 1757. These pieces were decorated with a beautifully controlled rose Pompadour ground reserving panels of painted flowers and gilding. The pink was named after Madame de Pompadour who, between 1757 and 1758, bought pieces decorated in this colour.
Above: Sèvres porcelain cup and saucer, c. 1760. They have blue grounds with caioutte gilding composed of circles of varying sizes. The figure subjects were finely painted by Viellard.
Right: Worcester porcelain soup tureen and cover, c. 1770. The vessel has a scale-blue ground reserving

panels of exotic birds and insects. The overlapping scales were painted on the piece after the first biscuit firing over a pale wash of cobalt.

THE CRAFT OF THE PORCELAIN ARTIST

The pigments used by the porcelain artist were derived from metallic oxides (often wrongly termed 'enamels'). They were supplied in powder form and were first ground by the painter with a palette knife on a tile. The longer the pigment was ground, the smoother and better the result.

As the medium the painter used fat oil, which he prepared himself in a 'fountain' – a pyramid of three or four pots in graduated sizes, the smallest at the top. Into the top pot was poured pure turpentine, which was allowed to evaporate to produce fat oil. The fat oil flowed over to the lower pots, becoming progressively thicker, while the top pot was regularly topped up with turpentine. The painter's fountain was an essential piece of equipment.

By adding fat oil to the pigment, a creamy paste was produced, and to keep it free and open a thin oil was used, the best being aniseed. Aniseed has a particularly strong smell and pervaded the painting department of a factory. Some painters found aniseed somewhat heady and alternatives such as oil of lavender (spike), or citron were sometimes used.

The artist painted with a brush directly on to the glazed surface of the piece, sometimes sketching the subject in pencil, sometimes working with a pounced-on pattern which reproduced the main outline of the decoration as a faint dotted line. A number of colours could be used at the same time provided that they all matured at the same temperature, and the piece was then fired in the decorating kiln for the first firing. There was usually a minimum of two firings and sometimes as many as four or five to obtain the desired effect.

There were several complications: one was that some colours – orange, for example – would only mature by fusing through another; another was that most colours underwent a change in the firing and the raw colour was not the same as the one that matured in the kiln. The painter had to learn the nature of the metallic oxides, and as much of his training was devoted to this as to the techniques of painting.

During the kiln firing, at temperatures ranging down from about 800° to 740°C, the metallic oxides were fused into the glaze, which loosened to accommodate them. The softer the glaze and body, the deeper the fusing. On eighteenth-century soft-paste porcelain and English bone china the metallic oxides sank in very much more than on hard-paste porcelain.

Metallic oxides were too low firing to withstand the firing of glaze on top so they were purely onglaze colours, prone to damage if the piece were badly treated, or from washing with rough soaps or soda, scratching by cutlery or contact with the juice from citrus fruits. High-firing oxide of cobalt could withstand glaze firing, however. It was painted on the biscuit and the glaze fired on top; hence underglaze blue. Some decorations have underglaze blue and onglaze colours, and these had to be fired in sequence.

Above: Worcester porcelain plate painted with a portrait of the actress Sarah Siddons in the character of the Tragic Muse by Thomas Baxter (1782–1821), c. 1814.
Right: Detail of the plate showing the painting in the form of hand-stippled dots of colour. The portrait is after a painting by Reynolds.

Above: Pair of Meissen porcelain bitterns modelled by Kändler and painted with naturalistic colours, c. 1753. Many of the early Meissen models were left white but painting, which was done directly on to the glazed surface, undoubtedly enhanced the decorative effect.

Right: Grainger Worcester porcelain vase and cover, c. 1900. The vase has a turquoise ground and was painted with a scene of peasants in woodland by James Stinton (1870–1961). Stinton specialized in such subjects during his lifetime of factory painting. In 1889 the firm of Thomas Grainger was absorbed by the Worcester Royal Porcelain Company.
Far right: Water-colour by the younger Thomas Baxter depicting his father's porcelain decorating studio at 1, Goldsmith Street, London, in 1810. It shows the painters resting their hands on boards to steady them as they worked, a fountain, pots of colour, bottles of turpentine and brushes.

Left: Chinese export porcelain dish made for Holland, K'ang Hsi (1662–1722). The hard-paste porcelain has a glittering white appearance and the metallic oxides stand hard on the surface.
Above: Frankenthal porcelain covered pot, mid-eighteenth century. The classical figure is typical of the work of the decorator Osterspray.

TRANSFER-PRINTING

Although some simple printing on ceramics using woodblocks had been practised by the Chinese, it was not until the early 1750s that transfer-printing started to become popular as a decorative technique. At Worcester transfer-printing from copper plates, which were etched, engraved, or etched and engraved, were applied to porcelain. The earliest prints were the 'smoky primitives', simple scenes of birds, ships and figures in a smoky brown colour, very much in the style of printed enamel boxes from Bilston, Wednesbury and Battersea. By 1757 the first of the successful transfer-prints – a depiction of the King of Prussia – had been introduced at Worcester by Robert Hancock. This was in a strong black colour known as 'jet enamel'.

The process involved the preparation of a flat sheet of copper either by etching with a needle through a resist and then dipping the copper into acid, which etched the design, or else by engraving into the copper with graving tools. Etching and acid-biting in succession produced great contrasts of perspective, and stronger lines could be produced by graving. Tissue-paper pulls charged with the ceramic colour were laid down upon the piece to be decorated and, after rubbing down, the paper was washed off and the piece fired in the kiln.

The earliest printing was onglaze in black, but from the late 1750s underglaze blue printing was possible and printing in England threatened to replace painted decoration, especially on the cheaper creamwares and pearlwares. Around 1800 a different method called 'bat printing', which produced a softer print, had a brief run. The process involved transferring the pattern in oil by a thin bat of glue and then dusting colour on to the oil, to which it adhered, before the piece was fired. Printing in underglaze blue reached its height in the early nineteenth century, when enormous quantities were produced for the American market, often printed with American scenes or with the famous Willow pattern – an English-invented Chinoiserie of which greater numbers must have been made than of any other scene.

Prints could be left in the colour in which they were printed or painted over by hand in several colours. Actual colour-printing was first produced by 'registering' bits of different-coloured pieces – rather like putting a jig-saw puzzle together – as done on the so-called 'Pratt pot-lids'. By the end of the nineteenth century full printing by lithographic transfers was introduced and nowadays this process, using sheets of coloured prints (or 'decals'), enables coloured scenes to be produced simply by squeezing them on to the piece before firing.

The 230-year-old technique of transfer-printing is still done in the traditional way in a few factories, and some superb work is produced. Because it is time-consuming and labour-intensive, the process is expensive: an elaborate copper plate can take more than 100 hours of engraving time, but then it can produce many hundreds of prints in the hand of a good and 'kind' printer. The printer will have two or three assistants, trimming, laying and rubbing down, and washing off; each print is then checked by the printer, who 'mends' any small piece that was missed.

Above: Scene in a printing shop in Staffordshire, 1884. The printer on the left is working at his stove, rubbing colour into a copper plate; his colleague operates the press while the girl rubs down a print.
Left: Staffordshire creamware tankard, c. 1790. The tankard was transfer-printed with Masonic emblems in black.
Right: Pratt earthenware pot and pot-lid, English, mid-nineteenth century. The scene transfer-printed on the lid is called 'The Truant'.

Left: Pratt pot-lid designed by Jesse Austen (1806–79), mid-nineteenth century. Austen, an engraver working for the Staffordshire firm of F. and R. Pratt, developed the method of polychrome transfer-printing. This example was decorated with a scene of a sea nymph riding on the back of a dolphin. The earthenware body has natural crazing of the glaze, which is very different from the harsh, large crazing of modern reproduction pot-lids made to look like old ones.
Above: Rogers of Staffordshire earthenware plate transfer-printed in blue, c. 1810–15.

TRANSFER-PRINTING
1. Ceramic colour was forced into the engraved lines of the hot copper plate.
2. Surplus colour was cleaned off, leaving the colour only in the pattern.
3. A wetted tissue was laid over the copper plate and the two were pressed together between rollers.
4. The tissue-paper 'pull', with the pattern printed in reverse, was removed from the plate.
5. An assistant trimmed away the excess paper and the print was carefully laid on to the object.
6. After hard rubbing down, the paper was washed off and the pattern fixed by firing.

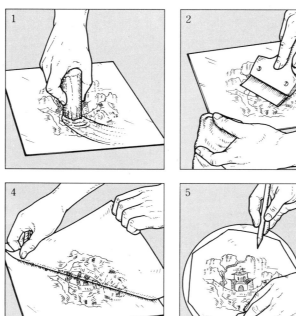
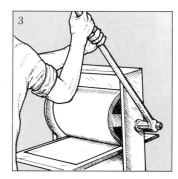

GILDING

Over the centuries many attempts were made to gild ceramics. In an early method gold leaf was applied with size and left cold on the surface. This was found to be unsatisfactory as the gold wore off during use. Chinese porcelain, early Meissen stoneware and English pottery were decorated in this way, but few pieces have survived with the gold in good condition. It was realized that some method of firing the gold was necessary to fuse it on to the body or glaze and make it permanent.

The first really successful process was probably the one developed in Germany at Meissen. They used a precipitated gold powder (made by adding a solution of ferrous sulphate to a solution of gold in aqua regia) and a lead silicate flux to lower the firing temperature. At Vincennes and Sèvres in France, and at Chelsea and Worcester in England, a fired gold-leaf method was used, known as 'honey gilding'. Gold leaf was ground up very slowly in honey and the honey washed away in hot water. After drying, the gold powder was fixed to the glazed ware with a mordant of oil of garlic, gum water and vinegar. The piece was then fired at a lower temperature than that at which the metallic oxide decoration was fired, and this produced a hard-wearing fused gold. Honey gold has a soft, brown appearance, and when looked at with a magnifying glass it will be found to be somewhat pitted and blistered. It was not possible to add another layer of gold on top as it could only be fired once.

Around 1780 the mercury method was introduced at Sèvres, and it was used extensively thereafter. Gold, dissolved in aqua regia, was precipitated by adding a solution of mercurous nitrate. This gave a much finer gold powder. It made a thin, bright film of gold which, when fired and burnished, was far superior to the old honey gilding. Some superb gilding was produced by specialist gilders and also by the great decorators, who were craftsmen able to carry out the complete range of decorative processes – ground-laying, painting, gilding and burnishing.

A young gilder began by practising over and over again the many different lines, strokes and curves that he would use until they became perfect and effortless. Gold was, of course, an extremely expensive material, and the practising would be done in a ceramic colour. Good gilding on ceramics, rather like a good frame around a painting, should not be obtrusive. Poor gilding, where strokes are not balanced or true, can ruin a piece.

Simple lines, such as those at the top or bottom of a piece, were done by using a 'whirler' – a wheel on top of a spindle. One hand turned the spindle while the other held the gold-laden brush. By this method fine or thick lines could be produced encircling the rim or centre of a plate or a saucer. With a piece that was not circular the gilder had to produce the line in short sequences.

Hand gilding could be built up upon the lines, as in the case of dentils – semi-circles of gold that look like rounded dogs' teeth. Strokes and elaborate patterns were produced, ranging from

simple flashes down a handle ending in a series of dots, to elaborate panels of gilding. The most complicated forms were raised gilding and jewelling, which were done by building up strokes or spots of thick ceramic colour over which the gold was applied. Elaborate hand-gilded pieces could take many days, or even weeks, to complete, as it was a much slower and more meticulous process than painting. High-quality gold – 22 carat – was fired on to the glaze at around 720°C, and several firings were often necessary for the most complex work.

Burnishing was the final process in the decoration of a fine piece. Basically, it was the polishing of the fired gold, which came out of the kiln very dull in appearance.

The simplest burnishing, on large flat areas, was done by polishing with very finely sifted silver sand held in a soft cloth. Rims of plates, saucers and the like were burnished with what is called a 'bloodstone' – actually a haematite – a rounded stone set in a wooden handle. This gave a very high polish to the gold. Awkward angles and crevices such as the insides and terminals of handles called for the use of a pointed agate.

A burnisher was often called upon to produce a much more artistic finish to the gold than could be achieved simply by polishing it. The agate could be used to draw patterns on flat areas of gold; the part drawn on by the agate point was bright and the area to either side remained matt, or dull. By such means quite complicated areas of decoration were built up. The process is called 'chasing', and in the nineteenth century the decorator would often do this work himself.

BURNISHING
1. Simple burnishing on flat areas was done with a soft cloth and silver sand, finely sifted.
2. A pointed agate set in a wooden

handle was used to hard burnish particular areas such as crevices or to incise designs in the gold. These areas were bright and contrasted with surrounding matt areas.

Left: Detail of a Derby porcelain plate, 1880. This shows the intricacy of the tooled gold and platinum decoration.
Below: Royal Worcester porcelain teapot, 1887. It was reticulated by George Owen and finely jewelled and gilded by Samuel Ranford. The droplets of gold and simulated pearls were meticulously done. This highly specialized type of decoration would have required many hours of work.

Left: Part of an 18-piece Royal Worcester dessert-service, 1921. The cobalt-blue ground and gilded decoration was much enlivened by the panels of fruit against a mossy background painted by Richard Sebright (1868–1951).
Above: Sèvres porcelain bonbonnière in the form of an egg, 1762. It has a blue ground with finely gilded decoration which was partially chased by the burnisher with an agate. After burnishing the piece was complete, having been through various different stages of production: it would have been handled by several craftsmen and undergone a number of separate firings.

METALWORK

The greatest technical step for mankind was the recognition that heat could be used to melt metals and make them malleable enough to be turned into tools, vessels and ornaments. Once heat was applied, metal could be cut, moulded, drawn, raised by hammering or cast, techniques which have been used by metalworkers for thousands of years.

The next crucial advance was the discovery that fire will fuse two or more metals to make an alloy with new properties. Copper, the earliest of the metals to be alloyed, is relatively soft and cannot take a cutting-edge, Once fused with tin, an even softer metal, bronze, was made, an alloy which could be as much as three times harder than copper. Gold and silver, too, highly valued for their qualities of colour, malleability and ductility, were alloyed to give greater strength and, for gold, to vary its colour. Other alloys included pewter and its later variants Britannia, or German, metal, and brass alloyed with zinc rather than the earlier calamine. The pace of discovery of alloys and of techniques of working metal was not steady and universal. In Japan and India steel was being produced well before 1000 AD, whereas the secret of its manufacture was still not fully understood in mid-seventeenth-century England.

Regional differences of techniques were considerable. In Saxony, a mineral-rich region, water power was in use to drive foundry hammers two centuries before it reached England in the fifteenth century. The casting methods introduced by the Huguenot goldsmiths from French workshops were far more refined than those practised in England at the time.

The basic equipment for working metals remained fairly constant over the centuries, whatever the metal to be worked. A hearth or furnace to melt the raw material or to anneal (heat) it while it was worked, bellows to control the heat, tongs, anvils, stakes and hammers, drills and files, and punches to work and shape the ingot, were common to all metalworkers' shops; to ornament and finish their products they used drills, files and punches. The most valuable pieces of equipment were moulds for forming the molten metal, casting patterns for components such as feet, handles, spouts or finials, and for applied ornament, and lathes for turning, to cut down on the labour of raising the metal with the hammer. Another important item, in use in Europe at least from the fifteenth century, was the crank-operated drawbench for pulling metal rods into wire.

Workshops were organized and supervised by the master, who also negotiated with his customers. Since the master was held responsible for the quality both of his metal and of his workshop's products, some mark of identification was usually stamped on pewter, silver and armour. Goldsmiths, pewterers and armourers also had marks of approval added by their respective craft organizations. Sheets of engraved ornament were circulated throughout Europe from the sixteenth century, often reprinted several times and remaining in use for many years. Designs were also transmitted by journeymen ('dayworkers'), who moved from one centre to another.

Between the early and the late eighteenth century new alloys, new techniques of smelting iron and new mechanized methods of rolling, turning and stamping transformed both the nature of the workshop and the scale of production in England, although traditional craft practices continued in certain European centres. The surface treatment of metalwares changed, too: improved coatings such as close-plating, tin-plating, japanning and the invention of fused copper and silver sheet (Old Sheffield Plate) meant that cheap base metals, formerly impractical for large-scale domestic use, could be disguised and so became both more practical and more decorative. Some of the traditional methods of working and ornamenting metals have died out; others, set aside by industrialization, have been revived or rediscovered, notably goldsmithing, blacksmithing and enamelling.

Left: French silver-gilt coffee-pot by Marc-Augustin Lebrun, Paris, c.1820. This piece illustrates various types of surface enrichment: the cast and applied vine leaves are set off by their textured background, which stands out against the plain burnished body.

Left: English lock and key made by Walter Bickford, late seventeenth century. The lock mechanism and the key are of chiselled steel and the case is of pierced gilded brass. The steel elements have been blued to contrast with the gilding.

GOLD AND SILVER

Gold and silver are the chief materials used in decorative art which are both inherently valuable and can be refashioned again and again without loss of the precious metal. They have been worked continuously since about 4500 BC, both as a form of currency and for ornament. Gold has always been scarcer than silver, and more highly prized. The two metals were worked by similar methods: craftsmen trained with gold could also handle the cheaper metal, and the term 'goldsmith' is traditionally used for workers in silver, too. The craft organizations which emerged in European towns during the Middle Ages called themselves goldsmiths. Members of these companies might be specialists in any branch of the craft from refining to chasing (see p. 154), from die-stamping (see p. 148) to engraving (see p. 156). Because of the need to protect the purity of their raw materials, and because of the interchangeability with currency, goldsmiths were strictly regulated and their wares marked (see p. 162).

Pure gold and silver are too soft to stand up to general use, whether for jewellery or tablewares. Since ancient times they have been hardened by alloying with small proportions of other metals, the most satisfactory for this purpose being copper.

In its native state, from whatever source, most gold naturally contains a proportion of silver. Gold with a large silver content produced the metal known as 'electrum', which was itself considered a precious metal and used in Ancient Egypt, Greece and Asia Minor. From early times craftsmen were able to refine gold to produce a relatively pure metal, using copper to harden it.

Most silver was extracted as a by-product of tin or lead. Traces of gold were usually to be found in the refined silver used by the Ancients, and, indeed, until the early years of the nineteenth century. They were unable to extract the gold as they did the other metals from the mix and, by rule of thumb rather than science, alloyed it with a small quantity of copper. In more recent times experiments have been made using metals such as zinc, cadmium and tin, mostly in a search for more tarnish-resistant silver.

The goldsmith's raw material was frequently old metal, purchased from his customers, cut up and melted to extract any gold left by gilding (see p. 168). The molten silver was then cast into an ingot. Before rolling mills came into being, the goldsmith had painstakingly to hammer out the ingot before any shaping could start. Once the ingot was flattened, the sheet was cut into the required shape. With the trimmings left over, the goldsmith could build up, for example, the foot and stem of a cup from many separate pieces. These would be soldered together (see p. 143) or slotted on to a central stem, a method used in England and Germany.

Far left: St Eligius in his Workshop *by Niklaus Manuel Deutsch the Elder (c.1484–1530), 1515. St Eligius was a goldsmith of legendary skill in the seventh century and the patron saint of metalworkers. The painting depicts the making of chalices in a typical sixteenth-century German workshop.*
Left: Flemish parcel-gilt beaker with a plain rim and engraved central band, Liège, mid-fifteenth century.
Below: French silver soup tureen and stand signed by Juste-Aurèle Meissonnier (c.1693–1750), Paris, 1734–36. The high Rococo moulds and casts were prepared by P.-F. Bonnestrenne and Henri Adnet.

A major advance in preparing the metal was the technique of rolling metal introduced into France from Germany more than 400 years ago, although not widely used until horse-driven mills were in operation early in the eighteenth century. There were advances, too, in European refining techniques, and by the 1750s there were many specialist refiners supplying prepared gold and silver to the local workshops, including the rolled sheet needed for the production of Old Sheffield Plate (see p.171).

Today, electrolytic refining ensures metals of constant quality, hardness and colour, produced in sheets of uniformly accurate gauge or in any other of the many forms required by the craftsman such as tube, grain for casting, wires and solders, and special alloys for spinning (see p.146) or enamelling (see p.195). Nevertheless, the goldsmith requires a knowledge of the properties of the metals and must still pay constant attention to the changes in the crystalline structure during working, even during polishing (see p.152). Annealing, to restore ductility and strength during making, remains an important process (see p.142).

Above: Silver-gilt pomander, probably English, c.1580. It has six compartments, four of which are shown open. Worn about the neck or at the waist, each of the loculi held perfumes or other aromatic substances (musk, civet, ambergris, hence the name pomander from pomme d'ambre) to protect the wearer from infection. Often Dutch and German examples are engraved with the names of spices within the four, six or, more rarely, eight separate compartments.
Left: The pomander shown closed. The chased scrollwork encloses black enamel.

ANNEALING

Because hammering and other working processes alter the crystalline structure of gold and silver, and make them brittle, the heat treatment known as 'annealing' was an essential operation, repeated several times during manufacture. Whether the separate elements were raised, spun, stamped, drawn or swaged, annealing was necessary to counter the effect of the internal stresses that were set up. This change is called 'work hardening'.

The need for annealing, though perhaps not the scientific reasons for it, had been recognized by metalworkers for thousands of years and it might seem almost a primitive process. In fact it needed considerable skill and a good knowledge of the properties of the alloy being worked to ensure that annealing was wholly successful, avoiding such problems as blistering, fire-cracking or 'firestain', a blackish deposit on the surface caused by overheating, leading to oxidation of the copper content of the alloy, and made worse by hammering. Overheating, which could damage the alloy, unequal heating and exposure to the atmosphere might all contribute to the failure of the process.

The craftsman placed the components he was working on in a special heavy iron pan, called a 'hearth', which he then rotated in the flame. The gold or silver was slowly brought up to a dull red heat (about 650°C), then lifted out with tongs and quenched in a cooling bath. The time taken was critical; obviously it was increased for larger objects, which took longer to heat through. Just as the pewterer smelled his metal to check the heat when casting (see p. 212), so the goldsmith generally judged by eye the exact depth of redness, which is why annealing was usually done in a dark corner of the workshop where it was easier to see the colour. Sometimes the piece to be annealed was coated with flux to prevent firestain which became fluid at a known temperature, an indication that the process was finished. After annealing, the work was plunged into a pickling tank, a solution of dilute sulphuric acid, to clean off dirt or oxide.

Left: Detail of a printed invitation to the working goldsmiths' feast at Goldsmiths' Hall, London, 6 February, 1701. Hammering and a variety of other processes employed to fashion and decorate gold and silver are illustrated on the card. All types of working caused alterations to the crystalline structure of the metal and made it brittle. To counter the effects of 'work hardening', the piece was 'annealed' from time to time during manufacture. The first stage in the process was to heat the metal slowly in a pan over a flame, and the fire shown here would have been used for the purpose.
Above: Goldsmiths' implements from Illustrations of Useful Arts *by Charles Tomlinson, 1867. The tongs would have been used in the annealing process to lift the heated metal from the pan and cast it into a cooling bath.*

SOLDERING

Soldering is the process of joining pieces together by fusing a 'solder', an alloy of the gold or silver, between them. Other than simple vessels such as bowls and tumbler cups (which, when tipped, 'tumble' back to an upright position), nearly all objects were assemblages of smaller parts soldered to the main body. Soldering was a highly skilled operation for, if possible, no trace of the solder was to be seen and the applied work had to be absolutely flat on the surface. The surfaces to be joined had to be meticulously clean.

For silver, the solder, like the rest of the work, had to be of at least sterling standard (see p.162). Today silver solder is usually alloyed with zinc to produce a hard solder with a melting-point of about 700° to 778°C; formerly the alloy metal was brass, also with a lower melting-point than sterling silver. The solder – in the nineteenth century in the form of a stick – was fed into the joint while the work was held in the hearth over a charcoal flame. The work was then plunged into the pickling tank to remove dirt and oxides.

At the rare points where old solder is visible, it has a distinctive colour which is unlike that of modern solder. Also, traces of it were seldom removed to the same extent as on modern silver. When it is visible, usually around the applied foot of a pot or cup, it can be a useful clue when forgery might be suspected. Sometimes crude repairs to old silver were carried out using lead solder, particularly on church plate.

The foot of a pot or cup was attached to the body by soldering on a collar wire and moulding just above the level of the base. On teapots and coffee-pots, kettles and spout cups, the spout was then soldered on, holes being drilled if required for teapots where the base of the spout was to be centred; otherwise a single hole was cut in the body of the pot. Cast handle sockets were likewise soldered in place for pots and cups, mugs and tankards, in early silver often on a small shaped plate, around 1700 often as a calyx of cut-card ornament (see p.160).

Left: Illustration of soldering from The Penny Magazine, *1844. Most hollow-wares, which include jugs, teapots, cups and trays, were assembled from several parts, which* were made separately, then soldered together.
Above: Photograph of a craftsman soldering, using a charcoal brazier and a blowpipe to increase the flame.

SOLDERING
1. Because of the expansion of the metal when heated, and the action of the bubbling flux, the pieces had to be bound together firmly. The bowl was inverted and tied with binding wire.
2. The bowl was protected with a flux and set on a grid over the revolving hearth to ensure an even heat.
3. The stick of solder was filed clean, charged with flux and fed into the joint. A flame was directed on to it from the reverse to pull the solder through.

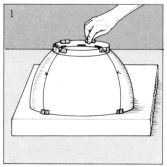

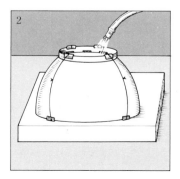

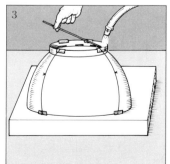

SINKING AND RAISING

Sinking and raising were two of the simplest and most common methods of working gold and silver. They were used to make hollow or dished objects, or parts of hollow-ware such as the covers, feet or spouts. Articles formed by sinking and raising have no seam, a particularly desirable factor in the manufacture of fine teapots, coffee-pots and goblets. Today, the processes have largely been superseded by spinning (see p.146).

First the craftsman cut a circle of flat silver, known as the 'blank'. He calculated the size of the blank by reference to the average diameter and the height of the piece to be made, as shown on the working drawing. Next he marked the centre of the disc. This centre point can often be discerned, even on the finished article.

Sinking, the simpler of the two processes, involved working the metal from a flat sheet, using various types of hammer, on a sinking-block. The part of the blank that was to become the outside of the piece was held down over the block. Using a blocking, or ball-faced, hammer, the goldsmith worked from the edge, row by row, towards the centre to produce a depressed rim, rather like a saucer, turning the blank as he proceeded. After each row, or 'course', the work had to be annealed to restore the ductility of the silver and to toughen it. For bowls and dishes further shaping was done by hammering the metal over a sand-filled leather saddle.

Deeper wares such as jugs, however, were formed over the raising-stake, which was firmly held in the 'steady block' or, for small wares, the bench vice. The blank was first hammered against a grooved stake to crimp the edge. The craftsman then inverted the saucer-shaped blank and held it at an angle over the raising-stake with one hand, while with the other he wielded the hammer on the outside surface, working row by row horizontally up from the base, alternately clockwise and anti-clockwise to avoid distortion. Here the centre marking and the inscribed circle became important, for the craftsman worked from that to the rim until the required width and height had been achieved.

With repeated hammering, row by row from the base upwards, the vessel gradually took shape. At each stage the piece was annealed again. As the diameter was reduced, the work was done over smaller stakes. Each time he reached the top, the craftsman hammered back the metal to thicken the edge – a process known as 'caulking', or 'corking' – to ensure a good, sound rim. In the making of tumbler cups, however, the silver was hammered back again to the base to ensure that the cup was base-heavy and would tumble properly without falling on its side.

When the body of the piece had been raised to the required shape, the roughness left by the hammering was removed.

Above: Mycenaean gold goblet, probably of Cretan workmanship, of a type made from about 1600 to 1550 BC. It has a stem foot and single handle, which would have been soldered on.

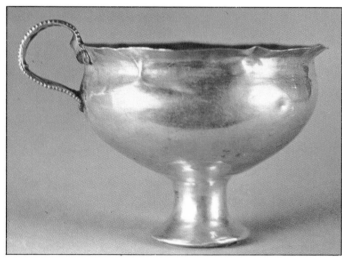

Above: Whiting Manufacturing Co. baluster-shaped jug, possibly made by a Japanese craftsman, Newark, New Jersey, c.1880. The Japanese taste swept Europe and America from about 1875 to 1885, after Japan had been opened up to the West. The hammered surface is applied with chased and engraved shells, reeds, a carp and a crab and lotus, highlighted with copper.
Left: Detail of the decoration on the jug showing the coppered finish that picks out the applied reeds.

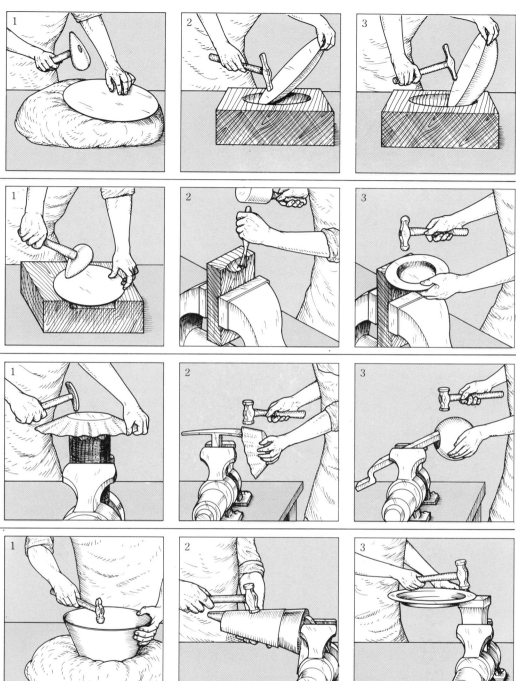

HOLLOWING
1. To make a simple bowl shape, the blank was blocked out with a doming mallet on to a leather-covered sandbag.
2. For smaller work the blank was held at an angle to a hollowed-out wooden block and hammered with the blocking hammer, working in a circle from the outside edge.
3. As the bowl deepened, the shape was checked against a template.

SINKING
1. To form simple shallow shapes, the blank was hammered into a pre-formed wooden block with a dome-headed mallet.
2. For shaping the rim of a vessel, a marked segment was chiselled out from a wooden block.
3. The blank was then rested on the curve of the wooden block and hammer blows directed on to the part of the metal that was resting on air, working round, row by row.

RAISING
1. The blank was hammered with a swaging hammer over a wooden block with hollows, working outwards from the centre to produce a pleated edge.
2. After annealing and pickling, the blank was hammered over a convex steel stake (transversely across its creases) using a raising hammer with a curved edge.
3. The last round of hammering was done with a wooden mallet so as to compress the edge.

PLANISHING
1. To planish a bowl with a curved base, the base was set on a sandbag and the bottom knocked out with a pear-shaped mallet.
2. To planish a cone shape, a square-faced collet hammer was used over a curved steel stake, the metal resting on the stake and hammer blows falling in overlapping sequence.
3. To planish a tray, the rim was placed on an absolutely flat surface and hammered evenly all over.

This was done, at least partially, by 'planishing', a process in which hammers with slightly convex, broad heads were used to smooth any unevenness on the surface and small irregularities in the thickness of the metal. Articles such as cups, bowls and dishes were planished over a round-headed stake; trays, salvers and other flat objects over a surface plate. As in all types of hammerwork of the goldsmith, evenness was essential. This ensured the regularity of curves and flat surfaces that gave gold and silver their subtle reflections and smoothness of line.

The making of trays, salvers, waiters and other stands involved a specialized branch of hand-raising that called for great skill. Once the piece has been shaped, and parts such as the edge mount and feet soldered on, the piece was flat hammered all over to ensure that the silver was firm and strong, and would not distort with use. The larger the tray or dish – and in the past great salvers, trays and sideboard dishes were often as much as 28 inches (71 cm) in diameter – the greater the strength required, and the piece had to be carefully hammered with a large flat-faced hammer while it was held over a perfectly flat wooden block. The process, as in all hammering, compressed the metal and did not extend it.

TURNING UP AND SPINNING

Because raising was slow, laborious and limited in its effectiveness, other methods of working the sheet were evolved. A method sometimes used to make simple, hollow objects inexpensively entailed turning up the sheet of silver into a cylinder or cone, then seaming it by soldering along the edges; for mugs or coffee-pots a flat base was soldered in, the joint being concealed by an applied foot-ring. The seam was not hidden completely but it was a speedy method, and it was eventually mechanized. The machine was formed of three parallel rollers, two working in the manner of a laundry mangle, the third deflecting the sheet as it rose from the first rolling process.

Especially in the larger workshops, silver hollow-wares were often made by spinning, a technique designed for production in quantity. It was first used for the manufacture of copper vessels in Ancient Egypt. As with raising, there was no seam. The sheet of silver (the gauge of which was critical for the metal to form satisfactorily) was held firmly against a fast-rotating wooden block, or 'chuck', and gradually shaped over it by using a long-armed forming-tool with a round-headed steel burnisher set in the top. This was made to resemble a tusk and it was sometimes called a 'finger-tool'. To complete the spinning process, the blank was burnished with a flat-faced forming-tool.

The principle of silver spinning was very like that of wood-turning (see p.22), though the tools were longer, being held under the arm, and much heavier. If the piece required further work – to shape the neck, for example – this was done with a raising hammer afterwards.

It was important that the chucks were firmly secured in the vice and remained in true, and a suitable wood was essential. The woods most favoured were boxwood and *lignum vitae*. Chucks for simple bowls were in one piece, but many were designed in sections so that if the object were, for instance, of baluster shape, the former could be removed without difficulty.

Compared with raising, with which the shaping of the body of a pot or cup might take half a day, spinning was much faster, and the metal had to be annealed more frequently: a piece such as a milk jug needed to be annealed about six times during spinning. Otherwise the assembly and finishing processes were the same, though of course spun wares were not planished. In recent times trade suppliers have produced standard spun blanks for finishing and decorating in the workshop. Ornamental wires (see p.158), various different styles of handle and cover, and other details, might be added from the workshop's own range.

The fact that a piece has been made by the technique of spinning can often be detected by the horizontal lines running round inside; certainly there are no hammered rows, which are usually faintly visible either inside or outside a hand-raised object.

Below: Roberts & Belk four-piece tea- and coffee-service of a design successfully made by spinning, Sheffield, 1877. For shaped work such as this the former, or pattern over which it was spun, had to be made in parts that were keyed together so that it could be removed easily. The best chucks were made of boxwood or lignum vitae.

Left: Photograph of a craftsman spinning. It shows how pressure was exerted on the rotating metal by using a long tool held under the arm.
Above: English drum-shaped mustard pot by W. R. Smiley, London, 1842. This was made by turning up from the sheet and soldering along the line of the handle; the foot and mouth wires were then soldered on.

SPINNING

1. The blank, or disc of greased silver, was slotted on to the spindle. The spinner then braced his forming-tool against a vertical peg so that its rounded face stroked the revolving disc on to the chuck.
2. As the bowl shape emerged, the peg was shifted to alter the angle between forming-tool and metal.
3. The blank was repeatedly greased during spinning to smooth the action.
4. The spinner held a wooden former against the slowly revolving bowl to ensure an even rim.
5. The spinner burnished the blank with the flat face of the forming-tool to remove any inequalities.
6. The blank was removed from the chuck ready to have the base soldered in.

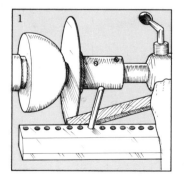

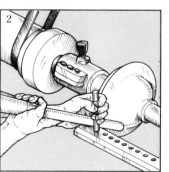

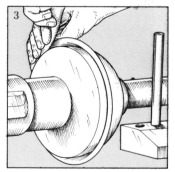

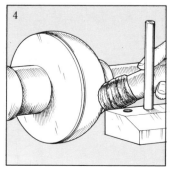

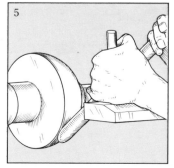

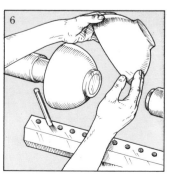

DIE-STAMPING, PRESSING AND HAND-FORGING

Before the eighteenth century die-stamping was a hand-process confined to decorating spoon-bowls, knife-handles, boxes, buttons and other smallwork, and used to produce ornamental strips to decorate the edges of bases and covers of cups, flagons and salts. The metal to be formed was hammered into the steel die, which was a block cut with a design in reverse. In the eighteenth century, once lighter rolled sheet silver, hardened steel for dies and water power had become available, all essential to large-scale silver production, die-stamping became mechanized. Matthew Boulton in Birmingham used light-gauge silver, die-stamped and then loaded to give strength, to make candlesticks; the same dies could be used to form both silver and Old Sheffield Plate (see p.171).

The quality of the machine dies had to be very high, and die-sinking was expensive; but it entailed fewer finishing processes and the metal was shaped with the minimum of attention, the shape being 'squeezed' on in a single operation. The sheet metal was repeatedly stamped into the die by means of a mechanical drop-hammer. This had a convex head which matched the concave pattern in the die. The same pattern could be repeated many times as the lower die was made of forged steel, strongly clamped down so that it would not move in the slightest during the stamping operation. Later the surfaces of the die were chromium-plated, the better to give a highly polished finish. Dies often incorporated relief decoration, and the definition of this could be improved afterwards by chasing, using a hammer and punches (see p.154).

Since it was just as easy to produce elaborate designs as simple ones, once the initial dies had been cut, an extraordinary variety of patterns for flatware was in use from the early nineteenth century. Two different dies could be used for the front and back, and part-dies for different sections.

Some customers such as the British Admiralty had their private dies cut. The crowned fouled anchor was found on navy-issue teaspoons from as early as 1838 and still remains in production, in electro-plate as well as silver.

Pressing was another method of forming thinner metal by compressing it into a die. The weighted fly-press was swung repeatedly to press the ram down into the silver to be shaped. In small workshops the press was an economical way of shaping silver sheet, saving time and effort where spinning was not feasible and casting inappropriate.

In the process of hand-forging, used for the manufacture of the finest flatware, a silver rod of the appropriate length and weight of the spoon or fork was prepared and shaped up roughly over a steel stake with a heavy steel hammer after heating it. Then the blank was pressed into the die by hammering or by a screw press, and the craftsman began work with the file, removing excess metal round the edges, truing up the spoon-bowl and cutting the prongs, also known as 'tines', of the fork.

Some patterns, such as King's, Queen's and Shell, were impressed in the die: others were added later, such as Bright Cut, which was hand-engraved on the finished product, or Bead Edge, which was done by hammering the edge with a special half-domed tool formed of two cups: the first was placed over the first 'bead' so that the next was exactly in position.

Below: English silver table-service in Queen's pattern by Mary Chawner of Chawner & Co., London, 1825/38.

This is an elaborated version of King's pattern. The pattern is 'double struck' – that is, stamped on both sides.

Right: Cartwright & Woodward cigar case die-stamped with a view of Crystal Palace in high relief, Birmingham, 1850/51.

Above: Emes & Barnard die-stamped silver decanter label, London, 1817. The lettering of 'Shrub' was pierced. Left: English snuff-box die-stamped with a view of Windsor Castle by Gervase Wheeler, Birmingham, 1840; English vinaigrette die-stamped with a view of Kenilworth Castle by Nathaniel Mills, Birmingham, 1837.

HAND-FORGING

1. To form a flatware handle, the workman cut a part-die.
2. He flattened the bar of silver into a spoon shape by hammering. The silver became harder with each blow and had to be annealed.
3. The spoon-shaped blank was inserted within a steel collar on to the lower die. The upper die was then put on top and the two pressed or hammered together. The spoon-bowl was hollowed out afterwards.

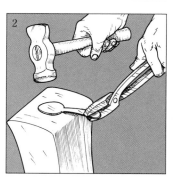
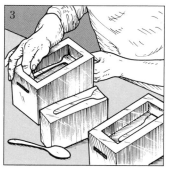

CASTING

There were several different methods for producing objects – or parts of objects – by casting. Of paramount importance in all of them was the design and finish of the original pattern and of the mould, the purity of the gold or silver and the heat to which it was brought before pouring. Using casting methods components of considerable complexity could be made, and with some techniques repeated as required. The techniques are to be seen to great advantage in some of the finest silver candlesticks, coffee-pots, salvers, and even wine cisterns, made in the eighteenth and nineteenth centuries.

Sand-casting of silver was similar to a technique used to cast iron (see p.180) and was used when a small number of reproductions was required. One part of a double metal frame was filled with the moulding material – a mixture of sand and clay – and up to half the depth of the model of the part or object to be cast was embedded in it. The upper half of the metal frame was then put into position and filled with more moulding material. Channels, known in the silver trade as 'gets' or 'gates', were cut into the mouldings, one for the molten metal, the other to allow the air to escape as the hot metal was poured in. The next stage was to separate the two halves of the mould and remove the original model. The two parts were then united, and the metal, heated in a crucible, poured in and allowed to cool. Then the casting was filed to remove rough edges, chased and polished.

Besides the more usual sand and clay moulding material, other substances such as cuttlefish bone, steatite and certain sandstones were sometimes used. The models themselves were of wood, metal such as brass, casting wax or plaster.

From the late seventeenth century sand-casting was used in England with exceptional skill, especially by French immigrant craftsmen. They used it not only for applied details such as handles, finials and mounts but even to make fine candlesticks, cups, coffee-pots and other elaborate objects, built up from several castings soldered together. Small parts such as salver feet, handle mounts, knobs and spouts are very often still cast in this way, as well as figures.

Lost-wax (*cire-perdue*) casting is a very ancient process, used by the ancient Chinese for casting bronze vessels. As with bronze casting (see p.202), a model was made in special wax. Then a mould was taken of it, leaving a get through which the wax would be melted out (and so 'lost') and the metal poured in. Finally the mould was broken and the metal cast revealed. This method was only feasible for small objects or for those where, even with a core set within, the wax could be melted out of the mould surrounding it.

Right: English oval soup tureen made by Paul Storr (1771–1844) for Rundell, Bridge & Rundell, London, 1807. The massive tureen is applied with cast and chased details – lion masks below the reeded handles and those at the sides further enriched with acanthus foliage, a laurel wreath enclosing a crest and four gryphon supports at each corner of the pedestal base.

Left: Detail of the richly cast and chased handle of a silver-gilt cup and cover by John Swift, London, 1738. The Rococo handle is harp shaped, with a bearded mask below the scrolling top; there is further applied foliage on the cover of the cup.
Below: English circular salt, one of a set of four, by Paul de Lamerie (1688–1751), 1743. The interior is gilded; the eagle rising from scrollwork is a tour de force of the Rococo caster's skills. It has been cast in several parts, soldered together and chased to conceal the joints.

SAND-CASTING

1. The bottom half of the cast-iron frame, or 'cope', was packed with a sand-clay mixture.
2. The mould, which could be made of wood, plaster or metal, was coated with graphite andd half embedded in the sand.
3. The upper half of the frame, or 'drag', was slotted on to the locating pins on the bottom half. Sand was then sieved over the model and packed down with a mallet.
4. The frame was reversed and the bottom cope lifted off, leaving the mould in the drag. Another cope was put on top; it was fitted with tightly packed sand and removed.
5. The model was removed and the 'gets', or channels, for the molten metal and the vents for gas and steam were cut in the sand.
6. The two faces of the mould were dried and coated with soot or 'torched'. They were then clamped together and the molten silver poured in to the mould, which was tilted at a slight angle to allow it to run in.

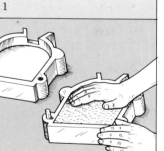

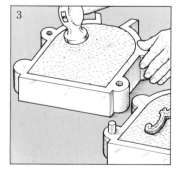
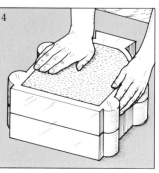
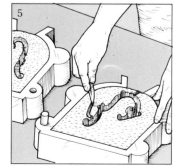
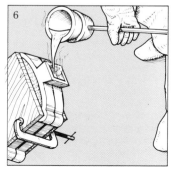

POLISHING, BURNISHING AND FINISHING

The appearance of an object, by whatever means it was manufactured, could be made or marred by the process of finishing. With complicated objects it was advisable to polish and finish the surfaces of individual parts before assembly in case they became inaccessible. It was also wise to send the parts to be assayed and hallmarked (see p.162) before assembling them so that the risk of damage to the completed article was minimized.

As a result of any of the processes used for manufacturing, whether by hand or machine, or a combination of both, there were inevitably scratches and file marks. The greatest problem, though, was firestain, a dark, cloudy discoloration, not to be confused with the greyish matt surface left by annealing. Removing the dark patches of firestain entailed stripping, thereby losing some of the surface metal. The first step involved stoning the surface with an abrasive such as water of Ayr stone, a natural soft slate which was bought in short sticks and used wet, pumice or Trent sand with colza oil. In modern workshops electrolytic stripping is sometimes employed, using the object as the anode so that it is virtually plated in reverse. Not only is this expensive but it can destroy the piece.

After any serious blemishes had been removed, the surface was buffed and made brilliant with finer abrasives; the friction melted the surface a little so that it flowed over the scratches. This was done with tripoli stone, rouge (red iron oxide mixed with grease and stearic acid) and whiting. These were applied to the surface on 'bobs' made of walrus or buffalo hide and felt cut into discs and screwed on to the polishing spindle, and soft mops of calico, wool and soft leather such as chamois. Bristle brushes were also used for irregular surfaces and the inside of hollow-wares, as well as brass wire brushes. Throughout the polishing operations the work had constantly to be cleaned to avoid scratches from filings, scraps of metal and even from the coarser polishing materials.

Burnishing, with rubbing tools of highly polished steel, agate or haematite shaped to the contour of the article, compressed the metal and gave it a highly reflective surface, which often contrasted effectively with areas of hand-matting (see p.155) or with frosting – a chemical surface treatment popular in the nineteenth century – and resisted scratches.

In the finishing process, after the surface had been made bright and reflective by burnishing, different effects and colours could be achieved by texturing or etching the surface.

Below: Illustration of polishing a large tray in Elkington's Birmingham workshop from The Illustrated Exhibitor and Magazine of Art, *1852. Absolute cleanliness was required at this stage since the slightest grain of dirt in the polishing mop would leave scratches on the surface of the metal.*

Right: Illustration of burnishing at Elkington's from the same magazine. The burnisher used a highly polished steel tool, which fitted the contours of the work. It was rubbed across in parallel overlapping strokes, lubricated with saliva. The final burnishing was done with a haematite stick.

POLISHING A GOBLET BY MACHINE
1. A Turk's head brush was attached to the spindle. The polisher turned the brush steadily towards himself.
2. The polisher held the outside of the goblet to the mop and worked from the centre outwards.
3. To polish the underside of the foot, the polisher used a pressed felt buff which was cut to fit the contour of the work. At each stage rouge was applied to the mop or brush.

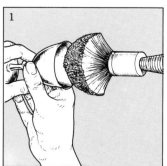

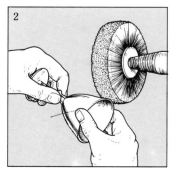

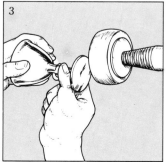

DECORATING GOLD AND SILVER

Apart from the use of contrasting colours, as in gilding (see p.168), goldsmiths employed three distinct types of decoration on their wares: either the surface was modelled or textured without loss of metal, as in flat-chasing and repoussé-chasing and embossing; or the metal was cut, by engraving or piercing; or the ornament was applied. Often two or more of these decorative processes were combined in a single object. The delicacy of piercing might be used to set off the massive cast and chased rim and foot mounts on a mid-eighteenth-century cake basket; the applied strapwork on a cup and cover might be enhanced with matted detail around the relief areas or with finely engraved borders and armorials contrasting with burnished surfaces.

'Chasing' describes all forms of decoration carried out with a hammer and a variety of punches where no metal was removed. With embossing, the simplest technique, the metal was domed from the reverse side; intricate designs of varying depth could be achieved with repoussé, a combination of embossing and chasing from the front; flat-chasing produced almost linear patterns, hardly distinguishable from engraving. The skill of the chaser was in creating the desired pattern, working from the front and the reverse.

Right: American silver tea-kettle and stand with lamp by Joseph Richardson, Philadelphia, c.1755. Besides the repoussé-chased scrolls, shells, flowers and lion pelts on the body, cover and even on the lamp, there are cast and chased motifs on the spout, the handle joints and the apron of the lampstand, which is supported on cast shell feet. The arms are those of Mary, widow of Clement Plumsted, a former Mayor of the city. Above: Danish silver beaker by Povl Ottesen Kiærulff (died 1716), Ringkobing. c.1713. The beaker is embossed and chased with scrolling foliage on a matted ground. The front has a wreathed reserve containing pricked initials and the date.

EMBOSSING AND CHASING

In the hierarchy of specialist craftsmen the chaser was the highest grade. He needed a draughtsman's eye for setting out the design and the knowledge of how to model and texture the metal to achieve high-relief, often sculptural, effects. Embossing was the coarser working of the metal from the reverse, and it required less skill.

The first stage of doming, or embossing, flat objects such as salvers, trays and open bowl shapes was done by setting the work on a bed of soft wood, wax or pitch and, using domed punches and a hammer, pushing the metal out into simple hemispherical or elongated shapes. With an enclosed shape such as a jug, two-handled cup, tankard, beaker or coffee-pot, however, the doming had to be done by 'remote control' using a 'snarling-iron'. This is a long piece of iron with a domed upturned end. It was fixed in a vice, and the iron tapped with a hammer so that the pattern (traced on the outer surface of the object) was bumped up from the reverse, the craftsman turning the ware as he worked.

Even what may seem bold and coarse decorative designs were seldom left without further finishing. The work was subsequently filled with pitch to support it and further detail added. This might only be the outline of the simplest of bosses; in the best work, though, considerable skill and effort was involved, and dozens, even hundreds, of different punches might have been needed to achieve an elaborate and intricate pattern displaying highlights, gradations in depth and such minute details as facial features, flower stamens and shells.

Embossing was often combined with further chasing from the front to improve the detail and definition. Since the middle of the nineteenth century relief work of this kind has been described as 'repoussé'. (In France the term is used for relief decoration done from the back of the object.)

Left: Photograph of a craftsman chasing a piece of silver. With the work supported on a bed of pitch, he models the metal to the desired pattern using a hammer and a wide variety of punches. No metal is removed in the process.
Below: English standing dish, maker's mark CB, London, 1631. The centre has flat-chased motifs at the angles of the lobed divisions; the border has repoussé-chased cherub masks between scrolls in matted panels in the 'auricular' style that had recently been introduced from Holland.

Above: Irish coffee-pot by John Wilme, Dublin, c.1758. It is decorated with embossed and chased flowers, seed pods, birds, dolphins and stylized lions.
Right: Detail of the coffee-pot. The rich contrast between the leaf scroll and animal forms is achieved by matting and other textured chasing.

FLAT-CHASING AND MATTING

Flat-chasing was surface decoration worked from the front in very low relief. The punches produced soft and undulating edges, as contrasted with the sharp cuts (even after long usage) of the engraver's tools. The work to be chased was placed on a bed of pitch, or itself filled with pitch (or a mixture of pitch, resin and plaster of Paris or brick dust), resilient enough to allow the chaser to control his tool yet strong enough to support the work however large and heavy it might be. In flat-chasing, as in most decorative processes worked by hand on gold and silver, the work was brought to the tool rather than the tool to the work. For this reason, the work was further supported on a sand-filled leather bag if it was itself filled with pitch; alternatively the pitch bed might be held in an iron bowl placed on a leather ring so that it could be turned as required.

The pattern to be flat-chased, often linear in theme, was first marked out using a chisel-like 'tracer', which was struck with a small hammer. This did not remove any metal but gently pushed it into an outline of the design, differently shaped tracers being used for straight lines and curves. Then, using various punches specially made for the job in hand, the chaser worked carefully and evenly over the design, making sure that the depth of the chasing was equal throughout. Parts raised by the punches could, if necessary, be reduced with the use of planishing punches.

Flat-chased ornament was often combined with a type of textured groundwork known as 'matting', a form of decoration also used on its own on seventeenth-century silver. The technique of matting involved slightly roughening the outer surface by striking it with small punches. The punch marks were made very close together and painstakingly evenly to produce an overall grained effect.

Left: Engish silver beaker, 1684. The beaker has a plain rim and foot; matting and the engraved armorials form the only decoration.
Far left: Detail of the matted and engraved decoration of the beaker. Matting was done by roughening the surface of the metal with small, evenly spaced punch marks.
Below: English silver toilet casket, maker's mark WF, 1683. Exotic birds, flowers and Chinese figures and buildings – Chinoiseries – were popular subjects for flat-chased decoration on silver from about 1680 to 1690.

ENGRAVING

One of the oldest forms of decoration on metal, as on stone and other materials, must surely have been engraving. It could consist of a few simple lines or a quantity of picturesque or armorial detail.

Engravers worked from printed sheets of ornament which were published and then copied and reprinted for many years throughout Europe. American goldsmiths such as Joseph Richardson of Philadelphia imported books of designs and cyphers from London. Engravers rarely signed their work, although the styles of Simon Gribelin and William Hogarth are easily recognizable.

The pattern to be engraved – lettering, a coat-of-arms, a crest or a decorative design – was carefully drawn out in black on white, then placed face down over the silver which had been coated with a thin film of beeswax. Rubbing firmly with a piece of bone or pricking brought the black impression out in the wax so that the engraver could draw the necessary outlines with the point of his scriber. Afterwards the film of wax was rubbed off and the engraver was left with the lightly scratched-on design as a guide.

The work was mounted on pitch, or held firmly against a sandbag on which it could be turned without damage, and the engraver brought the work towards his tool, turning it clockwise to the graver held against the palm of his hand and controlling it with the thumb. The surest control of the tool was essential and the choice of type of graver important in order to impart subtle suggestions of light and shade.

A special kind of engraving known as 'bright-cut' became fashionable from the 1770s onwards, an effective method of depicting festoons, urns and other Neoclassical motifs. It was done with a tool which had a very highly polished face and back. This picked out the silver as it cut into it, while the back burnished the cut as the metal was removed. Unlike flat-chasing, no impression appeared on the reverse.

Right: German beaker, Hildesheim, 1649. The three octagonal burnished panels enclosing armorials and the inscribed band around the rim contrast with the coarsely textured body, which has been struck repeatedly with a matting tool.
Below: Photograph of a craftsman engraving a commemorative plaque. The design was drawn to the exact size and setting-out marks lightly indicated on the plate.

Above: Norwegian peg tankard engraved with flowering plants and insects, Trondheim, c.1670. Scandinavian tankards of this form were made from about 1600 and copied in England at York, Hull and Newcastle.
Left: Detail of the decoration on the tankard. The botanical engravings were taken from the copperplate illustrations in contemporary books on natural history.

Above: German parcel-gilt ewer engraved with plaques depicting scenes from Genesis, sixteenth century.
Left: Detail of the decoration on the ewer. It shows the technique of cross-hatching to give modelling, a feature copied directly from the printed original. Engravers were capable of working either on copper for the printing trade or on silver for the goldsmith.

Far right: English bright-cut tea-caddy by Robert Hennell (1741–1811), London, 1785.
Right: Detail of the bright-cut decoration on the tea-caddy. With bright-cutting, the metal was burnished at the same time as it was cut, and the effect of faceting gave it an extra brilliance.

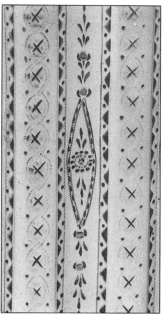

WIREMAKING AND FILIGREE

Wires were used in many forms and for various purposes, both practical and ornamental. At their simplest they were soldered on to strengthen the mouths of pots and jugs, the rims of cups, bowls, dishes, salvers and trays, and the feet of wares of many different kinds.

Wires to be used as mouldings were made in a steel 'draw-plate' in various profiles. The draw-plate, a fifteenth-century invention, had a series of holes of decreasing gauge through which the wire was drawn and shaped, gradually reducing in size. From about the middle of the eighteenth century a goldsmith working on the top of a vessel might throw it up straight for a short distance so that the wire could be sprung in. Once it had been soldered in place, the rim was trued up to be in line with the curve of the body.

Simple wires of circular, square, rectangular or hemispherical section were generally made in the draw-plate; more decorative patterns were produced by swaging – hammering the metal over a block or die – or casting. Both methods were used extensively from the beginning of the eighteenth century. Cast wires had, of course, to be chased up to sharpen the outlines and eliminate faults.

Silver and gilt wire was used for buttons, lace, fringes, spangles and epaulettes. To make silver thread, the flattened wire was wound tightly round a thread of silk.

Filigree is a specialized form of wirework that has been practised for some 4,000 years for jewellery and for decorating goldsmiths' work: notable finds from Troy and Mycenae date from about 1500 BC. There are examples of filigree toilet-services including boxes and candlesticks from almost every European country – Norway, Czechoslovakia, France, Portugal, Hungary and Russia. In England in the early nineteenth century the Birmingham workshop of Samuel Pemberton was noted for smallwares such as caddy-spoons inset with filigree in the bowls. Miniatures and toys, such as dolls' house furniture, were made in Sweden and Holland. The country of origin is often unclear since it was almost impossible to apply any marks, either of the maker or of an assay office, to filigree.

The technique consisted of forming fine-gauge wires into cables and shaping them into scrolls, coils, crescents, flower shapes or geometrical designs, then either soldering them at intervals into narrow frames – sometimes adding tiny beads at the junction of patterns – or mounting the wire designs on an equally finely cut backing. All this was very much on a miniature scale.

Left: Spanish silver filigree salver, probably second quarter of the seventeenth century. Vessels of this type, popular in the seventeenth century in various parts of Europe, were built up from innumerable silver threads shaped into coils and scrolls. Below: Swedish tapering beaker, seventeenth century. The twisted rope-pattern wire rings are suspended from an applied floral band, the lower part encircled with a ribbed wire supporting masks.

Left: Engraving of a goldsmith's shop in Augsburg by Etienne De Laune, 1576. All the large wares stored on the hanging shelf incorporate wire.
Above: Detail of the illustration showing the wire-drawing bench. A workman gripped one end of a silver rod while another turned the crank so that the wire was gradually drawn through the smaller and smaller holes.
Below: English silver-gilt covered dessert basket by William Pitts and Joseph Preedy, 1799. The wirework is overlaid with chased vine foliage and other naturalistic details.

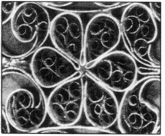

Below: English silver filigree pocket mirror with scrolling panels in the manner of late seventeenth-century engraved ornament, 1675.
Right: Detail of the pocket mirror showing how the wire cloisons enclosed even finer wirework.

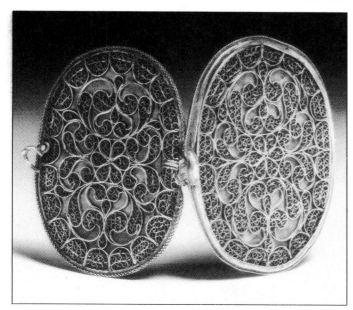

PIERCING AND CUT-CARDWORK

Another decorative technique where metal was removed in the course of embellishing the object was piercing. At its simplest it was a series of dot-punches made by hammering a punch into the surface of, for example, a caster top. In fact, using hammer and various small chisels, extremely complex patterns could also be achieved. This was the method used for all pierced work until the introduction of the piercing saw-frame during the second half of the eighteenth century.

The saw-frame consisted of a very fine blade set in a three-sided frame, the saw itself forming the third side of the rectangle. A hole was drilled through the metal to be decorated, the saw slipped through it and clamped into the top of the frame. The craftsman then made a series of exactly vertical cuts. Again, it was the silver rather than the tool which was turned. The tiny teeth of the saw gripped the thickness of the metal so that the finer the gauge of the gold or silver, the finer the saw that was required.

The difference between the two methods of piercing can be detected by examination of the edges of the cut. With an early eighteenth-century caster the metal has the outside edges turned into the cut, whereas serrated toothmarks would be visible on a later piece. The same applies to larger objects such as fruit and cake baskets. Pierced work was often enhanced by engraved detail around the cuts.

A type of decoration that combined piercing and applied detail is known as 'cut-cardwork'. It was introduced in the second half of the seventeenth century, became more complex in appearance during the first half of the eighteenth and is now more or less confined to wares reproducing the originals of those periods.

The 'cards' were thin sheets of silver cut into decorative patterns – usually based on leaf shapes in silhouette – soldered flat on to the silver or gold. They were applied around the base of, for example, a bowl or cup, or the handle sockets of a teapot or coffee-pot, along the edges of a casket or inkstand, on the underside of a footed salver or around the cover finial of a cup. The more complex the pattern, the more skilful the craftsman needed to be to ensure that the applied cards not only conformed absolutely to the curves of the piece but were attached in such a way that there was no trace of the solder visible in the pierced-out sections and no gap between card and object at the edges.

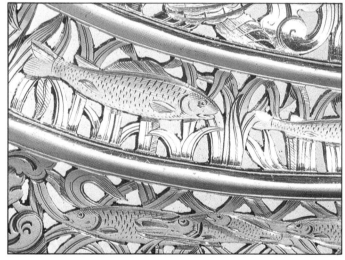

Left: English silver basket by de Lamerie, London, 1739. The openwork sides are pierced with scrolling foliage and fruit, picked out both inside and out with engraving below a border of shellwork and the elaborate applied cast and chased rim.
Above: Detail of the fluted fan-like blade of the slice from a pair of fish-servers by G. W. Adams, London, 1855. Each division is pierced with fish among reeds, probably after designs by the sculptor John Bell (1811–95). Piercing such as this was done with vertical cuts made with a fretsaw-type tool. Close inspection reveals the tiny upright saw marks.

PIERCING
1. The workman marked out the design to be pierced with a hammer and punch, then drilled holes in the sheet.
2. The blade of the piercing saw was fed teeth downwards through the hole to start cutting.
3. The saw-frame was pulled downwards to cut from one hole to another. When the design had been pierced, the sheet was turned over to remove the burr.

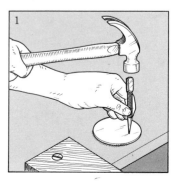

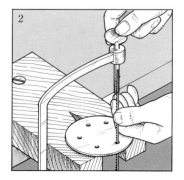

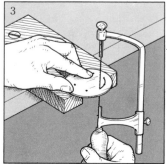

It was essential for the silversmith to have absolutely smooth sheets from which to cut his shapes, or cards. They were almost always of lighter gauge – thinner – than the body of the object to be decorated. Because of the difficulty of purchasing sheets of the right quality, goldsmiths in the colonies and in the provinces rarely used this form of ornament, although John Coney of Boston, Massachusetts, and John Elston of Exeter both did around 1700.

Well-performed cut-cardwork is often virtually indistinguishable from the applied cast and chased ornaments with which, in the first 30 years or so of the eighteenth century, it was often most successfully combined. Intricate patterns in high relief were built up, a practice that was later repeated in Rococo Revival pieces of the 1820s and more recently in good reproduction silver.

Some of the simpler designs of the seventeenth century were elaborated by tapered beaded details to suggest the veins and stems of foliage, especially along the spines of tankard handles. This type of decoration served the second purpose of adding strength to the part so ornamented.

Above: Set of three English silver-gilt casters by Philip Rollos, London, c.1705. The covers were pierced with small chisels and hammers. Above the waist a row of cast and applied shells echoes the piercing of the cover. Below the waist an applied openwork frame, a variant of cut-cardwork, encloses applied cast lobes. In the three zones of burnished applied decoration the chaser matted the surface to enhance the contrast.
Left: Detail of an English silver-gilt cup, 1715. This is an elaborate example of cut-cardwork.

HALLMARKING

For centuries it has been crucial both for the authorities issuing currency and for goldsmiths and jewellers to know the relative purity of their gold and silver. The oldest and simplest method of testing the precious metals was by the touchstone. With 'touch needles' of gold and silver of known alloy the goldsmith marked streaks on his touchstone and compared their colour with the streaks left by the metal under test. For gold, a later variation was the test with dilute nitric acid or aqua regia. By the fourteenth century the more accurate cupellation process of test by fire-assay was in use.

Testing and marking were originally introduced by the state as a means of controlling the use of gold and silver and providing some protection against fraudulent dealings. The modern system emerged in France in the mid-thirteenth century. In 1275, following an ordinance for the Paris goldsmiths of 1260, Philippe le Hardi ordered that every provincial goldsmith should adopt a town mark. Montpellier initiated both the obligatory maker's mark (in 1355) and the annual date-letter system (in 1427), both imitated in Paris within a few years. The purpose of the changing letter cycle was to enable the particular official responsible for testing and marking the piece to be identified and made responsible for any marked wares falling below standard.

The elements in the French marking system gradually came into use in England, too. From 1300 the leopard's head, later crowned, or King's mark was to be struck on gold of the 'touch of Paris', $19\frac{1}{5}$ carat (19.2 parts per 24 or 80% pure gold), and on silver which was of the sterling standard, that is, 925 parts, or 92.5%, of pure silver. Members of the Goldsmiths' Company were concerned with testing the coinage from at least the thirteenth century; it was but a small step for them to undertake the assay and marking of gold and silver. The supervision of the craft of the goldsmith by the Goldsmiths' Company in the City of London is the origin of the term 'hallmark', since it was at their Hall that the testing was, and still is, done.

The personal mark of the master goldsmith was required on English plate from 1363. At different times the mark has been a device, a play on his name or his shopsign, or a combination of his initials, within a shape which also could be varied. In 1478 the Company appointed their first Common Assayer, set up a permanent assay office and instituted a cycle of annual date-letters, a system that was only partially implemented in other English towns.

The fourth mark commonly found on English gold and silver, the lion passant, was introduced in 1544, when the coinage had been heavily debased below sterling standard. The sterling standard was replaced briefly between 1697 and 1720 by the higher Britannia standard (95.8% pure silver), identified by the different versions of the lion passant and leopard's head crowned (sterling standard) marks.

The official standard for gold has fluctuated considerably. In 1300 the 'touch of Paris' was ordered. Subsequently the English standard was set sometimes at 18 and sometimes at 22 carat; from 1854 the lower standards of 9, 12 and 15 were permitted, too.

The state imposed plate duty on goldsmiths' work in both France and England. From 1672 French plate bore the mark of the Fermiers-Généraux, or tax collectors. In England, duty was payable from 1720, and from 1784 to 1890 plate was struck with the sovereign's head duty mark.

The Medieval system of self-regulating guilds or companies of goldsmiths, in which each town had its own mark and most had date-letter cycles, was followed in most European

Left: Illustration of an assayer weighing gold in a balance from Description of Leading Ore Processing and Mining Methods, *1574. Ercker was control tester of coins in Prague from 1567 and wrote the first scientific account of assaying methods. It was essential for the assayer to determine the weight of the sample to be assayed, since assay by cupellation, the normal method from the fourteenth century at least, depended for its accuracy on a quantitative analysis. The sample was then wrapped in a thin sheet of lead and compressed.*

Right: Illustration of the cupellation process from De la Pirotechnia *by Vannuccio Biringuccio, 1540. The lead-wrapped samples of silver were put into bone-ash cupels, or small cups. These were heated in a muffle furnace to about 1100°C. The lead and the base metal in the sample were absorbed into the cupel after about 15 minutes, and the silver and any gold left in the cupel. After it had cooled, the small bead of precious metal was weighed and compared with the weight of the original to obtain the standard of purity.*

countries – the Austro-Hungarian Empire, Spain and Portugal, the Low Countries, Germany, Belgium, Denmark, Norway and Sweden. In North America, Canada, Australia, Jamaica and indeed all territories under European control or producing for the European market such as China, some form of personal marking as a guarantee of quality (although not standard) emerged, in direct emulation of some aspect of the French or the English system. Sometimes English official marks were improperly imitated, as in Canada, Australia and China. The term 'sterling' as distinct from 'coin' silver was sometimes used by North American goldsmiths to distinguish a standard.

Because of the long-standing and high reputation of hall-marking as a guarantee both of standard and of date, the official marks have from time to time been imitated – for example by provincial goldsmiths or, in the past 100 years or so, to deceive the purchasers of spuriously marked antique plate. The official punches were of hardened steel and gave a clean impression which could sometimes be detected on the reverse of the metal. The punches for forged marks were often copied from old plate, and the impressions from them were often soft edged and worn. Low-grade Dutch silver of the late nineteenth century was sometimes marked with a jumble of punches copied from earlier objects.

An earlier and rather different evasion of the hallmarking system, practised in England from 1720 until the 1750s, was 'duty-dodging'. Since duty was levied by the weight of the article to be marked, goldsmiths would send a small object to the Hall for assay and marking, and then cut the marks from it and insert them into a much heavier piece. Another practice was for the master to strike his personal mark three or four times, so that at a cursory glance the expected cluster of marks was to be seen.

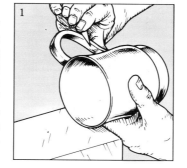

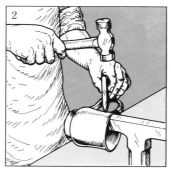

HALLMARKING
1. A sample of the metal was removed from a tankard for testing at an assay office.
2. The hallmark was applied to the tankard with a steel punch.
Below: Hallmarks for York on an English embossed sideboard dish, 1824. From the left, the maker's or retailer's mark for J. Barber & Co., the lion passant mark, the sovereign's head duty mark imposed in 1784, the leopard's head crowned and the date-letter n, both double struck, and the York town mark. Barber's were buying stock from Barnard's, a London firm; this may have been both made and part-marked in London for sale in York.

JEWELLERY

The term 'jewel' comprised all small decorative objects of precious metals, whether or not gemstones were present. The jeweller had to master all the techniques of the goldsmith on a small scale, and chainmaking in addition. His tools included many fine drills and chasing tools for delicate work, as well as casting equipment. Since jewellery often incorporated other precious materials, a good light was essential both for working and for judging gems. He needed to be able to assess the carat (weight) and colour of gemstones, and to have access to a stone-cutter, or lapidary, and to an enameller.

Sometimes materials of little intrinsic value have been mounted as jewels because of some other quality or association – amulets, talismanic and magical jewels, for example, relics, badges and seals, and memorial jewellery made of hair. Both precious stones and imitations or substitutes have been used by the jewellers for thousands of years. Egyptian faience beads imitated lapis lazuli; Medieval metalworkers cast base-metal rings, gilded them and set them with coloured glass; fishscale and glue balls imitated pearls; and glass pastes imitated diamonds. From the 1770s Wedgwood and James Tassie produced ceramic and paste cameos imitating classical gems. Since the 1870s man-made gems have been commer-cially available and widely used, but in earlier times gemsetters regularly painted or laid coloured foil behind their stones to enhance colour: Benvenuto Cellini in the sixteenth century described a method of varnishing diamonds with lampblack to reflect and throw back their brilliance to the viewer.

As well as gemstones and their imitations, the jeweller has incorporated many organic substances: coral, amber (fossil-ized resin), jet (fossilized wood), pearls – both marine and freshwater – shell and tortoiseshell. Imitations of all these have been produced in the past 100 years. Other less decorative organic materials such as toadstones (fossilized fish teeth), which were believed to detect poison, were often mounted in open settings to give close contact with the skin of the wearer.

The stone-cutter was a specialist whose work could be repeatedly re-used by jewellers in fresh settings. Because worked gems were small and easily transportable, jewellers often worked with stones imported from Brazil by way of Paris or Amsterdam (diamonds), or Naples (cameos), and much of their skill lay in their ability to devise new and fashionable settings for old stones; until vast new mines in Australia and South Africa were exploited, the greater proportion of the

Left: English emerald and diamond and ruby and diamond demi parures, c.1830. Both sets comprise a necklace and earrings. The technique of granulation employed in their manufacture entailed fusing small gold beads on to a base of gold without the use of solder. It was much practised by the Etruscans more than a thousand years before. The pieces are also examples of filigree work. Above: Illustration of a jeweller from The Young Tradesman or Book of English Trades, *1839. Hanging down from the workbench and covering the jeweller's lap is a piece of leather to cach filings and fragments of gold cut from his work. These would be collected and melted in the furnace on the left. The resulting bar would then be rolled to the required thickness in the mill behind him.*

Right: Enamel and gold link from a bracelet made in Geneva, c.1830. It depicts a lady in cantonal costume. The border, of three-coloured gold, is decorated with granulations.
Far right: English gold snake necklace with pavé-set diamonds, garnets and turquoises, c.1844. The turquoises were cut en cabochon *and mounted in simple rub-over settings. Cabochon-cut garnets with faceted diamonds make up the snake's eyes.*

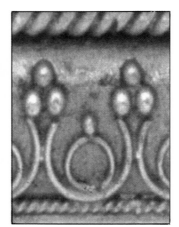

Far left: English octagonal gold brooch set with a Wedgwood jasper cameo, c.1860. The ceramic plaque with a frieze of putti is one of many designs produced at Wedgwood in imitation of classical gems.
Left: Detail of the gold surround of the brooch. The decoration is in the form of granulation, and plain and corded wire soldered to the ground.

jeweller's raw materials came set in old jewellery.

Settings for gems changed as cutting techniques became more complex and the beauty and colour of the stones more significant in the design. In early ring settings the simple straight-sided rim, or 'collet', encircling the stone was soldered to a backplate or directly to the shank, and the upper edge was rubbed-over to hold the stone in place. Small claws cut from shaped wire were soldered to the collet to grip the stone securely. An alternative, more elaborate, setting surrounded the plain collet with a decorative cusped quadrangular or hexagonal bezel. The cut-down setting enabled fine stones of complex cut to be seen to full advantage. The metal was fitted tightly around the stone, working up from the base.

Other settings included the so-called 'millegrain', in which the stone was gripped by tiny beads of metal pressed up from the mount or shaped with a nutted wheel, and the pavé setting, in which the jeweller drilled a series of holes in his mount. The setter then inserted the stones and raised with a graver segments of metal to hold them.

Jewellery components could be produced in relatively long runs using casting. Bezels were sometimes separately cast by the lost-wax process (see p.202) and sometimes cast all in one with the shank or hoop, but fine stones required individually tailored settings. Another technique adopted particularly for cheaper jewellery was stamping from a die. With the increased machine power of the industrial revolution die-stamping was the method best suited to exploiting the invention of rolled gold. This consisted of a block of gold bonded to copper which was then rolled out into sheet. An earlier gold substitute used by eighteenth-century jewellers was pinchbeck, an alloy which had a gold colour and did not tarnish. Chain was produced by hand-forging until machines took over, speeding up the process and supplying standard designs and sizes. By the late nineteenth century the trade had become highly specialized, with components being factory made and merely assembled by the jeweller. A handcraft revival was flourishing by about 1890 and continues to supply a significant section of the market.

Despite the introduction of machinery to reduce the labour

involved in the various manufacturing processes, jewellers continue to rely to a large extent on traditional practices.

Stones in metal mounts have been used not only for jewellery but also on vessels, sword-hilts and belts for thousands of years. Their colour and brilliance has been enhanced by foiling, and by cutting, which includes faceting or polishing. Since colour is not distributed evenly through a rough stone, the lapidary, or stone-cutter, had to assess where to cut to achieve the largest area of colour with the fewest inclusions. Before faceting was discovered, stones were polished into domed cabochons without angles. The lapidary had also to be able to cut and polish larger hardstones such as agate or onyx for spoon-bowls and small vessels, or for mounting as plaques.

Minerals are graded for their scratch hardness on a scale of 1 to 10, a system devised by Friedrich Mohs in about 1820. Diamonds are by far the hardest (10 on the scale), though their hardness varies according to the direction of the crystal lattice. Because of this, they are the most complex of all stones to cut. The ideal finished cut will reflect and refract light from every facet, splitting the light into its spectrum. Diamond-cutting is in three main stages: dividing the crystal, shaping – or 'bruting' – and polishing – or faceting.

The process of cutting diamonds on a wheel has been practised in Europe for at least 600 years. The stone-cutter first examined the stone to be cut through a magnifying glass, or 'loupe', to establish the cutting-line and marked it with Indian ink. Since a diamond will cleave readily along a line parallel to any octohedral face, the cutter then mounted the rough stone in a holder, nicked it at the line of cleavage with a sharp-edged stone and proceeded by tapping the nick hard with a blunted steel knife so that the stone fell in two along the cleavage line. The traditional cleaving process has now been superseded by the belt-driven diamond saw.

In the bruting process the diamond was set in a chuck on a revolving lathe. The bruter shaped it with a sharp-edged stone

held in a stick under his arm. The diamond in the revolving lathe was gradually ground into shape and the cutting-stone rounded, to be cut later in its turn.

The next stage, faceting, released the brilliance and fire of the diamond. The cutter, or polisher, worked on the 'scaife', a cast-iron disc on a spindle. Its surface was scored from the centre in curved lines with a carborundum stone and coated with a paste of olive oil and diamond dust. The diamonds to be faceted were mounted on 'dops', or holders, fixed in a bench-mounted clamp. A skilled operator could facet up to six diamonds at once, holding the faces to be ground in turn against the revolving scaife. The 'table', or topmost, facet was the very last to be polished to ensure that it remained unscratched. The stones were then checked, boiled in concentrated sulphuric acid to remove oil and dust, washed in methylated spirits and rinsed and dried. After this they were handled only with tweezers or tongs.

Other gemstones less hard than diamonds were cut by a similar process, although there were two distinct stages in the cutting. Since grinding left a surface on the stone that resembled ground glass, to improve their appearance the faces of the stone had to be polished.

Cameos and intaglios – with raised and relief carving, respectively – were worked with fine drills of hardened steel charged with diamond dust mixed with olive oil. Agate and other banded ornamental stones were cut on a vertical sandstone grinding-wheel. Stone beads were cemented on a board and drilled with a diamond point.

Diamonds were fully exploited in jewellery only from the seventeenth century as the possibility of multiple faceting became recognized, a development in which Renaissance mathematicians had played a large part. Long before this coloured gemstones which could be polished were highly valued. The largest 'family', and the most widely used, were the quartz minerals, which include amethyst, citrine and rock

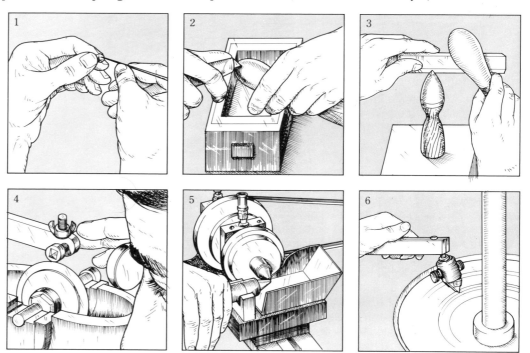

CUTTING A DIAMOND
1. The stone was marked where it was to be divided with Indian ink.
2. With the rough stone mounted in a holder, a 'kerf', or nick in the stone, was made by rubbing it with another diamond along the inked cleavage line.
3. In the traditional cleaving process a blunted steel knife was placed in the kerf and this was given a hard tap so that the stone fell in two along the cleavage line.
4. Another, modern, method of cleaving was by sawing. A revolving disc was used which was covered in a mixture of oil and diamond dust.
5. Forming the rough outline, or 'bruting', was done with the diamond set in a chuck on a revolving lathe. A sharp-edged stone was used to grind the stone into shape.
6. Polishing, or 'faceting', was the final stage. The diamonds, mounted in holders known as 'dops', were held against the revolving 'scaife', a cast-iron disc scored in circles around the centre and coated with olive oil and diamond dust.

crystal and, in another group, agates, cornelian, chrysoprase, onyx and bloodstone. Within this silica group, too, are the opals. The corundum family includes ruby and sapphire, distinguished by their hardness (9 on Mohs's scale) and their colour, due to trace elements: chromium oxide in rubies and iron and titanium oxides in blue sapphires.

The beryl group is dominated by emeralds, also coloured by chromium oxide, and aquamarines. Garnets have been valued for their warm red, often used *en cabochon* or as flat sheets, or in *cloisonné* settings (see p.196), for example by the Anglo-

Saxons. Tourmalines and topazes are both chemically complex stones which occur in a wide variety of colours.

Other gemstones include the jades – jadeite and nephrite – chrysoberyls and opaque stones such as turquoise, lapis lazuli and malachite. As new lands were discovered and conquered, so other gem materials were found and exploited.

The distinction between precious and semi-precious stones is a meaningless concept in gemmological terms since to the jeweller colour, clarity and size have always been the criteria by which he judged a stone.

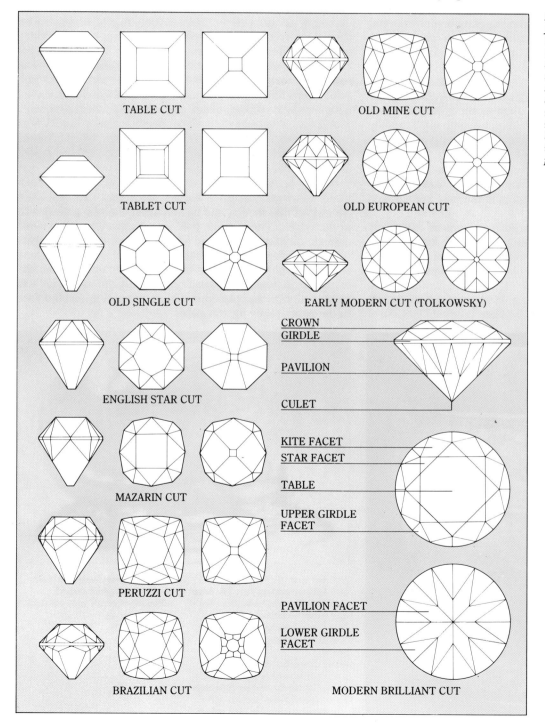

Left: The development of faceting, from the basic table cut to the modern brilliant cut, showing the stones from the side, the top and the bottom. The chronological order in which they were developed is: table cut, tablet cut, old single cut, English star cut, Mazarin cut, Peruzzi cut, Brazilian cut, old mine cut, old European cut, early modern cut (Tolkowsky) and modern brilliant cut. The modern brilliant cut is illustrated with the names of the parts of the cut stone and the facets.

TABLE CUT

OLD MINE CUT

TABLET CUT

OLD EUROPEAN CUT

OLD SINGLE CUT

EARLY MODERN CUT (TOLKOWSKY)

ENGLISH STAR CUT

CROWN
GIRDLE
PAVILION
CULET

MAZARIN CUT

KITE FACET
STAR FACET
TABLE
UPPER GIRDLE FACET

PERUZZI CUT

PAVILION FACET
LOWER GIRDLE FACET

BRAZILIAN CUT

MODERN BRILLIANT CUT

GILDING

Since gold was always the more expensive – and the scarcest – of metals, silver was often given a thin coating of gold to imitate its appearance at lower cost. Both for reasons of status and to give silver greater resistance to tarnishing, and to the effects of corrosive substances such as salt, vinegar and yolk of egg, tablewares were often 'double' gilded, that is given a second layer of gilding. Part, or 'parcel', gilding was especially used to protect the interiors of salts and egg-cups, for communion cups, the inside of boxes and caskets, and, not least, to produce contrasting areas of decoration.

Because there was a marked difference in cost between plain and gilded silver, clerks compiling plate inventories and goldsmiths in their bills distinguished between white silver, the cheapest, parcel-gilt pieces, and gilt or double gilt, the most expensive.

Before the introduction of electrolytic gilding (see p.175) the process known as 'mercury gilding', or 'fire gilding', was used. The technique was also used in the manufacture of ormolu (see p.204). Since much mercury gilding was gradually removed by heavy-handed cleaning, older objects have often been re-gilded using electrolytic gilding to restore the surface; the older method generally gave a more distinctive lemon-yellow colour. As well as for coating a piece with gold, the process could be used for inlaying gold in silver in engraved channels.

Mercury gilding, for whatever purpose, was an extremely dangerous process since the mercury gave off fumes highly injurious to the health of the worker. Without the use of specially controlled cabinets, the technique is forbidden by law in most countries today.

For gilding base metals, rolling gold was a process very like the one used for fusing Old Sheffield Plate (see p.171). Gold of the required standard (usually 9 carat) was sweated on to the base ingot, then the whole rolled out to the desired thickness. The base metal was usually a copper-zinc alloy known as 'gilding metal', or bronze, or the copper nickel alloy misleadingly known as 'German silver', or 'nickel silver'. Sterling silver which has been gilded would be hallmarked as though it were silver.

Gold leaf – extremely thin sheets of gold – has been used for decorating both metal and non-metallic surfaces such as wood (see p.52) for at least 4,000 years. The gilding was achieved by burnishing the leaves on to the surface so that they adhered, excluding all air. One or more layers of gold leaf could be applied, as required. It is a cold process, and one that was – and still is – very much a specialist craft.

The metal of 23¼ carat standard (in fact, almost pure) was rolled into strips 1¼ inches (32 mm) wide and 1/1000 inch (0.025 mm) thick. This was cut into squares and interleaved between sheets of fine vellum, each 4 inches (100 mm) square. The group of interleaved vellum sheets, called a 'cutch', was bound together with parchment and placed on a wooden block. It was then hammered for half an hour with a special 20-pound (9 kg) hammer.

Battery brought the gold out to the edges of the cutch. Each piece was then quartered and laid between more skins in a 'shoder' of 800 sheets, and beaten again until the gold spread to the edges. The leaf-like gold was removed with boxwood pincers, quartered again and filled into a mould of 1000 skins which was wrapped in parchment folders and beaten for as long as five hours. Now the gold leaf, 250 times thinner than the original strip, was laid on a calf cushion, cut into squares of 3¼ inches (83 mm) and placed in folders of rouged, sulphur-free tissue paper ready for the gilder.

Left: German silver-gilt beaker on foot, late sixteenth century. The areas chased in high relief with strapwork and foliage on the foot and lipband have been mostly heavily handled so that the gilding has worn away in patches.
Above: English shell salt, one of a pair, by Benjamin Smith, London, 1826. Gilding was extremely popular for the grand dinner-services of the Regency and later. The shell reflects the contemporary taste for Rococo marine forms which derived ultimately from late sixteenth-century Mannerism

Left: English parcel-gilt chalice set with amethysts and champlevé *enamel plaques made by John Hardman & Co., Birmingham, 1849/50, to a design by A. W. N. Pugin (1812–52). This chalice was shown in the Medieval Court at the Great Exhibition of 1851. Its bands of gilding contrast with the silver body, a conscious imitation of Medieval Florentine techniques.*
Above: English silver-gilt tea vase, one of a pair, by Emick Romer, London, 1769. The gilding, which is in excellent condition, has probably been renewed.

FRENCH PLATING AND CLOSE-PLATING

Similar to the technique of gilding with gold leaf, French plating entailed applying silver foil, brought to a high temperature and then burnished while still hot on to the cold object. Often the object was of copper, and makers of Old Sheffield Plate (see p. 171) used the technique to remedy faults in their work, as in the corners and knopped outer surfaces where the rolled-on silver had failed to join properly. By adding layer after layer of foil any desired thickness could be achieved.

French plating was not very durable, invaluable though it was for small repairs: relatively few objects retain this surface, although there was a large output with specialist retailers in the eighteenth and nineteenth centuries. It would not, for instance, have been practicable for the 'rubbed-in' shields of silver sheet on which armorials were engraved on Sheffield-plated objects since the layers would have separated as the graving tool cut into the foiled thickness.

For covering steel implements – knife-blades and -handles, snuffers, scissors, tongs, nutcrackers, skewers, fish-carvers and the like – close-plating was introduced by the cutlers of Sheffield very early in their history, and also used by armourers from the fifteenth century for plating bits, spurs and other accoutrements. Practically any metal that could be soldered was suitable for close-plating so long as the surface was perfectly clean and smooth.

The properly cleaned object was first dipped in sal ammoniac, then in molten tin. Silver foil of at least sterling quality (as laid down since no later than 1327, and reiterated in by-laws of 1625 by the Sheffield Cutlers' Company) was applied to the object and pressed down hard so that no air was trapped beneath. Next a heated soldering iron was passed over every part so that the tin melted and the silver adhered.

The chief drawback of close-plated articles in use is that excessive heat causes the silver to peel off, while damp atmospheres may penetrate the coating and rust the steel base so that the silver blisters. Once the metal has rusted or the piece is damaged, it cannot be repaired.

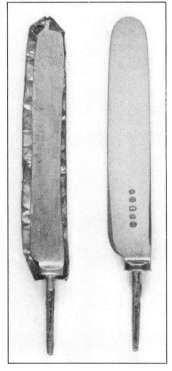

Left: Detail from an illustration of a French plater's workshop from Diderot's Encyclopédie. *English retailers advertised 'French plate' on their trade cards. The shape and decoration exactly followed silver but the cost was a third or less of the precious metal.*
Above: Two stages in the making of a close-plated knife-blade. The ground blade was wrapped in silver foil, which was then pressed down and heated with an iron. The plated blade was then struck by the manufacturer with his marks, in this case Aaron Hatfield & Son of Sheffield, which in size and arrangement imitated hallmarks.

OLD SHEFFIELD PLATE

Old Sheffield Plate was devised by the Sheffield cutler Thomas Boulsover around the year 1742. His method was to fuse a sheet of silver to an ingot of copper in a furnace and roll out the resulting plated metal block into sheet form, which could then be fashioned into articles. Fusion plating represented a great advance on previous methods of silver plating, which had involved applying silver by hand to base-metal articles. Boulsover's invention was adopted by other Sheffield cutlers, and soon there was an established plating industry in the town. Candlesticks and tablewares were the main products, and they were sold to a middle- and upper-class market.

A fused plate industry later developed in a few other towns, notably Birmingham, where Matthew Boulton introduced the trade in the 1760s, laying the foundations for an important nineteenth-century industry there. Examples of French, Russian and Swedish fused plate are also known.

When electro-plating was patented in Britain in 1840 (see p.174), fusion plating went into rapid decline, and in the later nineteenth century the older technique was retained only for items such as buttons and pub tankards which needed the more durable silver plating it afforded.

A sheet of sterling silver was placed on the copper ingot, the surface touching the copper having first been thoroughly cleaned. The cast ingot normally measured about 9 inches (23 cm) long, 2½ inches (6.5 cm) wide and 1½ inches (4 cm) deep. The gauge of silver varied according to the manufacturer's requirements, but a good quality metal might have ⅛ inch (3 mm) of silver on a 1½ inch (40 mm) ingot. A heavy iron weight, or 'bedder', was placed over the silver and the copper. One workman held it in place while his assistant struck it repeatedly with a hammer, thus expelling all the air between the silver and the copper and bringing the surfaces into close contact.

A copper plate, about ⅛ inch (3 mm) thick, was placed on the silver to protect it in the furnace. The inner surface of this plate had previously been whitewashed to prevent it fusing in the furnace with the silver. The three layers were then firmly

Left: Detail from an illustration of a fused plate workshop, c.1830. The workman on the left is casting an ingot of base metal. The workman on the right is filing and scraping the face of the cooled ingot to make it perfectly smooth and clean. In the centre the plating furnace is being loaded. After about 15 minutes the workman, watching through a peephole in the door, would see the silver flash as it began to melt. The block was then taken out.
Above: Old Sheffield Plate dish in the form of a shell, English, c.1800. Silver wire was often soldered to the rim to conceal the copper core.

MAKING THE PLATED METAL SHEET
1. A sheet of sterling silver was placed on the copper ingot.
2. To expel the air, an iron weight, or 'bedder', was placed over the silver and the copper and struck repeatedly with a hammer.
3. A copper plate was placed on the silver to protect it in the furnace, the inner surface of the plate having been whitewashed to prevent it fusing with the silver.

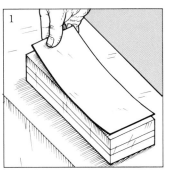

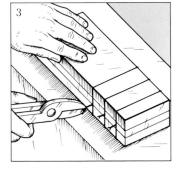

bound together with iron wire. A paste of ground borax was applied to the edges of the silver; this acted as a flux, melting at a low temperature and excluding air which might oxidize the two metals and prevent their union.

The block was put into the furnace, where it lay directly on the fuel, usually coke. When heated, the adjoining surfaces of the silver and the copper fused together, bonding the two metals. This occurred because an alloy of silver and copper was readily formed where the surfaces met. The melting-point of the alloy was lower than that of silver or copper, and this permitted the two metals to retain their integrity while their inner surfaces melted and fused. The block was then carefully removed from the furnace, the wires cut and the copper plate lifted off; the fused block was then cooled and cleaned. By about 1760 the Sheffield platers had begun 'double plating', or plating on both sides of the ingot.

The fused block was rolled out to a sheet by passing it through powered iron rollers. Since the silver and copper expanded equally when rolled or worked, fused plate behaved as a homogeneous metal.

Many of the objects made from Old Sheffield Plate were fashioned by raising. Die-stamping, which permitted a certain amount of mass production, was another method; although dies were expensive, they would generate quantities of stampings which could be assembled in various combinations to create a great range of designs. Spinning was introduced into the Sheffield fused plate trade around 1820. The various parts of a fused plate article were assembled by soldering, generally using a soft solder – a mixture of tin and lead; less frequently hard solder, a compound of brass and silver, was employed. Tall vessels were made by bending a piece of metal around a stake and soldering the seam, prior to raising or spinning. These seams, often dovetailed or 'cramped', were skilfully concealed by burnishing, but if they can be detected they may help to identify the material as fused plate. Electro-plated items are, by contrast, covered with a deposit of silver in which there are no joins.

One of the problems of fused plate was its copper core, which was exposed at any raw edge. Various methods were devised to deal with this. One early technique was to fold over the rim. Alternatively, a strip or wire of silver or plated copper could be soldered on to the raw edges. A method of silver-plating solid copper wire was introduced around 1768 and improved in about 1780. From about 1790 decorative mounts were stamped from thin silver, filled with soft solder and applied to the article. When positioned around the rim of the

Far left: Old Sheffield Plate soup tureen in the form of a turtle, English, c.1810.
Left: Detail of the soup tureen showing the silver wire applied to the raw edge of the fused plate.

Right: Old Sheffield Plate inkstand engraved with a crest, English, c.1780. The inkwell and sanders are secured by a pin passing through loops in the base of the stand.

Right: Old Sheffield Plate kettle and stand with lamp, English, c.1850. The fruit and vine decoration was stamped from silver, filled with soft solder and applied.
Above: Old Sheffield Plate salver with applied silver mount, filled with soft solder, English, c.1815.

article, the border of the mount could be lapped over the raw edge, concealing the copper.

Pierced decoration was fashionable in the 1770s and 1780s, but the silversmith's method of piercing, using a saw, was unsuitable for fused plate. The saw left jagged edges which had to be filed, and this exposed the copper core. Instead, the Sheffield platers used the fly-press, by which a steel punch with the desired outline was pressed through the metal into a matching depression in a steel bed. The force of the punch dragged the silver plate down over the copper core.

Engraving was another method of decorating Old Sheffield Plate. It was difficult to achieve without exposing the copper, and one solution was to solder a piece of silver or thickly plated copper to the article, providing an area suitable for engraving. Around the year 1790 the Sheffield platers introduced another technique, whereby a hole was cut in the article in the place where engraving was desired. Into this hole was soldered a piece of more heavily plated copper. The join, often masked with engraving, can usually be detected on the reverse.

Around 1810 these soldered-in shields were superseded by rubbed-in shields, which were achieved by heating a small leaf of silver and burnishing it on to the surface of the fused plate. Because it is made from pure silver, this rubbed-in shield tarnishes at a different rate from the sterling silver surface of the article. The presence of soldered-in or rubbed-in shields indicates that an object is made from fused plate.

Various finishing processes were necessary. The base or interior of most single-plated objects was coated with tin, poured on in a molten state to give an even deposit. This disguised the copper and prevented foodstuffs from coming into contact with it. Finally, the article was cleaned, burnished with steel and agate tools, and polished.

ELECTRO-PLATING

Birmingham was the home of electro-plating, a process of electrolytic deposition fully patented in 1840 by the brothers George and Henry Elkington. They are said to have learned of the discovery from a man called John Wright, who had developed it following experiments and the setting out of the laws of electrolysis by Michael Faraday in 1833. Already Alessandro Volta's electric pile had in 1800 enabled the experimental plater to use batteries, and only 14 years later the jewellers and goldsmiths to the Crown, Rundell, Bridge & Rundell, had claimed to have produced an electro-gilded, 'Galvanic', goblet. The Elkingtons' first patents of 1836 and 1837 appear, however, to have been the earliest attempts to protect the new development, and by 1843 the brothers were licensing the process to manufacturers elsewhere.

Silver was the first metal to be used for electro-deposition on a commercial scale, and the process has basically changed little over the last century and a half. A bath was prepared containing a solution of silver potassium cyanide (though sodium cyanide can be used) together with some 'free' potassium cyanide. This was dissolved in water and gave a clear solution. An anode of virtually 100% pure silver (less than 99.97% pure is unsuitable for plating) was used, and the work, perfectly cleaned and prepared, was suspended in the bath on copper wires. A low current was passed through the bath, which was kept at room temperature, and a voltmeter used to check that the terminals showed approximately 1 to 1½ volts, leaving the anode clean and white.

As in all finishing processes, the base object had to be chemically clean, absolutely free from grease and oxide films; once clean, they could not be touched by hand. After

Left: Padley, Parkin & Stamforth electro-plated coffee machine, Sheffield, c.1855. The firm abandoned the manufacture of fused plate for electro-plating after 1851, although the wares continued to be marked with the 'hand' mark which they formerly used on Old Sheffield Plate.
Above: Württemburgisches Metal Fabrik electro-plated mirror frame with a cast figure and lily pads, c.1900. The German firm of W.M.F. produced a number of innovative designs in Art Nouveau and Art Deco styles.

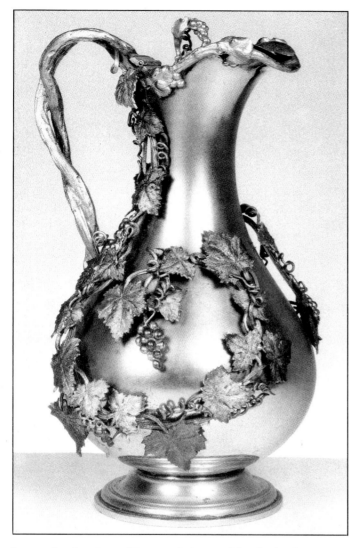

Left: Elkington & Co. gilt electro-plated ewer or claret jug with applied vine ornament, Birmingham, 1874. George and Henry Elkington were the first to patent fully the electro-plating process, in 1840. Almost all of their wide range of designs were available in both electro-plate and sterling silver.
Below: Elkington, Mason & Co. electro-plated wine-cooler, Birmingham, 1846. This is an early

example of Elkington's plate. Both the form and the ornament are typical of the Rococo Revival, rich in the flowers and C-scrolls that flourished in England from the 1820s. These were to be displaced by the motifs of Classicism and other historical styles in their later productions.

immersion for about 15 seconds in a striking bath, they were checked for adherence. This was a weak plating method, after which the objects were washed and friction-tested with scratch brushes to see that the plating had adhered properly.

Almost any base metal could be plated with silver, including iron, brass and copper. Today, the alloy of nickel-brass, misleadingly called 'nickel silver', is mainly used.

During deposition the operator kept the objects slightly in motion to ensure that the deposit was even. The pure silver could be applied to any required thickness, those parts closest to the anode naturally receiving the thickest layers. The interiors of pots and jugs, for instance, would receive much less unless special action were taken, and on a single object the variation in thickness could be as much as six times from maximum to minimum. Specially thick plating was done on the backs of the bowls of spoons, which received particularly heavy wear. For a good deposit, about the gauge of thin tissue paper, the object needed to be kept in the plating bath for between $1\frac{3}{4}$ and $2\frac{1}{2}$ hours.

It emerged looking like white china, unless a special electrolyte containing carbon bisulphate were used which left a brighter surface and so required less final polishing. The object

was washed, dried and the whiteness reduced, first by buffing with a composition paste on cotton mops, or 'dollies', then with rouge on felt mops and finally by hand-polishing with rouge.

Today, most gilding is done electrolytically, a process in principle very like that of electro-plating, though with variations in the temperature of the bath (about 60° to 65°C) and using between $\frac{1}{4}$ and 2 volts. The sheer cost of the gold potassium salts and the fine gold anode (if used) means that very light coats are generally deposited.

Full gilding was done by building up the layers in stages, gilding then scratch-brushing alternately. A frosted appearance could be obtained by sand-blasting the surface before gilding. Parcel gilding, for the interiors of egg-cups, salts and for the bowls of egg-spoons, for instance, or for decorative effect, was done by stopping off the areas not to be gilded with an impervious substance such as shellac.

The platinum group metal, rhodium, a hard, white and bright metal, is sometimes used to plate jewellery and silverware, and also base metals such as brass, bronze, copper and nickel. The anode is platinum, which is indissoluble, but nonetheless rhodium-plating is a costly protection and on silver gives a harsh, albeit untarnishable, finish.

IRON

Iron has been worked since prehistoric times and has proved a metal invaluable to man. While the majority of iron objects were, and still are, purely utilitarian, the metal has also lent itself well to the production of decorative work.

There are three basic types of iron: wrought iron, cast iron and steel. Of these, wrought iron is by far the oldest; cast iron dates from about 1400 and steel, in its present form, from 1856. Wrought iron is no longer made commercially, but small quantities of old iron can be re-rolled and re-worked. Mild steel is frequently used as an alternative.

The earliest uses for wrought iron were for simple tools and weapons, such as knives and spear-heads. The metal later found other practical applications, such as for nails and door hinges, and in due course ironwork began to serve an ornamental, instead of a purely utilitarian, purpose. By the eleventh century the plain flat straps of hinges were being formed into scrolls, and other flat patterns were applied to church doors. In the following centuries openwork screens and grilles were commissioned for churches, sometimes to surround and protect important tombs and monuments.

In the late seventeenth and early eighteenth centuries the craft of decorative wrought ironwork became an art form in its own right, as exemplified in Britain by the work of Jean Tijou, Robert Bakewell and the Davies brothers. In France (Tijou's birthplace, which he fled from to avoid religious persecution) important commissions were carried out for Louis XIV at Versailles. Later, in the 1750s, Jean Lamour created the architectural wrought ironwork for the Place Stanislas in Nancy, where scrollwork and relief decoration in the form of repoussé work were combined. Both Tijou and Lamour produced influential books of designs for wrought ironwork as well as practising the craft.

In the American colonies the earliest wrought ironwork was made with raw materials imported from Britain. By 1750, however, the position had been reversed and iron bars from the furnaces of New England, Pennsylvania and Virginia were being exported to Britain; from there, some of the manufactured objects were shipped back to America.

Wrought iron has a fibrous structure, not unlike that of wood. It is ductile and can be shaped by hammering, squeezing, rolling or bending; it is strong in tension, resisting forces that tend to pull it apart. Most working of wrought iron was done while it was red hot, but some shaping, such as repoussé work in sheet iron, could be done cold. If two pieces of wrought iron were heated to about 1350°C and hammered together, they would weld into a single piece.

The work of the craftsman in wrought iron, or blacksmith, has always been governed by certain fundamentals. Every wrought-iron object originated as a bar of iron, round, square or rectangular in cross-section, or, in the case of repoussé work, as a thin, flat sheet. The smith's raw materials were bought from iron merchants. They were only available in a limited number of simple shapes and sizes, and the smith usually had to do quite a lot of preliminary shaping before he could start on the more complex, and often delicate, forming needed in ornamental work. He may, for example, have had to taper an iron bar, convert all or part of it from round to square or vice versa, or swell it out locally at one or both ends, or somewhere in between.

The smith's tools were of a few basic types, varying in shape and size. There were bellows to blow the fire, an anvil, several hammers of various weights, a vice, numerous cutting-,

Left: Wrought-iron gates at Burghley House, Northamptonshire, probably by Jean Tijou (active 1689–1712), 1710. Tijou was a French Protestant who escaped religious persecution by living and working in England. A New Book of Drawing *published by him in 1693 is the earliest English book of designs for ironwork.*
Above: Design for a staircase by Jean François Forty (1744–80), c.1780. Forty was a renowned French designer, engraver and metal carver, who published eight volumes of his designs. This elaborate balustrade in the classical manner incorporates wrought scrolls, cast borders and repoussé central foliate motifs.

shaping-, and forming-tools – including 'swages' which could be fitted into holes in the 'swage block' – and a variety of tongs for holding the hot iron while it was being worked. Some of the items, such as bellows, anvil, hammers and cutting-tools, were bought from specialist manufacturers; others, especially tongs, were usually made by the smith. A piece of hot iron, were it to be hammered repeatedly in the same place, would spread more or less uniformly about that point; the art of the smith was in making it spread in the direction, and to the extent, he wanted. Alternatively, he may have intended not to spread it at all but merely to bend it.

The scroll, a common feature of ornamental gates and screens, is an example of plain bending. To make a scroll, the smith chose a piece of iron of the right size and cut off the necessary length by striking it with the hammer over the 'hardie', a chisel-shaped tool with a peg to fit in the 'hardie hole' in the anvil. He then heated it and shaped it with the hammer on the 'bick', or 'beak', of the anvil. If the work required a number of scrolls, the smith generally used a scroll former, a piece of iron specially shaped, around which the hot metal was wrapped. Scrolling might have smaller, branching scrolls.

Above: Wrought-iron gate forming part of the Fountain Screen at Hampton Court Palace, near London, by Tijou, c.1700. Tijou brought to the craft of the blacksmith the virtuosity of the goldsmith.
Top left: Scrollwork from the Fountain Screen. Scrolls could be made by wrapping the heated metal around a specially shaped piece of iron.
Bottom left: Repoussé work from the Fountain Screen. In repoussé work the metal plate was embossed from the back with punches and hammers.

These were formed separately and welded on by heating the two parts and hammering them together.

Much ornamental ironwork was based on natural forms – plants, birds and animals – and a variety of methods was used to make them. If the iron bar had to be tapered uniformly, this was done by hammering it on the 'fuller', a round-nosed tool held in the hardie hole. This left a series of dents in the surface which had to be removed by hammering on the anvil face or by using the 'flatter', a flat-ended tool held by the smith and struck by the smith's assistant, or 'striker'.

If the bar was to be round, the work was done with hollow-ended swages. One of these might be inserted in the anvil hardie hole, or a groove in the swage block. A hand-held swage was then placed on the iron and struck by the striker.

Some pieces of iron needed a local swelling. If this were at the end, it was done by heating the end and hammering, or 'upsetting', it. If the swelling were away from the end, the bar was heated at the appropriate place and the cold end repeatedly struck on the anvil; this was known as 'jumping'. Forming a thin, delicate shape, such as a leaf, flower, or mask

– repoussé work – was done by beating the shape with a special hammer while the sheet iron lay on a leather bag filled with sand.

Holes were punched by placing the iron over the 'pritchel hole' in the anvil, or over one of the holes in the swage block and hammering a punch through it. A heated bar could be twisted by holding one end in the vice and twisting it in a wrench. Shaping could also be done by cutting the iron with a hot chisel on the anvil. Final finishing was done with a file.

The smith worked either to his own design or to one prepared by an artist or architect. He used rules and calipers to check dimensions, but otherwise he was entirely dependent on judgement by eye, both for heating the metal to the correct temperature and for achieving the desired shape.

Steel has many of the physical characteristics of wrought iron, and it can be shaped in the same way. It found very little use for ornamental work in the past, but in recent years some craftsmen have employed it to good effect, using both the traditional wrought-iron shaping methods and some newer ones, such as electric arc welding, twisting, wrapping and gas

Far left: Illustration from De re metallica *by Agricola. It shows a typical forge of the sixteenth century with large, mechanically operated bellows to the left of the hearth.*
Left: Illustration from De re metallica *showing the conversion of pig iron into wrought iron. In the background is a hearth of a type common in the sixteenth century. Agricola's work is an important source of information about craftsmen's tools and practices. Other woodcuts from it are illustrated on page 64.*
Below: Nineteenth-century blacksmith's anvil. The beak, hardie hole and pritchel hole are features absent from the anvils illustrated by Agricola.

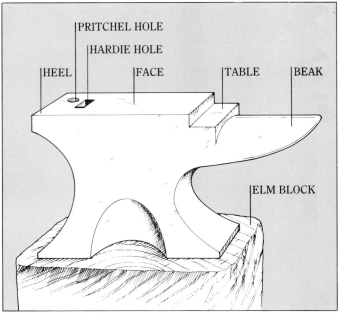

PRITCHEL HOLE

HARDIE HOLE

HEEL   FACE   TABLE   BEAK

ELM BLOCK

Left: Illustration of toolmaking from Diderot's Encyclopédie. *Shown here is a workshop for threading screws. On the left a workman traces out the pattern on a rod, while in the foreground a threading-tool is in use. On the right is a mechanical threader turned by a wheel.*

Below: German wrought-iron coffer, 1716. Made from bars and flat sheets of wrought iron, various blacksmithing operations were involved – bending, scrolling, hole punching, riveting, welding and decorative tooling.

cutting. Since the power hammer replaced the steam-driven hammer in the mid-nineteenth century, the speed at which steel can be worked has increased considerably.

Cast iron is crystalline but ductile, rather weak in tension and relatively brittle. It cannot be shaped by any of the methods used on wrought iron, but it can be heated and in a molten state poured into moulds.

From the Iron Age until the Middle Ages iron was produced in a bowl furnace that burned charcoal. Iron ore was burned with the charcoal, which formed carbon monoxide gas, reducing the ore to a spongy mass of metal called a 'bloom'. In the forging stage the bloom of iron was consolidated by hammering to beat out the impurities, or 'slag'.

Towards the end of the fourteenth century the development of the blast furnace revolutionized ironmaking technology. Iron ore and charcoal were burned together in a high conical furnace, absorbing so much carbon that it melted and could be tapped from the bottom of the furnace in its liquid state. It was then poured into a mould consisting of damp sand that had been impressed with a wooden pattern, slightly larger than the intended size of the casting to allow for shrinkage. Removing

the casting destroyed the sand mould, but the wooden pattern could be re-used.

This technique, known as 'open sand moulding', was suitable for a one-sided object, but in the case of an object in the round – a railing finial for example – a different method was necessary. Here, the wooden pattern was half immersed in sand in a 'moulding box' – open top and bottom – and a second box – also open top and bottom – was placed over the first one and filled with sand, which completely surrounded the pattern. The top box, or 'cope', was then removed from the bottom one, the 'drag', and the pattern lifted out. A hole was made in the cope sand to allow the molten metal to be poured in and the cope was replaced on the drag. Pegs and holes in the two box parts ensured that they were assembled correctly. There was now a two-part box with a cavity in it of the exact shape and size of the pattern, and the molten metal could be poured in.

With hollow castings damp sand was pressed into a wooden core box to produce a sand 'piece', or core, of the size and shape needed to produce the hollow in the casting. This core was inserted into the drag after the pattern had been removed and before the box had been closed with the cope. This left

Left: English cast-iron and paktong fire-grate, c.1800. The fire-back would have been made by the casting process known as 'open sand moulding'. This involved pressing a wooden pattern with the design on one side into a level bed of slightly damp sand, then removing the pattern and pouring molten metal into the shaped depression. After the metal had cooled, the casting was lifted out and any rough edges removed by filing, grinding, sawing or chiselling.
The bow front of the grate was made of paktong, an alloy of copper, zinc and nickel.
Below: Coalbrookdale Co. cast-iron cooking pots, English, eighteenth and nineteenth centuries. At the Coalbrookdale works, leased to Abraham Darby in 1708, molten iron was diverted directly from the blast furnace into sand moulds.

only a relatively thin 'skin-shaped' cavity to be filled by the molten metal. To cast a fluted column a more complex procedure was followed, since the flutes would have prevented the cope from being lifted up and the pattern from being lifted from the drag. The mould was made in four or more parts which could be drawn away from the pattern and then re-assembled.

The castings always had some rough edges, especially at the mould joints, and they also had 'gates', or channels, through which the molten metal was poured into the mould cavity, and these had to be removed. They were chiselled, sawn, filed or ground off in an operation known as 'fettling'.

The great breakthrough in ironmaking came in 1709 with the perfection of the coke smelting process by Abraham Darby of Coalbrookdale. This enabled coal rather than charcoal to be used as fuel. Throughout the nineteenth century cast iron was used extensively, for engine cylinders, bridges, building frames and the hulls of steamships, as well as a wide range of decorative components that included stoves, fire-backs and surrounds, and garden benches. It was sometimes used in combination with wrought iron on ornamental gates and screens.

Left: Illustration of an iron founder from The Young Tradesman or the Book of English Trades, *1839. The founder's tools included shovels, riddles for removing pieces of iron and other matter from the sand before re-using it, ladles – usually lined with clay – for collecting the molten metal from the furnace and various implements used for finishing.*

Above: Veritas cast-iron paraffin stove, English, c.1890. In the casting process the shaping and decorating of each piece of work was a single operation.
Right: American cast-iron armchair, second half of the nineteenth century.

Fern-pattern furniture was manufactured at several American iron foundries. Such pieces were frequently used as conservatory furniture, where, with their painted finish, they could withstand the humid atmosphere.

THE CRAFT OF THE ARMOURER

Armour in the Middle Ages was constructed, mainly from iron and steel, in the form of mail and plate. Armour of mail consisted of a garment made from interlocking rings of wire riveted together; plate armour consisted of a defensive garment formed of individual steel plates shaped to fit the body and held together by rivets and straps.

The manufacture of mail was a specialist craft. Iron wire was drawn through a steel draw-plate, as in the making of silver wire. The wire would then be wound round a circular rod and cut longitudinally to provide a group of open-ended rings. The rings were overlapped, probably with a punch, and swaged, the process involving the use of two steel dies which spread the section of the rings where they overlapped. This area was punched with a hole and a rivet hammered through it, and the individual rings could then be linked together to form a garment of the required shape and size.

The process of drawing the wire and hammering made it hard and liable to crack. By annealing the wire it became soft and could be worked again without difficulty. It is clear from contemporary illustrations showing mail-makers holding the mail with their bare hands that it was worked cold.

In certain forms of mail, particularly those produced in India, the mail links were butted together instead of riveted. Brass and bronze rings were sometimes used for decorative purposes. With some Turkish and Egyptian mail shirts of the fifteenth century each individual ring was stamped in relief with Arabic texts.

The development of armour entirely composed of steel plates dates from the fourteenth century. Several important centres of production, including Milan, Augsburg and Nuremberg, were established at this period and exported their wares to the rest of Europe. In the early stages of the craft's development the raw material for the armourer came in the form of rectangular ingots of iron which had initially to be hammered into plates. This was either done by hand or by using large mechanical hammers powered by water. In the fifteenth century, when the craft was well established, workshops generally imported their raw materials in the form of flat plates from centres such as Innsbruck.

A full harness of plate armour comprised a large number of plates carefully tailored to an individual's measurements, held together by hinges, rivets and straps. The plates were stretched and formed over specially shaped iron stakes using a series of hammers, and frequent annealing was necessary. Considerable skill was needed to make the plate thick at the front where protection was needed and thin at the edges in the interests of lightness. Helmets were raised from flat sheets by beating them down over a steel stake. Once the helmet bowl or breastplate had been shaped, the sharp edges were turned up over a wire. This was probably performed with a special type of vice which gave an even turn to the edge.

The most difficult parts of an armour to make were the defences for the legs known as 'greaves' – chiefly because there were so many different angles and raised sections. In order to allow for flexibility of movement, the joints were composed of narrow bands of metal fitting into each other like a

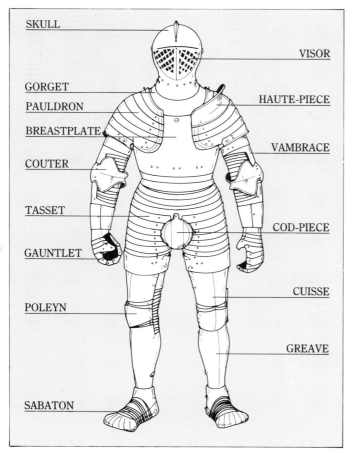

SKULL
VISOR
GORGET
PAULDRON
HAUTE-PIECE
BREASTPLATE
VAMBRACE
COUTER
TASSET
COD-PIECE
GAUNTLET
CUISSE
POLEYN
GREAVE
SABATON

Left: Henry VIII's armour for foot combat made at Greenwich, 1515–20.
Above left: Illustration of an armourer at work from a German book of trades by Jost Amman, 1568. The armourer is shown shaping a plate over an iron stake by hammering.
Above right: Illustration of a mail-maker at work from Das Hausbuch der Mendelschen Zwoelfbruederstiftung, *1425–1550. The mail-maker is shown using pincers to rivet the links of mail together. The links would have been made by first pulling the wire through a draw-plate, then winding that round a circular rod and cutting.*

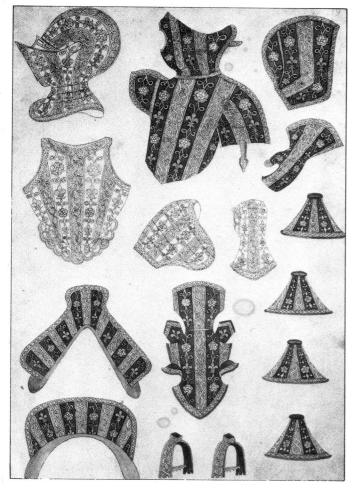

Above: Page of drawings for the armour on the right from the Jacobe Album. This was produced at Greenwich probably under the direction of the German Jacob Halder, 1556–87.
Right: English armour of etched, *blued and gilded steel made for George Clifford, 3rd Earl of Cumberland, at Greenwich, 1590. The workshop at Greenwich was established by Henry VIII, and a number of foreign workmen were employed there.*

telescope. These plates, known as 'lames', were riveted to vertical leather straps on the inside which allowed the knee, the ankle or the arm to bend.

The surfaces were elaborately decorated. In the fifteenth century decoration was often limited to embossed flutes and applied gilt borders in the Gothic style but, as armour became designed more for parade than for defence, other forms of decoration were employed: the entire surface might be oxidized in a flame or by using chemicals to a brilliant peacock blue – processes known as 'blueing' – bands of ornament etched with acid might be heavily gilded and the leather straps covered with velvet. In some sixteenth-century parade harnesses the surface was inlaid with silver, and portions of one armour have survived made in enamelled gold.

Some defensive garments were made from a combination of plate and textile. A type known as a 'brigandine' consisted of a short jacket formed of overlapping small iron plates riveted to a fabric base. The plates were often given a coating of tin to prevent rusting.

THE CRAFT OF THE SWORDSMITH

The manufacture of swords involved a number of specialist craftsmen: the blademaker who forged the blade, grinders and polishers who finished it, the hilt-maker who produced the hilt and craftsmen who specialized in binding the grip and making the scabbard which protected the blade. Once the work had been completed the sword was delivered to a sword cutler, who sold it to the customer.

The raw material for a blade was a 'billet' constituted of steel and iron. The composition of the alloy ensured that the qualities of both hardness and flexibility would be combined in the finished blade. There were many different shapes of blade, ranging from the short, single-edged blades used for hunting to long, narrow thrusting swords. The billet was stretched to the appropriate length and it was roughly shaped using large tilt-hammers.

A feature of most blades is a straight channel running along the blade near the hilt. This could be chiselled or forged into the blade, but German craftsmen developed a system of producing a shaped blade mechanically using steel rollers.

After some preliminary grinding the blade was heated to a specific temperature, which could be determined by its colour, and quenched in oil. After this the blade was re-heated to a lower temperature, tempered in a lead bath and then allowed to cool. This reduced any stresses in the blade. Next the 'tang' – a short projection forming the handle – was either welded to the blade or drawn from it, and it was then ready for final grinding and polishing. This was done on a series of grinding wheels linked by belts to a water-driven driving wheel. The craftsman generally lay on a bench behind the wheel holding the blade at right angles with a cloth. The blade was ground on revolving wheels of different grades, ending with a polishing compound to give the blade a 'mirror' finish. The blade could then be acid-etched or gilded. The delicate blue colour to be found on many blades was probably created by using special chemicals or by using molten lead baths.

Some swords were considered almost as costume jewellery and the most decorative part of them was the hilt. Hilts made of precious metals were cast in a mould in their separate elements. The hilt of a small-sword – the ornamental sword carried in the seventeenth and eighteenth centuries – consisted of a shell-guard, a knuckle-bow and fore-quillon, and a pommel with a grip of wood bound with wire. The main elements could be cast in two-piece moulds if they were to be made of precious metal or brass. Cast hilts were almost

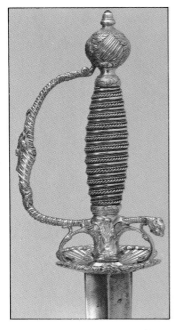

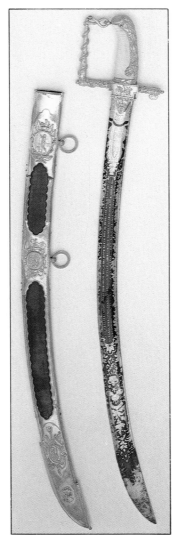

Above: English small-sword, with a hilt of cast and chiselled silver, bearing the maker's mark IR, c.1750. This is a fine example of work in the Rococo style.
Right: Lloyds Patriotic Fund Presentation Sword made by Richard Teed, presented to Lieutenant Bowen in 1803, English. The mounts are of gilded copper and the blade blued and gilded.

Above: Detail of an illustration of grinding and polishing sword-blades from Diderot's Encyclopédie. *The craftsman held the blade against revolving wheels of increasingly fine texture, linked by belts to a single driving-wheel powered by water. A noteworthy feature of the operation was the position in which some of the craftsmen worked, lying on a plank or bench behind the wheel.*

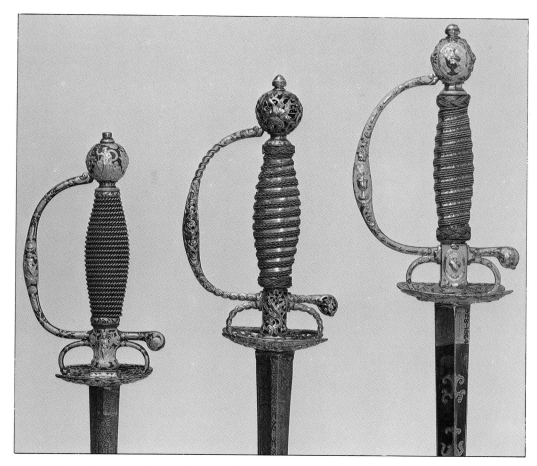

Left: French small-sword hilts of steel, decorated with gold overlay and chiselling, c 1730–80. The blades for these swords were usually imported from Germany, and the hilts were the work of a number of specialist craftsmen, each producing a different element.

invariably worked up afterwards with files and chisels, the ground of the design being matted with a hollow-headed punch. It is clear from an examination of brass sword-hilts that the same mould was used several times as many of the castings are extemely worn.

Some of the finest work on sword-hilts was carried out in iron and steel. It is likely that the work of chiselling, filing and piercing was executed in soft iron, then the completed elements were heated together with charcoal to convert the iron to steel. With pierced work the craftsmen had to be careful to subordinate the decoration of a hilt to its functional purpose. It was usually limited to very delicate lace-like scrollwork, and it is notable that chiselling was usually only used on the larger elements of a hilt.

A few hilts made from gold have survived. Some of the first are preserved in the dynastic armouries of Dresden and Vienna. They were generally cast, then worked up with chisels and chasing tools. Several are decorated with enamel or set with precious stones. When these and materials such as porcelain and tortoiseshell were used, the work was usually done by a jeweller. Of the silver hilts that survive, some are plain; others have elaborate pierced and relief decoration in the style of the Rococo.

At the end of the eighteenth century there was a vogue for highly polished steel hilts set with faceted studs. Fine examples of this form were made in the Soho (Birmingham) manufactory of Matthew Boulton. Some of the most intricate work in steel was done by sculptors and medallists, a few of

whom – such as Gottfried Leygebe, medallist, sculptor and coiner to the Elector of Saxony – signed their work.

A feature of the decoration of many sword-hilts was the use of applied and inlaid decoration. Some hilts were covered with silver sheet decorated with engraving, and another form of decoration widely used was 'damascening'. Damascening is a term used to describe two different techniques of inlaying precious metal. In the first technique the design was actually cut into the surface with a specially shaped engraving tool. The shape of the cutting-edge left a groove of dovetail section. Gold or silver wire was then tapped into this groove which held it firmly. The wire stood proud of the surface and was polished and finished off as required. Inlaid work of this form was very durable but was also very expensive, needing great engraving skills and a considerable quantity of precious metal. Because of this it is very rarely found.

Far more common was the inlay technique known as 'counterfeit damascening', or 'hatching'. The steel surface was first blued to darken it, using either fire or chemicals, then a series of fine lines were cross-cut deep into the surface using an engraving tool. The design was drawn on to this hatched surface, using a brass point, which showed up against the darkened surface. The craftsmen then took fine silver or gold wire and fixed it to the surface following the design, the wire adhering to the finely cut lines. The work was then polished. Although this technique did not require large quantities of precious metal, the work had the disadvantage of being easily worn and damaged.

LEAD

Lead occurs naturally in the form of lead ore (galena). The metal is obtained by reduction, by roasting the ore with coal. It is grey in colour, showing bright silver when cut or scratched; it has a low melting-point – 327°C – and is soft.

Lead has been used for building purposes since classical times because of its ductility and general ability to withstand weathering. During the Roman period it was widely used for water-pipes and coffins, which were generally cast in sand or plaster moulds. At that date lead came in the form of rectangular ingots stamped with the name of the reigning emperor and the source from which it was obtained. Roman piping was cylindrical and of a standard length and diameter, and surviving examples bear details of date and origin. Inscriptions are almost invariably in relief indicating that they were cut into the mould before the molten metal was poured in to it.

In the Medieval period lead was widely used, one of its better-known uses being for church fonts. A surprisingly large series of these has survived, especially in Britain. The usual form consists of a cylindrical basin, with a flat base, and some are as large as 6 feet (1·8 m.) in diameter. Nearly all are decorated on the outer surfaces, with designs in relief. Some, dating from the twelfth and thirteenth centuries, have figures set within pillared arcades. Abstract designs also occur, among them running floral scrolls, roundels and architectural motifs. Repeated designs seem to indicate that wooden patterns were used in the mould. These occasionally left an impression on the surface of the completed work in the form of a raised seam.

Small pierced lead plaques known as 'ventilating quarries' were used in windows to admit air. They are usually square or lozenge shaped with elegant pierced designs, usually in a pronounced Gothic style. The grilles were cast in fine sand moulds and it is possible to identify specific workshops by the

Left: English cast-lead fanlight, late eighteenth century. Lead's resistance to corrosion made it a suitable material for pipes, rain-water heads, fanlights and other external features on buildings.

Above: English cast-lead badge of a company of archers, fifteenth century. The badge would have been cast in a stone mould. It was probably worn in the hat.
Above right: English cast-lead badge of the Sun in Splendour worn by a supporter of the House of York in the Wars of the Roses, fifteenth century. Both badges were recovered from the river Thames.
Right: Illustration of a lead foundry from British Manufacturers. *Metal*

by George Dodd, 1845. The lead was melted in the furnace and any impurities, being lighter than the metal, rose to the surface. Near the bottom of the melting-pot was a valve, through which the molten metal flowed into a cast-iron mould.

design of the casting. They seem to have been used from the fourteenth to the sixteenth centuries.

Small lead castings were sometimes used as mounts for caskets and some fine examples from the fourteenth century, pierced in the Gothic style, have survived. The castings were widely traded, as examples clearly from the same mould have been found over a wide geographical area. When used for decorative objects the lead was usually gilded or painted, often over a layer of gesso (see p. 48).

Over the years large numbers of badges worn both by pilgrims and by retainers, dating from the fourteenth to the sixteenth centuries, have been recovered from river beds. They range from the mitred head of Thomas à Becket – a well-known Canterbury badge – to the Sun in Splendour badge carried by supporters of the House of York. A large number of the spurious antiquities produced by 'Billie and Charlie' – William Smith and Charles Eaton – in the 1840s, copying these badges, were cast in lead using plaster of Paris moulds.

Familiar items in lead include the elaborate rain-water heads used on the outside of buildings from the late Medieval period onwards to funnel rain-water into the lead down-pipes. They were elaborately ornamented with cast and pierced work, and many were cast with initials and dates. The designs vary enormously, from the castellated square boxes decorated with Gothic tracery of the sixteenth century to those decorated with classical columns and acanthus of the eighteenth century. Lead pipes and gutters were also decorated, usually with foliage patterns and scrolls.

Other familiar vessels associated with architecture are the large lead cisterns used to collect rain-water. Some large oval cisterns decorated with roundels in relief, thought to be French and from the fourteenth century, have survived, but the majority date from the seventeenth and eighteenth centuries. In these later examples the decoration often comprises relief strapwork incorporating figures and armorial subjects.

From the seventeenth century lead was widely used for garden sculpture and for fountains as it was found to resist corrosion. These large works were cast in sections, then assembled and soldered together. The best French work of the late seventeenth century was executed by sculptors, who worked on the castings with chisels to produce an exceptionally high finish.

Early illustrations of the workshops of lead workers show furnaces and ladles for transporting the molten metal. Also illustrated are various forms of mould, with long skimmers and rakes used to remove the dross from the surface when the metal was about to be poured. The castings were roughly finished with a file or trimmed with shears. In general the ductility of the metal obviated the necessity for much finishing, providing the mould had been properly prepared.

Goldsmiths often used lead for the preliminary models for decorated sections of bowls or cups; these were then copied by the chasers, and could be stored and used again and again. The softness and cheapness of the material made it ideal for modelling. Most of these models were discarded when the style changed, but some eighteenth-century patterns for jewellery, watch-cases and parts of snuff-boxes do survive and were sometimes re-used as models in the nineteenth century.

Above: Cast-lead statue of a shepherd boy and his dog in the gardens of Canons Ashby, Northamptonshire, probably by Jan van Nost, early eighteenth century. The figure would have been cast in several sections.

TIN

Tin, produced by smelting from cassiterite (tin oxide), does not tarnish and is resistant to organic acids; it can be polished to a silver-like surface. It has a comparatively low melting-point of 231·9°C, and it can be plated on a wide variety of base metals.

The use of tin as a protective coating against rust on iron was known in Roman and early Islamic times, and in western Europe in the Middle Ages. Examination of the wrought-iron straps used on Medieval chests often reveals the characteristic grey, silvery surface. Tin was also coated on copper vessels to avoid toxicity (see p.192)

Tinware – objects made from iron sheets coated with tin – was almost certainly first developed in Saxony and Bohemia in the late sixteenth or early seventeenth century. The production of tinware became of special significance in the seventeenth and eighteenth centuries in the town of Pontypool in South Wales with the development of the ironworks operated by the Hanbury family.

An essential part of the manufacture of tinware was the production of thin iron sheets. Iron bars which had been smelted with charcoal were heated and then hammered into flat plates using large tilt-hammers driven by water power. The plates were then placed side by side in a furnace and re-heated. In order to prevent the individual plates welding together, a separating mixture of sand and charcoal was used. The plates were worked on in large piles and, by a repeated process of heating and hammering, thin iron sheets were produced which were then trimmed to the required size using shears. After 1728 sheet iron could also be produced by rolling mills, which flattened the heated iron ingots between heavy rollers.

The iron sheets were first scoured, using sandstone, and then pickled in vats containing a fermented liquid to remove any scale. After further cleaning, they were plunged into cast-iron cauldrons containing the molten tin, which adhered evenly to the surface. The sheets were usually dipped twice to ensure an even coating. They were then polished with linen using oatmeal and sawdust.

During the eighteenth and nineteenth centuries a wide range of goods was made from tinned iron, at first by hammering the metal over a former. The best known are probably the lacquered wares which were produced at Pontypool and also in the Midlands. These centres produced a large number of shallow trays of various designs decorated with coloured lacquers. This decorative technique, known as 'japanning', is the same as that used on *papier mâché* (see

MAKING A TIN-PLATE BOX WITH WIRE
1. The outline of the box was cut out and the angles marked with a scriber on the surface of the tin.
2. The plate was inserted in a special iron vice and the ends turned over, using a wooden mallet.
3. The sides were turned up over an angular former, the workman again using the mallet.
4. The angles at the sides and corners were carefully formed with the mallet and block.
5. The ends were then soldered together.
6. A narrow strip was left at the top of each edge to hold the wire reinforcement.
7. Wire of an appropriate diameter was cut to the required length so that it completely surrounded the top edge.
8. The narrow strip was then closed over the wire using a wooden mallet.
9. Using a specially shaped hammer, the workman sealed the wire.

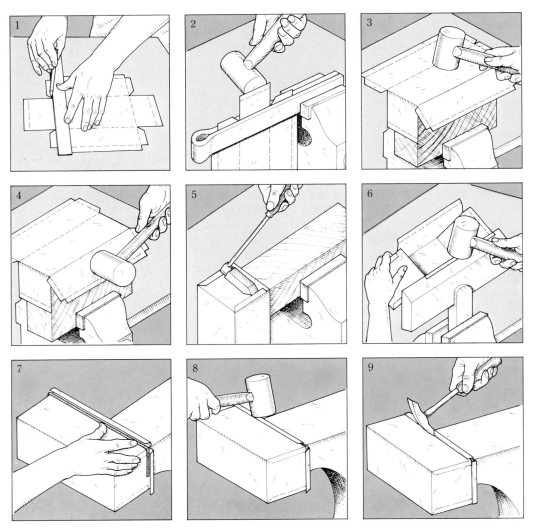

p.58). Similar japanned wares were made at the same period in France.

Plainer utensils such as plate-warmers, chamber candlesticks, coffee-pots and containers were also made in tin. These were constructed from sections of tin plate soldered together; the edges were usually rolled over iron wire to give additional strength to the wares. Machine manufacture was introduced in the mid-nineteenth century.

A substantial amount of tinware has survived in the United States, where it was extensively used for domestic articles in the nineteenth century. Berlin, Connecticut, became a centre of production of both plain and japanned tinware, some of the finest pieces being made by members of the Pattison family; the Pennsylvania Germans were also important producers.

Left: Tinsmith's workshop from Illustrations of Useful Arts *by Charles Tomlinson, 1867. The worker on the left is shown cutting a sheet of tin plate with 'snips', while the one on the right shapes the metal over a former. On the ground, mounted on a block of wood, is a polishing anvil and above the workbench is a row of punches, stakes and hammers.*

Right: American japanned tinware 'coffin' tray attributed to Frederick and Louis Zietz, 1874. Trays were made from two, one or half a sheet of tin plate, turned up around the edge. The 'japanning' consisted of layers of varnish, here mixed with asphaltum, dried in a stove after each application. This formed the ground for painted or stencilled decoration.
Below: Pontypool japanned tinware tea-caddy with painted decoration, late eighteenth or early nineteenth century. Pontypool, in South Wales, was an important centre both for the manufacture of rolled tin plate and of japanning.

Left: Pontypool japanned tinware chestnut urn decorated with painting of a landscape scene and gilding, early nineteenth century.
Above: Detail of the chestnut urn showing the gold contrasting with the black ground.

COPPER

Copper is found as a natural mineral or in copper ore, from which it has to be extracted by the smelting process. This involves roasting the ore at a sufficiently high temperature to melt the natural copper, which collects at the bottom of the hearth or furnace. When cut or scratched the metal is bright pink, rapidly oxidizing to a chocolate-brown colour.

Copper combines the qualities of toughness with malleability. It has a melting-point of 1083°C and is easy to work, although its hardness is increased by cold working. It is an important constituent of a large number of alloys, including brass, bronze, and pewter, and the principal constituent of Old Sheffield Plate.

Simple objects such as beads, pins and primitive tools made from copper have been found at sites in the Near East which can be dated to around 9000 to 7000 BC. The mining and exploitation of copper was widespread in the ancient world, in Sumeria, Egypt, Israel, Asia Minor, the Balkan peninsula and Cyprus. To the Romans it was known as '*aes cyprium*', an indication of the importance of Cyprus as a centre of production. In the Middle Ages copper was mined in Saxony, in Tuscany and at Falun in Sweden; the Stora Kopparberg mine at Falun was operating from the early thirteenth century and was the most important source of copper in Europe, though by the eighteenth century a significant quantity was being brought from Japan.

German miners dominated the copper trade, both technologically and economically. Much of the northern European trade was conducted by the Hanseatic League and, in the south, Nuremberg was an important trading centre. The wealth of the Fugger family of Augsburg was in part founded on the exploitation of minerals, and this family had a virtual monopoly in the early sixteenth century. German miners were prominent, too, in the two companies given rights to exploit the deposits of copper found in the Lake District area of Great Britain in the second half of the sixteenth century. A factory for smelting copper was established at Neath, in Wales, in 1582.

In 1800 Britain was the largest producer of copper in the world, but this lead was lost first to Chile in the 1830s, then to the United States and Spain. In America Benjamin Franklin had noted the importance of the copper mine of the Schuylers in New Jersey in 1750, and in 1798 Paul Revere offered to supply copper to provide sheathing for naval vessels. Baltimore became an important centre for refining copper in the middle of the nineteenth century.

Producers of copper went to considerable trouble to study their craft in order to improve methods of production and quality. Works such as *De re metallica* written by Agricola and published in 1556, were influential in spreading knowledge about the various techniques.

The techniques used for forming articles of copper were casting, stamping, spinning and raising. With raised wares – such as bowls and kettles – the gauge of the metal was generally comparatively thin. When the copper was hammered it became increasingly hard: lightness and rigidity were thus combined.

In the Middle Ages large numbers of apparently mass-produced wares were made in centres such as Limoges in southern France, especially in the thirteenth century, and crosses, reliquaries, candlesticks and a variety of objects for ecclesiastical use have survived. Much of the work was decorated with coloured enamels by the technique known as '*champlevé*' (see p.197), and some have figures or parts of figures in high relief. These were made separately and then soldered or pinned to the surface.

They seem to have been manufactured either by casting in a rough mould and then hammering up from the back, or by hammering up from sheet copper: nearly all the copper plaques which formed such a large part of the production of the Limoges workshops show signs at the back of some hammering. The features and finer details were later worked upon

Above: Illustration of a coppersmith forming a bowl by raising from a sixteenth-century book of German trades by Jost Amman.
Opposite: Illustration from Diderot's Encyclopédie *showing the manufacture of copper and brass cooking utensils and large vessels.*
Below: Illustration from the Encyclopédie *showing the manufacture of a hunting horn.*

The copper body of the horn was shaped round a former (Fig. 1) and a mouth was soldered on to it (Fig. 2). By filling the cavity with molten lead (Fig. 3), the craftsman was able to coil the tube without causing it to buckle (Fig. 4).
Right: English table lamp of cast and turned brass and copper designed by W.A.S. Benson (1854–1924), c.1895.

from the front using chisels and engraving tools. Some carry the roughly incised letters or Roman numerals which were to aid the craftsman during assembly. Vessels such as incense-boats or the cylindrical boxes made for ritual use known as 'pyxes' were made in several parts, then joined together using solder. Some show signs of having been turned on the lathe, presumably as part of a finishing process.

Cloisonné enamelling, and the painted enamels produced at Limoges, often had a copper base (see p.196). Gilding by the mercury process, as carried out in the manufacture of ormolu (see p.204), was another decorative technique used on copper, sometimes in combination with enamelling.

A wide range of copper wares were produced by Italian coppersmiths during the sixteenth and seventeenth centuries. The wares included a distinctive footed ewer with a prominent spout and various forms of deep bowl, and large chargers were also fashionable. These were lower-priced versions of the finely engraved brass and bronze wares of the period. The surfaces were almost invariably decorated with punches.

The punches used on copper were generally made of brass or steel. A tracing punch was used to outline the design on the metal, an embossing punch to bring certain areas into relief and a planishing punch to impart a smooth, flat surface, each of these having a different shape of head. Matting punches produced dense clusters of impressions on the ground. With

skill it was possible to achieve a clear pattern with a single blow of the hammer.

Incense-burners, braziers and warming-pans were pierced to allow heat to escape. The gauge of the metal was usually so thin that holes could be made using a sharp punch. These holes were then enlarged to the required size using a saw or specially shaped file.

Because copper is a soft metal, it is easy to engrave. The design was usually drawn on to the surface and then gone over with a scriber with a needle-like point which lightly scratched the design into the surface. For the actual engraving process the object had to be set into pitch or sealing-wax; more commonly it was supported on a bag containing sand. As with engraving on silver, the design was then cut into the surface using a graver. The ground of a design might be covered with fine intersecting lines, or 'cross-hatching'. This could be done by simply using a graver with a narrow blade and a straight edge. A more convenient method of producing the same decorative effect was to use a tool called a 'liner', the head of which was cut with a series of parallel lines. Errors in the engraving process could be corrected by stoning out the line and revealing a new surface.

Many copper vessels were tinned. As tin was resistant to many organic acids, it was used as a coating to avoid toxicity, especially for vessels used in cooking and serving food. Many

Above: Warwick Ciborium, English, late twelfth century. The copper vessel, used for the reservation of the Eucharist, was originally gilded, enamelled and engraved. The bowl would have been formed by raising and turning.

Above: English tinned copper cooking utensils, nineteenth century. Copper vessels used for food and drink were generally plated with tin to prevent corrosion and to avoid toxicity.
Right: Detail of a French copper plaque decorated with champlevé *enamelling, gilded silver filigree and cabochons, probably from the side of a house-shrine, c.1290–1310. Made in Paris, it is in the manner of work produced at Limoges. The applied figures of the Virgin Mary with the Infant Christ and St John the Baptist were cast in copper and decorated with chasing and gilding.*

Far left: Back of a Dutch gilded copper book cover, set with panels of painted enamel in high relief, c.1670. The edges of the cover are engraved with a pattern of diagonal bars alternating with circles against a hatched background.
Left: Detail of the book cover showing the floral ornament on the back.

eighteenth-century stew- and boiling-pans – now polished bright – show traces of the original tinned surface in the corners and on the under-surfaces.

To fix tin to a copper surface, the copper vessel was thoroughly cleaned, usually by immersing it in acid. The vessel was then heated to a temperature above the melting-point of tin – 231.9°C. A 'flux', or fluid to help fusion, such as ammonium chloride was applied over the surface and the surface was then rubbed with a bar of pure tin which immediately adhered to it. Vessels could also be dipped into a bath of molten tin which gave a thicker, more even, coating. This was the process used to coat iron.

Tinned surfaces are usually an unattractive matt grey colour, but when highly polished resemble silver. Particularly finely engraved tinned copper wares were produced by the craftsmen of the Near East. The engraved design on the grey tin surface was usually heightened by filling the engraved lines with a black compound.

In the past various methods were employed to alter the chocolate-brown colour to which copper patinates naturally. A range of surface colours were produced by the application of chemicals: pickling in arsenic turned copper grey or black; copper carbonates produced brown or green. Domestic articles such as stew-pans or kettles were kept constantly scoured so that they remained pink. Craftsmen of the nineteenth-century Arts and Crafts Movement, who produced some fine articles in copper, applied clear lacquer to the plain surfaces to give them a bright finish.

ELECTROTYPING

An interesting technique which was developed from the principle of electro-plating was the perfect copying of an object by a galvano-plastic process. The process was demonstrated as early as 1838 by Professor Jacobi, using the battery invented by Dr William Hyde Wollaston in his experiments in 1800 and 1801. It is recorded that one Thomas Spencer of Liverpool deposited copper on a copper penny by immersing it in a battery cell, and, on peeling off the deposited copy, found it bore an exact counterpart of the face of the coin.

It was a process much used from the 1850s, when Elkington's had a contract to produce a number of replicas of historic silver and other art objects for the South Kensington – now the Victoria and Albert – Museum. These included some of the most famous pieces of English silver in the Russian royal collections, now in Leningrad. Elkington's continued to produce commercial electrotype copies of historic objects well into the twentieth century, offering alternative finishes in silver, gilt or bronze.

From the 1860s electrotyping was a normal means of production in both Europe and the United States. Although the early electrotypes were of antique or natural objects, the process was increasingly used to reproduce important contemporary work such as the exhibition pieces of the Frenchman Léonard Morel-Ladeuil, who was employed by Elkington's from 1859 to 1888.

The process entailed taking a mould of the object in a plastic substance such as gutta-percha, beeswax, sealing-wax, plaster of Paris, printers' compo (the first use of the process was, in fact, for reproducing type-faces), gelatine or some other softenable material. Since the moulding material had to be of the highest quality – each mould being a 'one-off' job – the reproduction of works of art in this way was costly, though supremely effective.

The mould was coated with a film of conductive material, connected to the suspension wires, then hung in a vat of copper sulphate solution. It was connected to the negative pole of the battery, the anode being a plate of copper. The mould was then plated with the copper to a reasonable thickness, removed from the vat, washed and dried, and separated from the copper layer.

The reverse was then covered with soft solder grain to support the copper shell, and backing material soldered in. The exterior was usually electro-plated with silver or gold.

The models to be copied could be of any substance: besides metal originals, plants, seashells, fishes and other natural objects could be faithfully reproduced.

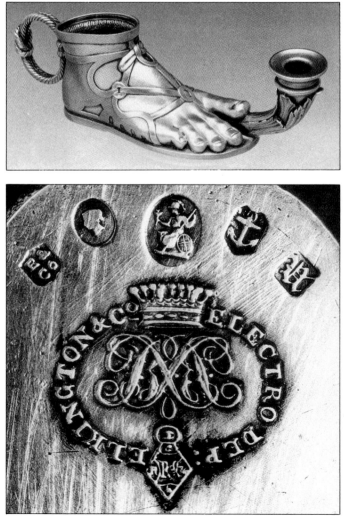

Above: Elkington, Mason & Co. silver electrotype of a Pompeian two-handled cup, Birmingham, 1851. The body is decorated in high relief with putti and centaurs on a matted ground. This remained a popular pattern for some years.
Above right: Elkington & Co. taperstick in the form of a Roman sandal from a design by Benjamin Schlick, Birmingham, 1844. Schlick, a Danish-born architect, was employed by Elkington's in the year that this design appeared. It was one of the firm's most successful patterns.
Right: Marks on the taperstick.

The design was registered at the Patent Office, as can be seen by the lozenge-shaped part of the firm's stamp below the Birmingham hallmarks for 1844. The model was also made up in 1857 in an electrotype copy by the Swedish silversmith Christian Hammer.

ENAMELLING

The term 'enamelling' properly describes the decorative process of applying to metal a glass-like substance in opaque or transparent colours and fusing it on by heat. Similar vitreous 'enamels' were used for painting on glass (see p.94) and ceramics (see p.132). The molten enamel adhered to the base material after firing at a moderate temperature; too great a heat distorted or melted the piece. To prevent mixing during firing when one colour was applied over another, the successive applications of enamel had progressively lower melting-temperatures: some pinks and turquoises could only be fired at a low temperature, for example, so these might be the last to be applied.

Little is known of the formulation of the earliest enamels; the manufacture of an opaque white enamel was described by Antonio Neri in 1612 in *L'Arte Vetraria*. Roughly equal proportions of tin and lead were mixed together and calcined. The oxides thus produced were purified and mixed with a similar proportion of soda crystal frit (see p.62), and a little tartar was added to lower the melting-temperature. The mixture was heated in the furnace for ten hours in a pot glazed with white glass, to protect the enamel from impurities, after which it was cooled and powdered ready for use. Coloured enamels were made by adding metallic oxides to the white enamel powder; the mixture was melted several times, each time being cast into water and powdered.

By the nineteenth century decorative enamels mostly had a transparent, colourless, lead-borosilicate type of glass base, confusingly known as 'flux' (see p.61), the composition of which was varied according to the melting-point that was required: a hard enamel for use on a gold base might have contained silica, red lead, saltpetre and borax in the ratio $3:3:2\frac{1}{2}:0$, while for a soft enamel the proportions would have been altered to $10:15:4:1$. Enamels for use on silver and copper were obtained by adding more borax to the same mixture. Five grades of fusibility became commercially available but many craftsmen would have prepared their own enamels. The flux was made opaque with oxide of tin or antimony, or with phosphate of lime, and coloured in the same way as for hard enamels. The enamel mixture was fused, cooled, crushed and then finely ground with water in an agate mortar. The powdered enamel was carefully washed in running water and stored under water in a covered vessel.

The enamel was generally applied to the piece as a damp paste and dried near the furnace. For firing, a muffle furnace was used which shielded the work from direct contact with the heat source. The actual melting in the furnace took only a few

Left: German saucer with enamel painting on copper, mounted in silver gilt, by Elias Adam, first half of the eighteenth century. Adam worked in Augsburg, which, in the eighteenth century, was noted for the production of painted enamels.

minutes, and this was followed by careful cooling; the process might be repeated several times to modify the design or correct defects.

Enamelling has always been an experimental art as the enamel is very sensitive to furnace conditions and may blister, discolour or fail to adhere to the base. The best adhesion was obtained on glass, glazed porcelain and pure gold. The presence of copper in gold alloys gave rise to firestain, to which the enamel would not adhere, and this had to be cleaned off by abrasion or with chemicals. Similar problems arose with silver, though not with bronze. The surface might be roughened with a sharp tool to facilitate adhesion. Some thin, or sheet, metal – used for the Limoges process, in particular – was enamelled on both faces, the backing being known as 'contre-émail'. The two layers counteracted any distortion or cracking that might be caused by the expansion and contraction of the metal during heating and cooling.

With the earliest forms of enamelling the pattern was achieved by containing the natural flow of the molten enamel within 'cells'. In cloisonné enamelling the partitions, or 'cloisons', were made of strips of metal attached to the base, generally by soldering, following a design previously drawn or scratched on the base. After all the cloisons had been filled with several coats of enamel and subsequently fired, the surface was ground flat and polished. Gilding of the exposed edges of the metal – which both enclosed and separated the areas of enamelling – increased the rich, jewel-like effect.

The earliest surviving enamels have a base of gold, electrum or bronze – metals that have, incidentally, suffered the least with age. Mycenaean craftsmen developed the cloisonné technique in the thirteenth to eleventh centuries BC, and by the third century BC it was practised in western Europe, where the Celts were later to become masters of the craft.

The great period of European cloisonné manufacture is associated with religious patronage in the Byzantine Empire between the ninth and twelfth centuries. St Mark's, Venice, is richly endowed with examples from this, literally, golden age. The altarpiece known as the 'Pala d'Oro', installed there in 1105, is considered the outstanding example. In its present form the screen is decorated with 137 enamels of various styles and dates. The earliest have relatively few, boldly drawn cells with deep, brightly coloured enamels. Later additions, or replacements, have smaller, more detailed cells, and there was a greater use of pale colours.

Above: Pair of Chinese cloisonné *and gilded bronze long-tailed birds, eighteenth century. In* cloisonné, *the earliest type of enamelling, different coloured enamels were contained within cells made of narrow strips of metal attached to a metal base.*
Far left: English snuff-box, Staffordshire, c.1770. The design was transfer-printed in brown and overpainted with enamels.
Left: English needlecase with enamel painting and raised gilding, Staffordshire, late eighteenth century. A variety of domestic and decorative articles were produced in Staffordshire, the designs executed in transfer-printing or hand-painting, or in a combination of the two.

Left: English japanned casket with two enamel tea-caddies and a sugar-canister, Birmingham, c.1770. Each of the enamel containers was painted with bouquets of flowers and summer insects to produce an effect of great delicacy. Birmingham was an important centre for the manufacture of metalware. The blanks were either enamelled there or sent elsewhere to be decorated.

Below: German pendant in the form of a fabulous bird comprising Baroque pearls and rubies mounted in gold with émail en ronde bosse, *sixteenth century. This type of encrusted enamelling on three-dimensional objects was used especially by jewellers. The pendant, measuring 3³/4 inches (9.5 cm) in height, is reproduced larger than actual size.*

A variation of the *cloisonné* technique in which the partitions were made of twisted wire was known as 'filigree enamelling'. The wire was typically raised and did not form a continuous, flat surface with the enamelling. It was particularly favoured in Ancient Greece and, from the time of the Renaissance, in Hungary and Russia.

With the *champlevé* technique the enamel was again contained within cells, but here the cavities to be filled with enamel were formed by indentations in the base, rather than by a framework attached to the base. A greater thickness of metal was required than for *cloisonné* enamelling – from which it can be distinguished by variations in the width of the cell walls – and for this reason base metals were commonly used. The indentations were made by casting the metal, chiselling it away or, later, removing it by acid etching. Enamelled-bronze medallions and brooches were manufactured in the Roman period, and the technique was revived, at Limoges and in the region around the river Meuse in particular, in the twelfth century.

The development of transparent enamels led to a modification of the *champlevé* technique known as '*basse-taille* enamelling'. Details of the pattern were chased on to the underlying metal and showed through the enamel so that modelling of the folds of a garment, for example, was achieved by varying the depth of enamel. Great brilliance was achieved by the light penetrating the enamel on a gold, silver-gilt or silver ground. The technique originated in Italy in the thirteenth century, and spread to Spain, Germany, France and England.

Plique-à-jour was essentially a *cloisonné* process. Either the metal partitions were attached to a temporary base made of a material such as fireclay, to which the enamel would not adhere, or the enamel was built up gradually without a backing.

This use of transparent enamels to create, in miniature, the impression of a stained-glass window dates from the late fourteenth century, but it is principally associated with the jewellery trade during the nineteenth century and the inventiveness of René Lalique, the designer Fernand Thesmar and the Falize family in France, the Italians Fortunato Pio Castellani and Carlo Giuliano, and Marcus & Co. in New York.

Enamelling of a three-dimensional object was known as 'encrusted enamelling', or 'émail en ronde bosse'. From the late Middle Ages, at first in France and then elsewhere in Europe, the technique was used in the manufacture of jewellery and for figures and other sculptural details on reliquaries and altar-pieces and other larger objects.

The invention of painted enamels in which the colours were applied side by side, without any metal partitions to separate them, is attributed to Limoges in the fifteenth century, although examples from Burgundy and Venice are also known. The plaques, usually of silver or copper and slightly domed, depicted religious scenes in polychrome enamels. Another technique known as 'grisaille' enamelling, involved applying a layer of white enamel over a dark ground. Applying the enamel thickly or thinly varied the depth of ground colour which showed through; the effect of the modelling might be enhanced by incising and refiring.

Brush-painting in polychrome enamels on candlesticks, snuff- and patch-boxes and a variety of other domestic objects

CLOISONNÉ ENAMELLING
1. *Wires were soldered or glued to the outline of the picture, drawn on the domed metal plate, to form* 'cloisons'.
2. *Lumps of enamel were powdered under water in a mortar and pestle.*
3. *The powdered enamel was washed repeatedly to remove dust.*
4. *The underside of the plate was coated with moist enamel; then the cloisons were filled using a brush or spatula. The surface of the enamel was pressed to a firm layer just above the cloisons.*
5. *The enamel was thoroughly dried, melted in the furnace for a few minutes only, then withdrawn and cooled.*
6. *The enamel was ground flush with the cloisons and polished.*

CHAMPLEVÉ ENAMELLING
1. *Acid etching was here used to create recesses to receive the enamel. The design was drawn on a thick copper plate.*
2. *Acid-resist was applied to the lines separating the recesses, and to the back and other areas to be protected from the acid.*
3. *Exposed areas of the plate were eaten away with nitric acid.*
4. *The plate was washed and inspected for depth of etching, another acidizing perhaps being found necessary.*
5. *The resist was removed and a clean finish given to the work with a brush ready for enamelling.*
6. *The etched areas were filled with moist enamel to just above the surface of the metal. The work was then dried, fired, cooled and polished as for cloisonné enamelling.*

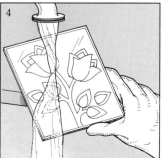

became popular throughout Europe in the eighteenth century. Notable centres in England were Battersea in London, Birmingham and Bilston in Staffordshire and, in Germany, Augsburg and Berlin. Parisian enamellers produced some fine work, too; earlier, some of the most delicate painted enamels had been executed by Jean Petitot and a group of enamellers from Geneva. Decoration of mass-produced items was effected from the mid-eighteenth century by transfer-printing on an enamel ground, a technique similar to that used on ceramics (see p.134). The printed design was often coloured by hand afterwards.

Niello was a type of decoration produced by fusing a powdered alloy of silver, copper, lead and sulphur on to a metal base by heating. The process, although non-vitreous, may be compared with enamelling. With one method the design was incised in the surface with a graver and the molten black material rubbed into it. An alternative method was to niello the background, leaving the design in silver or silver gilt.

Above: French plique-à-jour *enamel and gold bowl designed by Fernand Thesmar (1843–1912), probably made by the firm of Thirné, 1892. Plique-à-jour was a* cloisonné *type of enamelling but without the metal backing so that the partitions formed an openwork pattern. When translucent enamel was used, the effect was of stained glass in miniature.*

Left: Eltenburg Reliquary, Rhenish, c.1180. This remarkable example of Medieval craftsmanship is of oak mounted in copper and gilded bronze, with figures carved in walrus ivory and champlevé *enamelling on the roofs and pillars. With the* champlevé *(literally 'raised field') technique the metal base was gouged away to form recesses for the molten enamel; a later technique was to form the recesses by acid etching.*

Below: Byzantine silver-gilt pectoral cross with plaques of gold and cloisonné *enamelling on each side. The gold partitions, or* 'cloisons', *are clearly visible.*

BRONZE

Bronze, which was manufactured as long ago as 3000 BC, is an alloy of copper and tin. Its uses have varied from gun barrels and machinery castings to sculpture, for which it has always been the most popular metal. It was also used for architectural features such as capitals, window-frames and door-furniture. The proportions of the two metals in antique bronze varied widely, from 67% to 95% copper, but by the Middle Ages this had stabilized: the ratio of one to the other was in accordance with the purpose, 8 parts copper to 1 part tin being used for bronze gun metal, for example.

Techniques used to form bronze include both sheet work and casting. Sheet metal could be cut into an appropriate shape and bent to form vessels, and the seams soldered or riveted. As in silver manufacture, the technique of raising over a stake using a hammer with a hemispherical head was used, and bowls could be formed by spinning, a circular sheet being brought into contact with a revolving former. The sheet of metal was sometimes ornamentally embossed with punches and hammers, working from the reverse in the repoussé technique and on the surface in chasing. Mass production of embossed ornament would be achieved by hammering the sheet into a mould made of hardwood.

Bronze is superior to all other metals for casting, expanding as it solidifies to enter every crevice of the mould, then contracting slightly as it cools, facilitating separation from the mould. A little added lead or zinc improves bronze as a casting metal, and the proportion of tin may then be as small as 1 part in 10.

Early bronzes were cast solid by pouring the molten metal into moulds of stone or baked clay. The solid casting process,

Left: Roman bronze, coral and enamel flagon from Basse-Yutz, France, fourth century BC. The detail on the handle, lid and spout would have been achieved with a tracer, producing a line hammered into the metal.
Below: Greek equestrian bronzes attributed to Lysippus which surmounted the central arch of St Mark's, Venice, and are now inside the basilica. The horses are thought to have been brought to Rome by Augustus. They were removed to Byzantium by Constantine and brought to Venice following the Latin conquest of Constantinople in 1204. They were cast in sections and then carefully soldered together before being gilded by the mercury process.

Above: The Creation of Man by Lorenzo Ghiberti (1378–1455), 1425–52, a bronze relief from the doors of the Baptistery in Florence. Along with the nine other scenes on these doors, the panels were cast in very low relief, the figures being disposed to convey accurately a sense of perspective. Ghiberti's careful calculations depended on the recent researches into perspective of Brunelleschi and Donatello.
Right: Detail of The Story of Joshua from the Baptistery doors. Ghiberti's training as a goldsmith would have assisted him in producing work in bronze of such delicacy. To carry out the reliefs on this and an earlier pair of bronze doors for the Baptistery, Ghiberti employed a large number of assistants in his workshop.

Left: Bronze figures of Bacchus and Ceres attributed to Michel Anguier (1613–86), French, seventeenth century. These were cast by the cire perdu, or lost-wax, process. The pieces have a dark-brown patina.

with moulds in three or four pieces, was highly developed in Mesopotamia by 2500 BC. In Britain two-part stone moulds for axe heads have been found which date from the first half and middle of the second millenium BC.

To produce an object such as a wine container in bronze, the lower part of the core was shaped in clay, thrown on a potter's wheel, dried and covered with wax of the thickness desired for the bronze. The upper part was then similarly modelled and covered with wax. The surface of the wax was carved in relief, successive layers of clay of increasing roughness being painted over, to about 1 inch (2·4 cm) in thickness. This had both vertical and horizontal divisions so that it could be removed in wedge-shaped sections to scrape the wax off the core, leaving

a free passage for the molten metal. This piece-moulding process left ridges on the surface of the bronze, corresponding to the joins between the pieces; the ridges were usually chiselled away during finishing.

The *cire-perdue*, or lost-wax, process differed in that the mould around the wax and core could not be opened up, and the wax had to be driven out by heat. Casting by this process was known to the Sumerians, in the Indus Valley in the third millenium and in Egypt by the eighteenth dynasty, after 1573 BC. In China, it may have been known by the Shang dynasty (1523–1028 BC).

Three forms of lost-wax casting are known. In the first a solid model of wax was employed, over which a mould of some refractory material – capable of great heat resistance – was formed. The wax was melted out and the liquid bronze run in, to make a solid cast. With the second method an object in wax was modelled over a refractory core. The mould was then formed over the wax. The core was held in position by bronze pins, and the wax melted out. Bronze was then poured into the space between the mould and the core, which was chipped away with chisels, leaving a hollow cast. Both methods involved the destruction of the original model.

A third method, employed by the Greeks, required a mould formed over an original model, which might be either in wood or stone, or sometimes of clay or alabaster. The surface of the mould, after the removal of the prototype, was covered with a layer of wax and filled with a core of refractory material. The wax could then be melted out as before, and the bronze poured in. This preserved the model for later use, enabling casts to be multiplied from the same original work. Piece-moulds were used, which had to be removed from the original in sections.

Wax modelling in sections for decorative purposes existed by the sixth century BC; the best description of the technique is given by the Italian Renaissance sculptor and goldsmith Benvenuto Cellini in connection with the casting of a statue of Perseus.

The lost-wax process was the principal method employed for forming objects of bronze until the nineteenth century, when the process of electrotyping was devised. This has been used to produce facsimiles of antique bronzes.

Surface corrosion of old bronze creates a 'patina', an incrustation produced by oxidation. This may be green, blue, brown or even black in colour, according to the circumstances in which the bronze was kept or buried. Copper sulphate has been used to create a bluish green patina; bronze with silver, or a high proportion of tin, in its alloy often acquires a black patina. A number of recipes for patination have been evolved by recent experiments.

Above: Italian bronze handle, sixteenth century. Bronze was widely used for door-furniture and household objects as well as for statuettes and works of art on a larger scale.

LOST-WAX CASTING
1. The wax figure, modelled over a clay core, was encased in a framework of sprues and risers in preparation for casting.
2. A plaster mould was built up around the model and its framework. Fine plaster was then poured in, to coat the model's surface.
3. The completed mould, strengthened with wire, was smoothed prior to firing in a burn-out kiln, to empty out the molten wax.
4. The molten bronze was poured from a small crucible into the hollow mould, embedded in a wooden frame of earth.
5. Once the metal had cooled, the casting was freed from the mould, which was destroyed with a hammer and tools.
6. The waste metal gated assembly, including runners and sprues, was removed with sharp tools, leaving the casting free to be sand blasted, patinated and finally waxed.

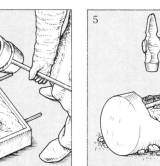
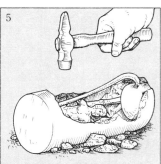

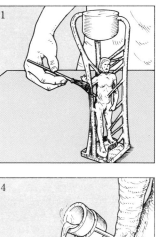

Above: French bronze figures of hounds by Pierre Jules Mène (1810–79), mid-nineteenth century. Mène was one of a group of sculptors specializing in the modelling of animals to be cast as small bronzes. Because they were manufactured by sand-casting – a process in which the shape of the object was impressed in half-moulds of packed sand – an unlimited number of casts could be made of the same pattern.

Left: Illustration of casting cannon from Diderot's Encyclopédie. *A fire was built on the floor of the workshop for drying the model and the mould, both of which were made of clay.*

Below: Illustration from the Encyclopédie *showing a two-part mould and the channels through which the molten metal was poured.*

ORMOLU

The term 'ormolu' orginated with the French description for a group of metal works of art that were gilded by the mercury process. The phrase from which the word derives is '*d'orure d'or moulu*' (gilding with gold which has been ground up). In the mercury process an 'amalgam', or mixture, of mercury and gold was prepared which had the consistency of a paste.

Ormolu is now used to describe elaborate gilded decorative wares produced from the latter part of the seventeenth century until the nineteenth century, the range of which was considerable. It included mounts for furniture, door-handles, decorative vessels such as vases, every form of light-fitting from candlesticks to sconces, clocks and the elaborate fire-dogs known as '*chenets*'.

The particular alloy from which these objects were made varied, but seems to have been analogous to brass: it usually contained a large proportion of copper, with smaller proportions of zinc and sometimes tin. Characteristic of all ormolu is the heavily gilded surface produced by the technique known as 'fire gilding', or 'mercury gilding', the process used to coat silver and other metals with gold before the introduction of plating by electricity in the nineteenth century.

A ladle or crucible was prepared by covering it with a thin coating of whitewash to prevent the metal from adhering to the surface. Mercury was then poured in and heated until it boiled – at 357.25°C. Gold, usually in the form of sheets, was heated and then let into the mercury, which immediately absorbed it, forming an amalgam. The amalgam was poured into cold water, then strained through a leather bag to remove any excess mercury. The object to be gilded was carefully cleaned so that the gold would adhere to the surface, either using acid or an abrasive. An amalgamating fluid was sometimes used to prepare the surface for gilding. This was made by dissolving mercury in nitric acid. The object was then heated and the necessary amount of gold amalgam spread evenly on the

Left: Avignon Clock designed by Louis Simon Boizot (1743–1809), the work in ormolu by Pierre Gouthière (1732–1813/14), French, 1771. Boizot provided the original model, and from this Gouthière made the cast. By chasing the surface with increasingly fine tools, he gave detail and texture to the surface. After depositing the gold on the metal by the process known as 'mercury gilding', or 'fire gilding', certain areas of the piece were given a high polish by burnishing.
Below: Perfume burner of red jasper and ormolu made by Gouthière, 1772–82. A container for the perfume pastille is set within the neck of the bowl. Gouthière became a maître-doreur in 1758, and by 1770 he was recognized as the most skilful creator of elaborately chased and gilded decorative works of his time.

surface using a damp wire brush. The object was then heated to drive off the mercury, which evaporated, leaving the gold adhering to the surface. The gilded surface was then polished with a burnisher such as an agate or a bloodstone, or with a mild abrasive.

Objects made in ormolu were usually cast using the lost-wax method and the surface worked on using punches and chasing tools. With the aid of a hammer the metal was pushed into the required shape, and afterwards the tools were used to indent the surface to provide different textures and finishes. In high-quality ormolu work matt surfaces were carefully chased to contrast with the highly polished gilded areas.

Ormolu is principally associated with France, where refined methods of production evolved in the middle of the seventeenth century. The manufacture of objects in ormolu was treated as a special craft and was carried out by members of the Corporation des Fondeurs (founders) and the Corporation des Doreurs (gilders).

Some of the finest producers of ormolu wares such as Charles Cressent were trained as sculptors, and there was always a close link between sculptors and craftsmen who worked in ormolu. As well as mounts for furniture and clock-cases, fine porcelain and Oriental lacquer were sometimes mounted in ormolu. The mounts usually consisted of an elaborate frame set around the vessel, held together by screws or bolts. In spite of the heavy material in which they worked, the best 'bronziers' were able to produce works of art of extraordinary lightness and delicacy. Most of the more skilful artists, such as Pierre-Philippe Thomire and Pierre Gouthière, worked for the French royal family.

Almost as well known as a manufacturer of fine ormolu was Matthew Boulton, who produced some exceptionally high-quality pieces at his factory in Soho, Birmingham. A large proportion of his output consisted of mounts for vessels carved from marble and bluejohn – a variety of fluorspar found in Derbyshire – and fine clocks mounted with classical figures in ormolu.

From the mid-nineteenth century the technique of electro-gilding replaced the mercury process. Although a wide range of wares continued to be cast in the traditional manner, the colour and the insubstantial nature of the gilding distinguishes gilded brass and bronze wares from true ormolu.

Far left: Ormolu wall light, one of a set of four, made by François-Thomas Germain (1726–91), French, 1756. Decorative objects such as this are described as 'bronzes d'ameublement'. Germain employed up to 80 assistants in his workshops manufacturing works of this kind.
Above: Detail of an ormolu mount on a kingwood bureau plat, or flat-topped writing table, attributed to Charles Cressent (1685–1768), French, c.1735. The fine chasing of the metal is here clearly visible. Contrary to guild regulations, Cressent employed both founders and gilders on his furniture-making premises.
Left: Detail of an ormolu mount on the leg of the bureau plat. Matt, textured surfaces contrast with areas that have been burnished.

BRASS

Brass is an alloy of copper and zinc. The proportion of copper to zinc has varied from 55% to 90%, depending on the type of metal required. The colour of brass is related to the proportions of other metals in the alloy but it is usually a golden yellow. Brass is hard and will take a high polish; it can be cast in a mould or wrought by hand.

The manufacture of brass in Antiquity involved the use of calamine, which is zinc carbonate. The calamine was ground and mixed with charcoal and granules or fragments of copper. The mixture was put into a crucible and heated to a temperature sufficiently high to reduce the zinc in the calamine ore to a metallic state, but not so high as to melt the copper. Zinc is volatile and, because copper will absorb gases at high temperatures, vapour from the zinc permeated the copper, thus converting it to brass. The brass was then heated to melting-point and poured into moulds.

Brass was first used by the Romans for making coins and commemorative plates, and it was in reasonably common use by the first century AD. They imported calamine from various parts of the Empire, including the Ardennes in Belgium and the Mendips in Great Britain.

The first accurate account of the manufacture of brass appears in a text by the German monk Theophilus, *De Diversis Artibus*, which dates from the first half of the twelfth century. In it he describes heating '*calamina*' and copper together in a crucible. An account of a seventeenth-century brassmaking furnace describes it as being dug below ground level, fitted with a canopy and a chimney, and having a series of crucibles. The furnace was blown by bellows to generate sufficient heat. Initially these furnaces used wood for fuel, but by the eighteenth century coal was sometimes used, notably in Britain.

The molten brass was taken from the furnace and poured into two-piece moulds made from sandstone, or a similar material, held together by iron clamps. The brass plates were then shaped and flattened using large tilt-hammers powered

Left: English brass dome-topped tankard, c.1720–30. The body and lid were formed by raising or casting; other features such as the handles and the foot were attached by 'brazing', a technique comparable to soldering silver.

Below: Illustration of a German brassmaker's workshop from Amman's book of trades showing basins being formed by the hammer. The furnace was used for annealing the brass while it was being worked.

Above: Dutch brass timepiece in Art Nouveau style made in the workshop of Onder Den St Maarten at Zaltbommel, c.1900. The pendulum is a decorative rather than a functional feature. The case shows a variety of decorative techniques including engraving, punched work and stamping.

Left: Pair of English brass candlesticks, c.1690–1700. These would have been cast and turned. Below: English brass kettle and kettle stand, mid-eighteenth century. The body of the kettle would have been raised, the spout then brazed on to the body. The elegant stand would have been cast in sections and brazed together, then finished by turning.

by water. This process, which was known as 'battering', necessitated the use of a furnace to soften the brass after it had been hammered.

In 1738 William Champion of Warmley, near Bristol, developed a technique of producing metallic zinc by using a vertical retort. During the eighteenth century this method was increasingly used, although until the middle of the nineteenth century the calamine method continued to be used by those who thought it supplied brass of a better colour.

In Britain important centres of brassmaking included Isleworth in Middlesex and Tintern in Monmouthshire, operated by the Society of Mines Royal. This enterprise was first established in the sixteenth century in the area around Bristol where calamine had been discovered. The brass industry at Baptist Mills near Bristol was operating over 30 furnaces by the early eighteenth century.

On the Continent the best-known areas for the manufacture of brass from the Middle Ages onwards was around Liège, Aachen and Dinant, the latter city giving its name to a whole group of brass wares known as 'Dinanderie'.

Before the eighteenth century the American colonies had to import nearly all their brass wares. German miners were brought in to exploit the copper mines in Connecticut and New Jersey, and it is possible that brass was being made in America by the middle of the eighteenth century. There is reliable evidence for the establishment of a brass button industry in Waterbury, Connecticut, by the early nineteenth century, and Baltimore had developed a substantial trade in brass production by the mid-nineteenth century.

A large part of the brassmaking industry was devoted to the manufacture of brass wire, used for pins and for binding the grips of sword-hilts. Alternatively, it was supplied to workshops in the form of sheets which had to be shaped or cast by the craftsman. A feature found early in the brass trade is the simplification of production by casting, turning and stamping.

Casting was the process commonly used to form objects. Small articles such as frames for buckles, or items that were decorated on one side only, could be cast using open moulds. An impression was pressed into the face of the mould and the molten metal poured in. Items such as candlesticks were cast in a two-piece mould. A pattern would be made of the piece required, usually in a hardwood such as boxwood. The mould consisted of two halves, each side bearing half an impression of the object to be cast.

Another casting technique, used to produce complex wares with hollow interiors such as the brass ewers known as 'aquamaniles', was the lost-wax process. This was the method used to cast bronze as well as silver.

In the Middle Ages narrow bands of ornament were sometimes produced by the stamping process. A group of brass dishes and basins made in Nuremberg from the fourteenth century onwards have designs produced by stamps, and their manufacture was recognized as a specialized craft.

Punching and embossing are techniques that were often used to decorate brass wares. A craftsman would possess a number of punches of different designs and sizes to give his work variety. The vessel to be worked on was usually held against a block of lead or pitch which allowed the brass to stretch without cracking. Embossing was extensively used on brasswork in the Low Countries, especially during the Baroque period.

Far left: Egyptian kursi *in brass overlaid with silver and copper, Mamluk style, nineteenth century. A* kursi *serves as a holder for the Koran and at the same time as a lectern. The construction consists of a framework supporting sheets of pierced brass held together by rivets.*
Left: Detail of the kursi *showing the fine piercing on the door and the combination of brass, silver and copper.*
Below: Dutch brass tea-caddy, early eighteenth century. This was decorated with pierced and engraved work, executed with a saw, file and burin.

Because brass can be easily cut and filed, it was a suitable medium for openwork. Examples range from the finely pierced dishstands produced by specialized craftsmen in Nuremberg in the fifteenth and sixteenth centuries to the ornate designs fretted out on the lids of eighteenth-century Dutch warming-pans and the sides of tea-caddies.

Before the discovery of electro-deposition the mercury gilding process was used on brass. Brass wares close-plated with silver are to be found, too, sometimes carrying spurious marks imitating the hallmarks of sterling silver. The plating is often worn away, but traces can usually be discerned on those areas of an object not exposed to wear.

In the eighteenth and nineteenth centuries brass was often treated with coloured lacquers to act both as a preservative and as a colouring agent. Electro-gilded brass, as used for clocks or furniture-mounts in the nineteenth century, was coated with tinted lacquer which gave it an 'antique' appearance. If, today, the lacquer is removed, a bright surface is nearly always revealed beneath.

The techniques of damascening, as practised by the sword cutler were also employed on brass. Inlaid brass and bronze was a speciality of Near Eastern craftsmen, and some excellent work was produced in the first half of the sixteenth century by craftsmen working in Venice and its colonies.

Below: Pair of French brass chenets, or fire-dogs, in seventeenth century style. Burning logs would have been supported on the iron bars, while the elaborate uprights served a purely decorative purpose.
Right: English horse brass commemorating the Coronation of George V and Queen Mary, 1911. This was produced by casting.

THE CRAFT OF THE LOCKSMITH

The lock is almost certainly a Near Eastern invention. A sophisticated wooden lock, working on a system of wooden pegs operated by a key fitted with vertical pins, was excavated from Khorsabad, near Nineveh, and is likely to be about 4,000 years old.

The earliest surviving locks, mostly from Egypt, are nearly all of wood. Locks made from metal – generally iron – were first developed by the Romans. Roman locksmiths almost certainly invented 'wards', the projections around the lock which ensure that the lock will only operate if the correct key is inserted. The locking mechanism usually operated a simple square bolt, but it is possible that some Roman locks had spring-operated bolts. In size and technical detail Roman locks differed little from those made by Medieval locksmiths and it is likely that the tools employed were similar.

To make a wrought-iron lock for mounting on a chest a locksmith in the fifteenth century started with a piece of iron sheet, which he hammered to the required thickness and then trimmed with shears. The mechanism was then built on the inside of the lock.

The mechanism was usually attached to the lock-plate with iron pins or rivets, which were 'burred over', or flattened at either end, to fix the mechanism securely. Except in the best-quality work, the inside of the lock would generally be coarsely finished; by contrast, the surface of the lock that could be seen was often elaborately decorated. Embossed, pierced and filed decoration was common, though the design in some instances incorporated long rectangular panels of openwork. These were fretted out with files and saws and then pinned to the surface, sometimes over panels of textile or gilded brass. In some locks the hasp was chiselled to represent a human figure and the key-hole concealed behind a hinged cover.

By the late fifteenth century locksmiths had developed sophisticated springs, and by the sixteenth century it was common to have chest locks with a large number of bolts. In the finest work the mechanism would be attached to the lock-plate by screws, and small cover plates were fitted over delicate spring-work for protection.

German locks of the sixteenth and seventeenth centuries were decorated with etching. Popular designs were of figures, strapwork and minute scrolls. Craftsmen working in centres such as Nuremberg seem to have supplied flat iron plates cut to size and already decorated.

By the second half of the seventeenth century locksmiths were fitting the mechanical part of the lock into a deep-sided rectangular box made from heavy-gauge iron plates. These

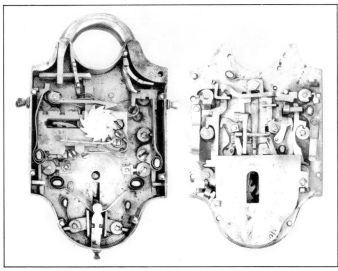

Far left: Photograph of a locksmith in his workshop, 1905. The part of a lock or key which he is in the process of filing is held firm in a vice. At the back of his workbench is a small anvil.
Above: German steel padlock, seventeenth century. This is a puzzle padlock and probably made as an exercise of skill. By operating marked dials on the back, the key could be released and the padlock opened.
Left: English steel key, seventeenth century. The bow was fretted out with a drill, then filed and engraved.

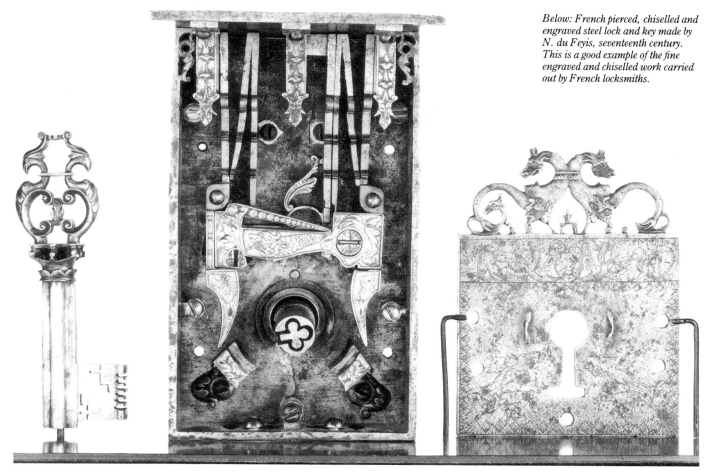

Below: French pierced, chiselled and engraved steel lock and key made by N. du Feyis, seventeenth century. This is a good example of the fine engraved and chiselled work carried out by French locksmiths.

were decorated with engraved work, often incorporating the locksmith's name, or, especially with French locks, they might be finely pierced and chiselled. The design on the lock was almost invariably reflected in the design of the key. The more elaborately decorated locks are said to have been made as tests of skill – masterpieces to gain admission to the craft guild.

In the sixteenth century brass was used for key-hole covers and as decoration on locks. In the second half of the seventeenth century cast-brass cases were made for locks, notably in England where they were extensively used by the Birmingham maker Wilkes. The very fine locks marked with the name of Bickford (see p.139) are distinguished by the use of gilded-brass in openwork, usually fitted over a lock of blued steel. Both these makers produced locks fitted with indicator dials which showed how many times the lock had been used.

Modern lockmaking may be said to have begun in 1778 with the invention by Robert Barron of the double-acting tumbler lock. This lock was fitted with two levers, or 'tumblers', which had to be raised by different amounts to permit the bolt to operate. Further improvements were made by makers such as Chubb and Bramah. Bramah sought the assistance of the engineer Henry Maudsley to make the parts for his patent lock by machine. The well-known lock patented by Linus Yale in 1848 worked on a system of raising pins by means of a key – like the earliest Egyptian locks. When the pins had been correctly aligned, the cylinder could be turned. The locksmiths of the nineteenth and twentieth centuries concentrated their efforts almost entirely on the security of locks rather than on their decorative qualities.

An important part of the locksmiths' trade in the sixteenth and seventeenth centuries was the manufacture of padlocks. Designs varied from massively built plain box padlocks to small locks of spherical form. A flat, shield-shaped padlock was widely used throughout Europe during the eighteenth century. Puzzle padlocks, which required a series of complex operations to open them, were made for the locksmith's own amusement or to demonstrate his skill.

The bronze keys of the Middle Ages were cast in a two-piece mould, then roughly finished with a file. Early iron keys were also very crudely forged, then roughly shaped and pierced. By contrast, the steel keys made from the fifteenth century onwards are masterpieces in their own right. The best examples were forged and chiselled, often by turning them on a lathe.

The tools used by a locksmith included a series of small hammers, a small anvil on which the iron bars and plates could be forged, and a furnace to heat the work. A large part of the craft required the use of cutting-tools such as drills, saws and files. Punches and dies were used to form the parts of a lock, and a draw-plate was necessary to produce the pins holding the mechanism to the plate. Lathes were used to make keys and a workshop would, as now, have a series of blanks from which keys could be cut. Very fine saws were necessary to cut the appropriate wards in a key.

PEWTER

Pewter is an alloy, the principal component of which is tin. The metals forming the alloy have varied considerably over the centuries but analysis of English pewter flagons has indicated that the alloy used there for fine pewter was composed of 92% tin, 1% copper and 3% to 5% lead. Pewter of cheaper quality contained a larger proportion of lead – rendering it dangerous if used for eating- or drinking-vessels. Antimony was introduced in the late seventeenth century, and for pewter produced today the alloy consists of 94% tin, 4% antimony and 2% copper or bismuth.

When polished, pewter has a silvery surface which varies in patination from grey to matt black. The metal is comparatively soft and has a low melting-point – 300°C. It can be worked in the form of flat sheets, shaped by the hammer, but the process more commonly used was casting. This was one of the earliest methods employed to make vessels and it has been established that Roman pewter was almost certainly manufactured by casting in moulds of limestone. Sand and plaster moulds were also employed for casting in early times. Later, the moulds were usually constructed in two sections and were made from gunmetal (an alloy of copper and tin or zinc).

Pewter ingots were melted in a furnace and the inside of the mould treated with a wash consisting of red ochre, pumice and egg white to prevent the molten metal from sticking to the inside surfaces. The pewterer judged by smell whether the metal was the correct temperature. The mould was heated and molten pewter poured in with a ladle; it was tilted, then brought to the vertical as it was filled to ensure that the metal flowed into the furthest recesses and produced an even casting. Because of its low melting-point, the metal set rapidly. After the mould had been opened, the casting was 'cleaned up' to remove any excess metal, or 'sprue'.

Certain larger vessels such as chargers and basins were generally hammered up from the sheet, but small plates and dishes, candlesticks, salts and most of the other articles known by the name of 'sadware', were cast and then finished by hammering or turning on a lathe. Hammering compacted the metal, making it stronger. Large and complex vessels such as flagons had to be assembled from a number of castings: feet, handles and lids were cast separately, then soldered to the main body of the vessel, a process needing very precise judgements about temperature to prevent excess heat melting the individual elements. Wares of simple form such as bowls and porringers could be cast in their entirety.

In finishing pewter by lathe-turning, tools of various shapes were held against the rapidly revolving piece, cutting and shaping it to the required design and thickness. The lathe was driven by a wooden treadle, as in wood-turning (see p. 22). In

Left: English broad-rimmed pewter charger, c.1660–65. The well has a shallow central boss, or protuberance, and the rim is engraved with continuous scenes of the hunt. Above: American pewter lamp with bull's eye reflector, nineteenth century. This would have been cast in a mould.

the late eighteenth century spinning was introduced. The vessel was formed on a lathe by pressing sheet pewter over a chuck. This enabled large quantities of cylindrical and hollow sections suitable for mugs and bowls to be produced quickly and cheaply.

Much pewter is plain and its appeal lies in the excellence of the line, colour and construction. However, some pewter vessels made for display were very elaborately decorated. *Edelzinn* was a type of relief decoration introduced, probably in France, during the first half of the sixteenth century. The best known exponent of this method of decoration was François Briot, a medallist from Lorraine, who produced a series of moulds for ewers and dishes in the Mannerist style. Some dishes made from these moulds incorporate allegories of Temperance; hence the name given to the ware of 'Temperantia dishes'.

Casper Enderlein, a pewterer working in Nuremberg during the early seventeenth century, produced versions of these dishes as well as an important series of tankards. Nuremberg was the centre of production of relief pewter work during the seventeenth century and among the best-known examples of these wares are a series of small circular dishes decorated in relief with medallions depicting the Seven Electors. Another well-known group is cast in relief and incorporates the arms of the Swiss cantons.

A form of vessel which was also made purely for display purposes was the guild tankard. Guild tankards were ceremonial vessels of great weight and size used as display plate at the formal occasions of individual guilds. Examples from northern Europe survive from the fifteenth century, and they are among the most impressive objects created in pewter.

One of the most celebrated makers of these large-scale tankards in the sixteenth century was Paul Weise, who worked in Zittau in Saxony. A tankard produced by him incorporates bands of relief known to have been taken from models by Peter Flötner, the German artist. The Briot dishes and Flötner plaquettes seem to indicate that patterns for designs were widely distributed, often long after they had

Left: English pewter ale pitcher, early nineteenth century. The body would have been cast and the other elements soldered on.
Below: WMF green glass decanter mounted in pewter, German, c.1900. The pewter base in the form of a maiden and lily pads was cast. The firm of Württembergisches Metal Fabrik produced fine pieces in the Art Nouveau style.
Bottom left: Two pewter measures. On the left an English baluster measure, c.1700; on the right a Scottish tappit hen measure, late seventeenth century.

been originally made. It is likely that the designs for the Temperantia dishes were still being employed during the nineteenth century.

Pewter was sometimes used in combination with other materials. The main body of a tankard or bottle might be of glass or earthenware with the lid of pewter. Pierced work, in which the design was fretted out with a file or saw revealing the main body of the vessel underneath, is found on tankards from Germany. This decorative technique was often used on the type of tankard known as a '*Pechkrug*', which was constructed like a barrel from a series of closely fitting wooden staves.

A method of engraving widely employed on pewter was known as 'wrigglework'. By moving the engraving tool from side to side when cutting the design into the surface a zig-zag line was produced. The technique was used extensively in the last quarter of the seventeenth century, especially in England and in the Low Countries. Many tankards and dishes of the 1690s are decorated with the figures of William and Mary set amidst foliage in a delightfully naïve style. A more sophisticated use of this type of decoration is to be seen in the large commemorative chargers produced by London pewterers in the latter part of the seventeenth century.

This period also saw the use of coloured enamels applied to pewter. These enamels were usually in blue, white and red and in the *champlevé* technique, where the ground of the design was cut away, filled with enamel, then fired and polished. The decoration was almost exclusively armorial, and confined to the central bosses of dishes and chargers.

Casting was widely used for pewter in the Art Nouveau style fashionable in the early 1900s. Attenuated shapes with relief decoration could be produced easily in a mould. Some of the best cast work of the period was produced by the German firm of Württembergisches Metal Fabrik. Modern pewterers employ centrifuge moulds in which the molten pewter is pressed into the pattern by centrifugal force, allowing very finely detailed work to be produced.

Pewter was often employed for the more practical wares such as serving-dishes, tankards and measures, used alongside silver plates, cups and flagons. It was much cheaper than silver but still far more expensive than the alternatives in ceramics and wood. Pewter wares closely followed silver forms and, as the craftsmen lived in close communities, styles and techniques were very quickly disseminated.

From the fourteenth century onwards pewter vessels became more common. As with precious metals, only a few of what must once have been a great variety of wares have survived. Pewter was easily damaged and, once the trade had become well established in many centres, customers could take their damaged wares to be melted down and re-fashioned. This almost certainly accounts for the comparatively small number of pieces that have survived from before the sixteenth century.

National styles and forms first began to emerge in the fifteenth century. Earlier, the forms of International Gothic were to be found throughout Europe: pewter flagons with short, squat, bulbous bodies, often with faceted sides, are known from many sites.

Throughout Europe, beginning in the fourteenth century, guilds of pewterers were formed in the major cities. These strictly regulated the manufacture and sale of pewter wares. Samples of the alloy were taken at the hall of the guild and carefully weighed against a measured quantity of pure tin to assess its quality.

Like silver, the items were stamped with marks indicating

Left: Illustration of a pewterer's workshop from Diderot's Encyclopédie. *Two of the craftsmen are shown turning a vessel on the lathe (Figs. a and b), while another shapes a handle (Fig. c). Close to the furnace solder is being applied with a hot iron (Fig. d), and in the foreground molten pewter is poured from a ladle into a mould (Fig. e).*

Far left: German pewter flagon, thinly plated with silver, made by Paul Weise (c.1535–91), c.1570. The handle bears the impressed town mark of Zittau, in Saxony, together with the maker's mark. The flagon was made for a butcher's guild and would have been intended for display.
Left: Detail of the flagon showing a figure from the upper of the two bands of ornament. The reliefs, made in a series of separate moulds, were, with the figure of Lucretia on the handle, based on designs by Peter Flötner (died 1546).
Below: English pewter tankard, dated 1698. The zig-zag pattern, known as 'wrigglework', was executed by rocking the engraving tool from side to side as the design was cut into the surface of the metal.

standards of quality and with the name of the maker or workshop where the piece had been made. Certain officers were appointed with a right of search. They had powers to enter workshops and seize work that fell below acceptable standards or was produced by craftsmen working outside the authority of the guilds.

Some idea of the pewterer's workshop and stock in trade can be gained by looking at wills and inventories. As well as ingots and sheets of the metal, workshops would have lathes, moulds and a special bench to support the moulds. Known as a 'horse', this had two posts at opposite ends – one fixed, the other movable – held by a wedge and clamp. The mould was held in position by a rod fitted with a screw-thread which could be tightened as necessary. Specially shaped hammers with a double head, known as 'planishers', were used to flatten out irregularities in the surface of the metal. A curved steel burnisher with long handle was used to polish the surface after casting.

One of the most important items in the workshop was the stake, usually made of hardwood, on which the pewter could be formed with the use of various hammers. There would also be several types of engraving tool to decorate the surface. To enable the pewterer to cast and solder his work, the workshop would be fitted with a furnace and blowpipe. A group of pewterer's tools of the eighteenth century has been preserved at the Hall of the Worshipful Company of Pewterers in London. These include burnishers, bouge hammers for hammering the 'bouge', or curved section, of plates and dishes, and a 'grater' with a spear blade used for turning the insides of hollow-ware.

The range of wares made in pewter is enormous, ranging from ordinary domestic articles to elaborate display plate emulating the magnificence of silver.

BRITANNIA METAL

Britannia metal is a pewter alloy containing a proportion of antimony. There has been considerable discussion as to its composition because of the similarity of Britannia metal to other alloys. A recipe given in 1837 describes it as an alloy of tin with antimony and small amounts of copper and zinc.

Britannia metal is traditionally thought to have been developed in Sheffield: in 1769 a filesmith in the cutlery trade, James Vickers, acquired a recipe for what was described as 'white metal', and he used it to cast spoons.

At first it was raised by hand over a stake or formed cold by pressing or stamping from rolled sheet, and solid elements such as handles and knobs were cast in bronze moulds and then soldered to the main body of the vessel; manufacturers of

Britannia metal were quick to take advantage of the many improvements in methods of production that had taken place in the Old Sheffield Plate trade. These improvements included the use of rolling mills to produce sheet metal from the ingots, drop-hammers and steel dies, which enabled ornament to be stamped.

Contemporary descriptions of the die-stamping machines, especially those powered by steam, indicate that they were capable of producing from flat discs of metal complicated forms such as salvers, dishes and meat covers. Some decorative treatments such as fluting and ribbing could be rolled into the sheet metal before die-stamping.

The range of wares made in Britannia metal was enormous. As early as 1787 James Vickers was using it for measures,

Left: English Britannia metal tea-caddy made by Richard Constantine, c.1800. Britannia metal is a tin-based alloy which has similarities with pewter, though a more lustrous polished surface could be achieved. The Britannia metal industry is said to have been introduced to Sheffield by James Vickers, and Constantine was one of his principal competitors in the manufacture of tableware and other domestic articles. This piece is comparable in design to contemporary tea-caddies in silver and fused plate. Above: Broadhead & Atkin Britannia metal cream jug with a ceramic lining, English, c.1840. The metal body was made in two parts by the stamping process, the handle and footring were cast and applied.

Left: Illustration of James Dixon &
Son's factory in Cornish Place,
Sheffield, c.1825. Dixon's was
established in 1805 to manufacture
Britannia metal and cutlery.
Below: American Britannia metal
candlesticks made by Henry Hopper,
c.1845. In the eighteenth century
Britannia metal was imported from
England, but by about 1810
American manufacturers had begun
to produce their own wares.

teapots, casters, frames, salts as well as spoons. Because of
links with the Sheffield plating industry, several of the forms –
especially for candlesticks – were copied directly from those
used by the makers of Old Sheffield Plate.

A technical development which was to influence the design
of vessels made in Britannia metal was the invention of
spinning. The ovals and octagonals, which were the earliest
shapes, could not be made by spinning, but Dixon's catalogues
from the middle of the nineteenth century show large numbers
of wares with cylindrical bodies which could have been – and
almost invariably were – produced by this method.

Elkingtons had patented electro-plating in 1840 and by the
last quarter of the nineteenth century electro-plated wares had
overtaken the production of the better-designed unplated
Britannia metal pieces. Mechanical methods of decoration
such as engine-turning, widely introduced in the middle of the
century, led to the standardization of decoration, and this was
also a contributory factor in the decline of the trade.

Although the Britannia metal trade was concentrated in
Sheffield, a few articles such as spoons and small boxes were
made in Birmingham and London. The wares were being
exported to the United States before the end of the eighteenth
century and by the first quarter of the nineteenth century firms
such as Trasks in Beverly, Massachusetts, and Boardman in
Hartford, Connecticut, were producing teapots and other
vessels in the alloy. As in Sheffield, mechanical production
methods were used extensively. Tea-sets, communion sets,
candlesticks and spitoons were all included in the repertoire of
the larger firms. In due course the American trade, too, was
overtaken by manufacturers of electro-plated wares.

BIBLIOGRAPHY

GENERAL
Connoisseur, The, *The Connoisseur Complete Encyclopedia of Antiques*, 1985
Fleming, John, and Honour, Hugh, *The Penguin Dictionary of Decorative Arts*, 1979
Osborne, Harold (ed.), *The Oxford Companion to the Decorative Arts*, 1975

WOODWORK
Beard, Geoffrey, *The National Trust Book of English Furniture*, 1985
Chinnery, Victor, *Oak Furniture: The British Tradition*, repr. 1979
DeVoe, Shirley Spaulding, *English Papier Mâché of the Georgian and Victorian Periods*, 1971
Edwards, Ralph, *The Shorter Dictionary of English Furniture*, 1964
Goodman, W. L., *History of Woodworking Tools*, 1964
Hasluck, Paul N. (ed.), *Revival of Traditional Woodcarving*, 1978
Hayward, Charles H., *English Period Furniture*, 1984
Hayward, Helena (ed.), *World Furniture*, 1965
Hoadley, Bruce R., *Understanding Wood*, 1981
Huth, Hans, *Lacquer of the West, 1550–1950*, 1971
Joy, Edward, *English Furniture, 1800–1851*, 1977
Joyce, Ernest, *Technique of Furniture Making*, 1980
Lincoln, W. A., *The Art and Practice of Marquetry*, 1971
Macquoid, Percy, *History of English Furniture*, 4 vols, repr. 1972
Montgomery, Florence M., *Textiles in America, 1650–1870*, 1984
Sparkes, Ivan, *The Windsor Chair*, 1975
Symonds, R. W., *English Furniture, Charles II to George II*, 1929
Thornton, Peter, *Authentic Decor: The Domestic Interior, 1620–1920*, 1984
Toller, Jane, *Papier-Mâché in Great Britain and America*, 1962
Walton, Karin-M., *The Golden Age of English Furniture Upholstery, 1660–1840*, 1973
Watson, F. J. B., *Wallace Collection Catalogue, Furniture*, 1956
Wills, Geoffrey, *English Furniture*, 2 vols, 1971
Wolverhampton Art Gallery and Museums, *Georgian and Victorian Japanned Ware of the West Midlands*, 1962

GLASS
Agricola, G., *De re metallica*, repr. 1950
Angus-Butterworth, L. M., *The Manufacture of Glass*, 1948
Arwas, V., *Glass Art Nouveau to Art Deco*, 1977
Bailey, K. C., *The Elder Pliny's Chapter on Chemical Subjects*, 1982
Biser, B. F., *Elements of Glass and Glass Making*, 1900
Charleston, R. J., *English Glass*, 1984
Drahotova, O., *European Glass*, 1983
Duthie, A. L., *Decorative Glass Processes*, 1982
Elville, E. M., *English Tableglass*, 1960
Gardiner, P. V., *The Glass of Frederick Carder*, 1971
Glass Circle, The, vols 1–4, 1972–1982
Goldstein, S. M., Rakow, L. S. and J. K., *Cameo Glass*, 1982
Grehan, I., *Waterford: An Irish Art*, 1981
Harden, D. B., Painter, K. S., Pinder-Wilson, R. H., and Tait, H., *Masterpieces of Glass*, 1968
Ingold, G., *The Art of the Paperweight*, 1981
Manley, C., *Decorative Victorian Glass*, 1981
Matcham, J., and Dreiser, P., *The Techniques of Glass Engraving*, 1982
McGrath, R., and Frost, A., *Glass in Architecture and Design*, 1961
Mentasti, B., and Toninato, T., *Glass in Murano*, 1984
Morris, S., *Victorian Table Glass and Ornaments*, 1978
Neri, A., *The Art of Glass*, 1662
Northwood II, J., *J. Northwood*, 1958
Oppenheim, A. L., Brill, R. H., Barag, D., and von Saldern, A., *Glass and Glassmaking in Ancient Mesopotamia*, 1970
Pellatt, A., *Curiosities of Glass Making*, 1849

Revi, A. C., *Nineteenth-Century Glass*, 1967
Tait, H., *The Golden Age of Venetian Glass*, 1979
Vavra, J. R., *Five Thousand Years of Glass-Making*, 1954
Warmus, W., *Emile Gallé, Dreams into Glass*, 1984
Williams-Thomas, R. S., *The Crystal Years*, 1983
Woodward, H. W., *Art, Feat and Mystery: The Story of Thomas Webb & Sons, Glassmakers*, 1978
    The Story of Endinburgh Crystal, 1984

CERAMICS
Bradshaw, Peter, *Eighteenth-century English Figures*, 1981
Charles, Rollo, *Continental Porcelain*, 1964
Charleston, Robert (ed.), *World Ceramics*, 1968
Cushion, J. P., and Honey, W. B., *Handbook of Pottery and Porcelain Marks, 1745–1795*, 1980
Godden, Geoffrey, *Encyclopaedia of British Pottery and Porcelain Marks*, 1964
    Staffordshire Porcelain, 1983
Pugh, P. D. H., *Staffordshire Portrait Figures*, 1970
Sandon, Henry, *British Pottery and Porcelain*, 1980
Savage, George, *Porcelain Through the Ages*, 1961
    Pottery Through the Ages, 1963

METALWORK
Abbey, Staton, *The Goldsmith's and Silversmith's Handbook*, 1952
    Enamels, 1983
Anderson Black, J., *The History of Jewels*, 1974
Bates, K. F., *Enamelling: Principles and Practice*, 1952
Benjamin, Susan, *English Enamel Boxes*, 1982
Blair, C., *European Armour*, 1958
Bradbury, Frederick, *A History of Old Sheffield Plate*, 1912
Bruton, Eric, *Diamonds*, 1978
Campbell, Marian, *An Introduction to Ironwork*, 1985
Cotterell, H., *Old Pewter: Its Makers and Marks*, 1963
Cuzner, Bernard, *Silversmiths' Manual*, 1935
Frégnac, Claude, *Jewellery from the Renaissance to Art Nouveau*, 1969
Gentle, R., and Field, R., *English Domestic Brass, 1680–1810*, 1975
Gooden, Robert, and Popham, Philip, *Silversmithing*, 1971
Goodison, N., *Ormolu: The Work of Matthew Boulton*, 1974
Graeme Robertson, Edward, and Robertson, Joan, *Cast Iron Decoration: A World Survey*, 1977
Grimwade, Mark, *Introduction to Precious Metals*, 1985
Haedeke, H., *Metalwork*, 1970
Hughes, G., *A Pictorial History of Gems and Jewellery*, 1978
Lecoq, R., *Serrurerie Ancienne*, 1978
Mackay, J., *The Animaliers. Animal Sculptors of the Nineteenth and Twentieth Centuries*, 1973
Maryon, Herbert, *Metalwork and Enamelling*, 1971
Michaelis, R. F., *Antique Pewter of the British Isles*, 1971
North, A. R. E., *An Introduction to European Swords*, 1983
Rawson, Jessica, *Ancient China: Art and Archaeology*, 1980
Royal Academy, The, *The Horses of San Marco*, 1979
Savage, George, *A Concise History of Bronzes*, 1968
Schiffer, P. N. and H., *The Brass Book*, 1978
Scott, J. L., *Pewter Wares from Sheffield*, 1980
Selwyn, Arnold, *The Retail Silversmith's Handbook*, 1954
Smith, Ernest A., *Working in Precious Metals*, 1971
Southwork, Susan and Michael, *Ornamental Ironwork*, 1978
Tylecote, R. F., *A History of Metallurgy*, 1976
Weaver, L., *English Leadwork: Its Art and History*, 1909

ACKNOWLEDGEMENTS

Roxby Art Publishing Limited would like to thank: Roger Dodsworth, Broadfield House Glass Museum, Kingswinford; Rosemary McBeath, Phillips Son & Neale; Roger Keverne, Spink & Son Ltd; Paul Tear and the Conservation Department, Wallace Collection; Metalwork Department, Victoria & Albert Museum; Colonel William-Thomas, Stevens & Williams Museum; Stan Eveson, Thomas Webb Museum; John P. Smith, Asprey PLC; John Culme, Tessa Aldridge and the Furniture Department, Sotheby's, and David Beasley, Goldsmiths' Hall.

AMB American Museum in Britain; APC Antique Porcelain Company, London; BAL Bridgeman Art Library; BL British Library; BM British Museum; BHG Broadfield House Glass Museum; CMG Corning Museum of Glass, New York; FM Fitzwilliam Museum, Cambridge; HFPW The Henry Francis du Pont Winterthur Museum; NT National Trust, London; SCM Sheffield City Museum; V & A Victoria & Albert Museum; WC Wallace Collection, London; WCG Worshipful Company of Goldsmiths; Photographs: (T) top, (B) bottom, (C) centre, (L) left, (R) right.
Front cover: Giraudon; Spink & Son Ltd; Phillips Son & Neale; Christie's; Pilkington Glass Museum; Spink & Son Ltd; Phillips Son & Neale.
Back cover: Sotheby's.
Page 6 WC. 8 Scala/Palazzo Vecchio, Florence. 9 City of Edinburgh Museum and Art Galleries. 10 V & A. 11 (T) Museum of Fine Arts, Boston; (L) Bantock House Museum, Wolverhampton; (R) V & A. 12(L) FM; (R) V & A. 13 WCG. 14 Christie's. 15 A & E Foster. 16 London Library. 17(T) Phillips; (B) Christie's. 18(L) Smithsonian Institution, Washington DC; (R) Phillips. 19(T) Christie's; (C) Phillips; (B) Sotheby's. 20(L) Giraudon; (T) Leonard Lassalle/BAL; (B) Sotheby's. 21 Sotheby's. 22(L) V & A; (R) A & E Foster. 23 (L) A & E Foster; (R) V & A; 24(L) Sotheby's; (R) BAL. 25(T) Sotheby's; (B) Christie's. 26 Israel Sack, New York. 27(L) Christie's, New York; (R) Cheltenham Art Gallery and Museums. 28(L) Sotheby's; (R) Christie's. 29(TR)V & A; (BL) Sotheby's; (BR) Temple Newsam House, Leeds/BAL. 30 V & A. 31(L) Bowes Museum, Barnard Castle; (R) Sotheby's. 32(L) Sotheby's; (R) V & A. 33(L) Fratelli Fabbri/Gallery Etienne Levy, Paris; (R) Sotheby's. 35(TL) FM; (TR) Museum of Fine Arts, Boston; (B) V & A. 36(L) Asprey PLC; (R) Christie's. 37(L) Phillips; (TR) Sotheby's; (BR) Christie's. 38(L) V & A; (R) Sotheby's. 39 V & A. 40(L) and (B) Asprey PLC; (TR) BAL. 41(T) Fratelli Fabbri/Palazzo Pitti; (BL) Phillips; (BR) Sotheby's. 42 WC. 43 WC. 44(L) and (BL) Christie's; (R) Sotheby's. 45(L) Scala/Ca' Rezzonico, Venice; (B) Scala/Castello Sforzesco, Milan. 46(T) Sotheby's; (B) Phillips. 47(TL) NT/Petworth House; (R) Christie's. 48(TL) AMB; (TR) V & A; (B) Scala/Palazzo Davanzati. 49(L) and (B) Christie's/BAL; (R) V & A/BAL. 50(TL) V & A; (BL) Phillips; (R) Smithsonian Museum of Art: Gift of Kenneth O. Smith. 52(L) and (BR) Sotheby's; (TR) Asprey PLC. 53(TL) and (BR) Sotheby's; (TR) V & A. 54(L) Sotheby's; (R) Phillips. 55(L) Christie's; (R) V & A. 56 Christie's. 57(TR) and (B) Sotheby's; (TL) Phillips. 58(L) Halcyon Days; (R) V & A/BAL. 59(T) Phillips; (C) Bantock House Museum, Wolverhampton; (R) V & A/BAL. 60 Asprey PLC. 61 Sotheby's. 62 Christie's. 63(TL) Staatliche Sammlung Ägyptischer Künst, Munich; (TR) Christie's; (B) Sotheby's. 64 V & A. 65 John P. Smith. 66 BL. 67(L) V & A; (R) BL. 68(L) Christie's; (TR) CMG; (BR) Delomosne & Son. 69(L) CMG; (R) BL. 70 David Watts. 71(L) Durrington Corp (Isle of Man Ltd)/Asprey PLC; (R) BM/BAL. 72 BAL. 73 BM/BAL. 74(L) BM; (C) and (R) Sotheby's. 75(R) Sotheby's; (L) Christie's. 76 Sotheby's. 77(L) Sotheby's; (R) Delomosne & Son. 78(L) Christie's; (R) Bristol Museum & Art Galleries. 79 CMG. 80(L) BM; (R) and (BR) CMG. 81 CMG. 82 BM/BAL. 83(T) Asprey PLC; (B) Christie's; (R) Sotheby's. 84(C) Stevens & Williams; (L) Science Museum; (R) CMG. 85(T) CMG; (B) Pilkington Glass Museum. 86(TL) BL; (R) BM/BAL; (BL) Christie's. 87(TL) and (C) Christie's; (R) BHG. 88(B) Thomas Webb Museum; (TL) BHG; (TR) Sotheby's. 89 David Watts. 91(L) BHG; (BR) Stevens & Williams. 92 Pilkington Glass Museum. 93 Christie's. 94 Sotheby's. 95(TL) and (BL)

Sotheby's; (R) Phillips. 96(L) BHG; (R) Asprey PLC. 97(L) Cecil Higgins Art Gallery/BAL; (C) and (TR) V & A/BAL; (CR) V & A. 98 V & A. 99 C. Elsam, Mann & Cooper Ltd. 100 Sotheby's; (TR) Bristol Museum and Art Galleries/BAL; (B) Ronald Inch and Michael Blicq. 101(R) Christie's; (L) Phillips. 102 V & A. 103 V & A. 104(BR) Spink & Son Ltd; (TR) Phillips; (L) BM. 105(R) BM; (BR) V & A/BAL; (L) Christie's. 106(L) V & A; (R) Phillips. 107(L) Christie's; (R) Sotheby's. 108 Spink & Son Ltd. 109 Spink & Son Ltd. 110 Christie's. 111(BL) Phillips; (R) and (TL) APC. 112(L) APC; (R) Phillips. 113(TR) APC; (B) Phillips. 114 V & A. 115(L) Bluett & Son Ltd./BAL; (R) Sotheby's. 116 BM. 117(L) Mansell Collection; (R) Spink & Son Ltd. 118(L) V & A; (R) Spode Museum. 119(L) Dyson Perrins Museum, Worcester; (R) V & A. 120 BAL. 121 Josiah Wedgwood & Sons Ltd. 122 Mansell Collection. 123(TL) V & A; (R) and (C) Mansell Collection. 124(R) NT/Waddesdon Manor; (L) Phillips. 125(BR) Phillips. 126 V & A/BAL. 127(R) Minton Museum, (L) Alistair Sampson Antiques; (BL) Rouslench Collection. 128(R) V & A/BAL; (L) Spink & Son Ltd. 129(R) Phillips; (L) V & A/BAL. 130 Sotheby's. 131(L) Sotheby's; (TR) and (CR) Phillips. (BR) Private collection, U.S.A. 132(TL) and (B) Dyson Perrins Museum; (R) Sotheby's. 133(TR) V & A; (TL) Dyson Perrins Museum; (BR) Phillips; (BL) Spink & Son Ltd. 134(TL) Mansell Collection; (BL) Bonhams/BAL; (R) Phillips. 135 BAL. 136 Phillips. 137(L) S.J.Phillips/BAL; (B) and (R) Phillips. 138 Phillips. 139 V & A/BAL. 140(L) Kunstmuseum, Bern; (T) Christie's; (B) Christie's/Cleveland Museum of Art. 141 Asprey PLC. 142(L) WCG; (R) Westminster Reference Library. 143 (L) V & A; (R) Colonial Williamsburg Foundation. 144 (L) BM; (R) Phillips. 146 Christie's. 147(L) C.J. Vander; (R) Phillips. 148 Christie's. 149 Sotheby's. 150 Christie's. 151(TL) Brand Inglis; (R) Asprey PLC. 152 V & A. 153(L) Phillips; (R) HFPW. 154(TL) and (BL) Phillips; (B) Spink & Son Ltd. 155 Christie's. 156(TL) Phillips; (TR) and (BR) Christie's; (BL) Judith Banister. 157 Christie's. 158(L) and (R) V & A. 159(T) John Freeman/Fotomas;(BL) Brand Inglis; (BR) Christie's. 160(L) Spink & Son Ltd; (R) BAL. 161(T) Sotheby's; (B) WCG. 162 WCG. 163(T) WCG; (C) Phillips; (B) V & A. 164(L) Sotheby's; (R) London Library. 165(TL), (BL) and (BR) Sotheby's; (TR) Cameo Corner/BAL. 168(L) Phillips; (R) Museum of Fine Arts, Boston. 169(L) V & A; (R) Phillips. 170(L) Mary Evans Picture Library; (R) SCM. 171(TL) Sheffield City Libraries; (TR) SCM. 172(T) SCM/BAL; (B) V & A. 173(TL) SCM; (R) Phillips. 174 Sotheby's. 175(L) Sotheby's; (R) S.J. Shrubsole. 176(L) BAL; (R) V & A. 177 David Pearce. 178 V & A. 179(T) and (B) V & A. 180(L) Christie's; (R) Ironbridge Gorge Museum Trust. 181(L) Science Museum; (R) Metropolitan Museum of Art, Edgar J. Kaufmann Charitable Foundation. (T) London Library. 182(L) London Library (R) Stadtbibliothek, Nuremberg. 183(L) V & A; (R) Metropolitan Museum of Art, Museum Fund 1932. 184(L) and (R) V & A; (C) Phillips. 185 V & A. 186(T) V & A; (L) and (C) Anthony North; (R) London Library. 187 NT/ Canons Ashby. 189(T) V & A; (C) HFPW; (BL) Mallett/BAL; (BC) and (BR) BAL. 190 V & A. 191(TL) London Library; (TR) and (B) V & A. 192 V & A. 193(TL) Angelo Hornak; (TR) Keir Collection; (B) V & A. 194(L) Sotheby's; (TR) and (BR) Birmingham Assay Office Collection. 195 V & A. 196(T) Christie's; (BL) Sotheby's; (BR) Christie's. 197(T) Sotheby's; (B) S.J. Phillips/BAL. 199(T) Phillips; (BL) and (BR) V & A. 200(TL) and (BL) BAL; (TR) BM/BAL; (BR) Scala/St Mark's, Venice. 201 Phillips. 202 V & A. 203(T) Phillips; (B) V & A. 204 WC. 205(L) J.Paul Getty Museum; (TR) and (B) Christie's. 206(L) Phillips; (TC) Alistair Sampson Antiques; (B) London Library. 207 Alistair Sampson Antiques; (R) Mallett. 208(L) Christie's; (BR) V & A. 209(T) (Phillips; (B) Mallett. 210(L) Racal Chubb; (R) and (B) V & A. 211 V & A. 212(L) Phillips; (R) AMB. 213(L) V & A/ BAL; (TR) Phillips; (BR) Sotheby's. 214 V & A. 215(L) and (R) V & A. 216(L) SCM(TR). 217(T) BAL/SCM; (B) AMB.

Every effort has been made to trace copyright holders. It is hoped that any omission will be excused.

INDEX